Web Page Design

Adobe Seminars: Web Page

LISA LOPUCK

SHERYL HAMPTON

DESIGN

ADOBE PRESS
San Jose, California

Library of Congress Catalog No.: 97-73666
ISBN: 1-56830-426-9

10 9 8 7 6 5 4 3 2

Managing Editor: Hans Hansen
Copy Editor: Karen Whitehouse
Text design: David Bullen

Printed in the United States of America by GAC Shepard Poorman, Indianapolis, Indiana.

Published simultaneously in Canada.

Adobe Press books are published and distributed by Macmillan Computer Publishing USA. For individual, educational, corporate, or retail sales accounts, call 1-800-428-5331, or 317-581-3500. For information address Macmillan Computer Publishing USA, 201 West 103rd Street, Indianapolis, IN 46290. Macmillan's World Wide Web page URL is www.mcp.com.

Contents

	Foreword	*vii*
CHAPTER A	The Web Design Workflow	*1*
CHAPTER B	Input and Illustration	*17*
CHAPTER C	Web Animation Techniques	*45*
CHAPTER D	Creating Interface Elements	*67*
CHAPTER E	Navigation and User Interface Ideas	*95*
CHAPTER F	Preparing Graphics for the Web	*115*
CHAPTER G	Using a WYSIWYG HTML Editor	*135*
CHAPTER H	HTML: So Much More Than Just Text	*153*
CHAPTER I	Adding Animation to Web Pages	*169*
CHAPTER J	Adding Audio and Video to your Site	*189*
CHAPTER K	Creating PDF Files with Adobe Acrobat	*211*
CHAPTER L	Behind the Scenes	*225*

Foreword

The idea for this book came during the middle of one of those endless, mind-throbbing seminars I had the displeasure of attending—hot, boring, and never to the point. I kept wondering why I had paid several hundred dollars to be there. In the end, I received a binder of black-and-white printouts and a free CD with product demos. I thought, "Why not deliver a book expressly with the seminar concept—short sessions, to the point, a mix of how-to and techniques, and all color—centered on a topic of immediate interest?"

Adobe Seminars: Web Page Design is a seminar-in-a-book. It offers as many hands-on solutions as possible. Lisa Lopuck and Sheryl Hampton, its hard-working authors, cover the gamut of Web page design and production from A-Z. Their combined years of conducting real seminar and conference sessions is immediately apparent. We've tried to keep their voices unique, almost as if they were speaking in front of you. So you will find that proper names of screen elements may be described as "the wand-like looking icon," or the text peppered with personal observations and opinion.

Other seminar-like enhancements are the 100 or so sessions. We purposely created a book with very little required reading—just jump in and start wherever you want.

The Image Club© has contributed to a wonderful CD that accompanies this portable seminar. They have generously provided the graphics so you can practice along with Lisa and Sheryl in the step-by-step sessions. On the Image Club CD are some great ideas and demos about Image Club products that you can use to extend your Web page concepts.

And, finally, like any good seminar, there are sessions for both intermediate and semi-advanced users. There are creative shortcuts and productivity enhancing techniques for users of all skill levels. If, by chance, a session gets too hard, back off and start over; or put it down for a while. You always can come back to this book's concept and remember where you left off.

Adobe Seminars: Web Page Design is the first of many solutions-oriented books in this the first of the *Adobe Seminar Series.* Solutions that cover the needs of people who create, produce, refine, and explore today's digital communications.

—Patrick Ames, Publisher

Adobe Press, Adobe Systems, Inc.

Chapter A

THE WEB DESIGN WORKFLOW

Before you begin diving into production, it's a good idea to step back and take a look at the big picture—the overall process of designing a Web site from start to finish. By understanding the creative process of building a Web site, you have a better chance at ensuring its success—from planning to design, production, and marketing. This chapter focuses on the Four-Step Design Process, a process that covers everything from initial client contact to information architecture, visual design, and final implementation. In addition, we'll look at the roles of the primary participants, the responsibilities involved in common Web production projects, as well as how to track and manage them. In the final session, we'll discuss various methods to ensure that potential users know about your site once it is finished.

CHAPTER SESSIONS

A1 *Definition of the Project*

A2 *Information Architecture*

A3 *Visual Design*

A4 *Web Production Roles*

A5 *Project Tracking*

A6 *Marketing Your Site*

FOUR-STEP DESIGN PROCESS

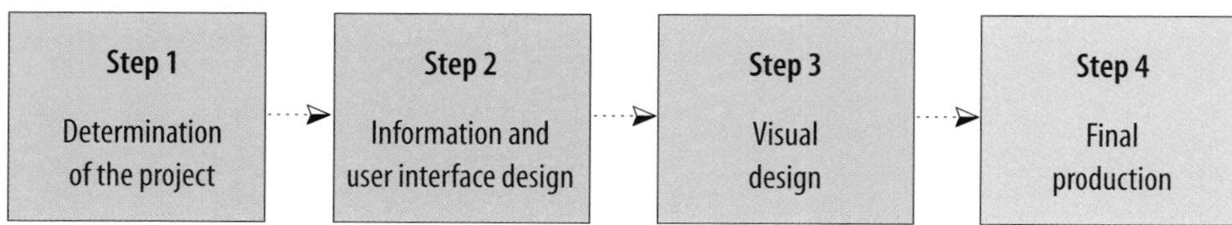

There are many ways to organize the Web site creation process. We prefer to break it into four coherent development stages ideal for project management. Over the past four years, we have refined this process and applied it to Web sites of all scopes. We believe it to be a crucial part of our Web design business.

STEP 1: PROJECT DEFINITION

In most cases, the definition of the project takes place before and during the creation of a proposal and budget for the project. Everyone involved, including the client, must understand the size and scope, schedule, and goals of the site. See Session A1 for a detailed analysis of this step.

STEP 2: INFORMATION DESIGN

After the project has been clearly defined for all team members, you can begin organizing the content. Information architecture, or information design of a project, defines how content is organized, and how the user will find and access information they want on your site. See Session A2 for a discussion of information architecture.

STEP 3: VISUAL DESIGN AND USER INTERFACE

Now that the goals and information architecture of the sitehave been outlined, you can address the visual design and user interface. In many cases, design of a Web site is simply an extension of a company's current branding and design strategy. In other cases, a company's Web site can be a radical departure from an older visual style that the client wants to update. See Session A3 for a further breakdown of visual design and user interface.

STEP 4: PRODUCTION

After the information architecture and visual design are approved, implementation of the site can begin. This step usually takes the most time and includes the following tasks:

- Generating, linking, and testing HTML pages.
- Creating and processing graphical elements into palettes and appropriate file formats.
- Integrating additional content such as QuickTime movies, Shockwave and Flash animations, audio files, panoramas, PDF files, and so forth.
- Performing back-end programming with CGI and Java scripting for secured transactions and other site enhancements.

During this step, upload the site and make sure that it is functional on its server. Once the site is online, you should allocate two to ten working days for testing it on different platforms and in different browsers. Not until the completion of Step 4 is a site ready for launch—with a champagne toast!

Session

A1 *Definition of the Project*

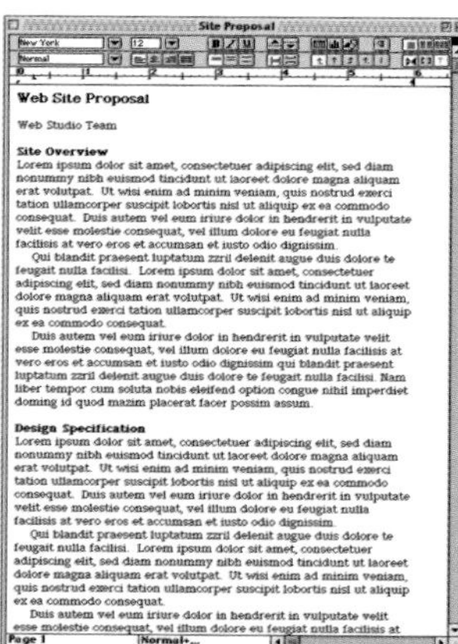

Before you initiate the design or production of a Web site, you must first define the project. In fact, this step generally begins during the client proposal stage. After all, how do you know what you are committing yourself to unless you know what the project entails? Everyone involved, including the client, must understand the size and scope, schedule, and goals of the site.

QUESTIONS THAT HELP DEFINE THE PROJECT

In order to understand the scope of a project, as well as its goals, ask your client and your team the following types of questions:

- What is the content of the site?
- Is your company expected to design or supply any original content?
- What will make this site successful? Hits? Publicity? Revenue?
- Who is the user? Young? Conservative? Wealthy? Why will a user visit the site?
- What are the bandwidth and technical considerations? Can you rely on plug-ins? Which browsers will you support?
- Which platform and modem speed will the site support? Should you design for the lowest common denominator?
- Is there a particular event driving the launch date?

Once these questions are answered, and you have generated a project schedule and budget, you can create a proposal that will act as on overall roadmap for the project.

CREATING THE PROPOSAL

Once you have a good grasp of the project's scope, you can draft a proposal or contract so that the client and your team have the same vision moving forward. In general, try to address all of the following issues in your proposal:

- Your understanding of the project to ensure any miscommunications are resolved immediately.
- If you are in a bidding situation, outline your company's key selling points and why you should be awarded the contract.
- Create a schedule of milestones and deliverables. In many cases, a schedule also includes deadlines for the client.
- Estimate the budget for the project.
- Discuss the ownership issues of content or design.
- Address the issue of credit and the potential for a link back to your Web site.
- Include the names and contact information for all the key team members.
- Include any added expenses that are not covered in the estimated budget such as travel expenses and applicable sales tax.

Session

A2 Information Architecture

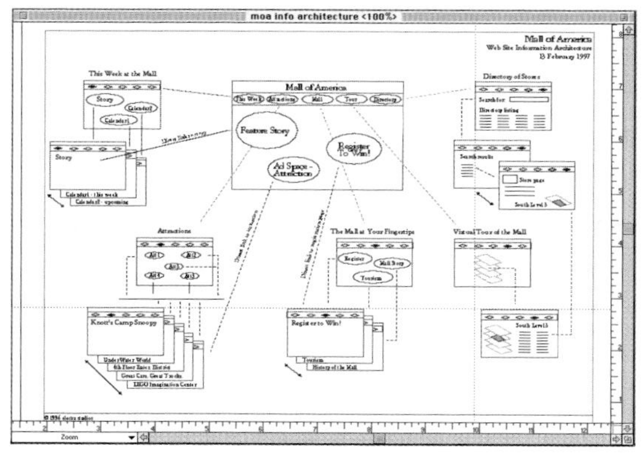

Information design is the organization of content within a Web site, and how a user finds and accesses that information. Even if your site boasts award-winning visuals, users will leave if they cannot find what they're looking for quickly and intuitively.

Begin the information design process, by categorizing and prioritizing the information that you will include in the site. What are the five to seven main categories? Weigh the importance of the information to be presented. Without addressing any visual styles, draw outlines and diagrams that show how information is grouped together. For instance, product and company information could be grouped together, but perhaps kept separate from functions like search and feedback. Furthermore, think about which groups of information should be given the most prominence on the screen, and draw those items larger in your diagrams.

WHERE TO START?

The following questions and suggestions can guide you in designing the flow of information throughout the site:

- What are the five to seven major groupings (or categories) of information?
- What information or functions should users be able to access from wherever they are in your site?
- You should group like-information. For instance, don't group a feedback function with product and company buttons, treat it differently.
- What information will visitors want to see first? Do you want to highlight different products or events each week?
- What kind of user experience do you want to provide: a practical hierarchical presentation, a linear story, or an exploratory environment?
- How do users get from one place to another and back? Do they need to travel back to the home page in order to choose a different category?

CATEGORIZING AND PRIORITIZING CONTENT

Before you begin the process of categorizing and prioriting content, be sure that you have a complete list of all the site content. There is no greater development challenge than to accomodate late-coming information. Once you have a list of all the content, create a simple text outline. Look for ways to group like-information—categorizing the information into no more than five to seven categories. Designing an interface to accomodate more than seven categories is difficult, and you can potentially overload your users with information. After generating a simple text outline, begin to prioritize. Decide which information should be given most prominence on the screen and which information should always be accessible to the user.

NAVIGATION AND USER INTERFACE

You can begin to think about navigation and user interface after you have categorized and prioritized the site content. How does the user get from one category to another? After the user makes a navigational choice, how does he get back to where he started?

The best way to work out preliminary user interface and navigation decisions is on paper. Take your text outline and turn it into a flowchart diagram. Represent each top-level category as a rectangle (the shape of a Web page). Then, within each rectangle, draw shapes that represent buttons to other catogories and functions. This diagram will become the "site map," or blueprint, for your Web site.

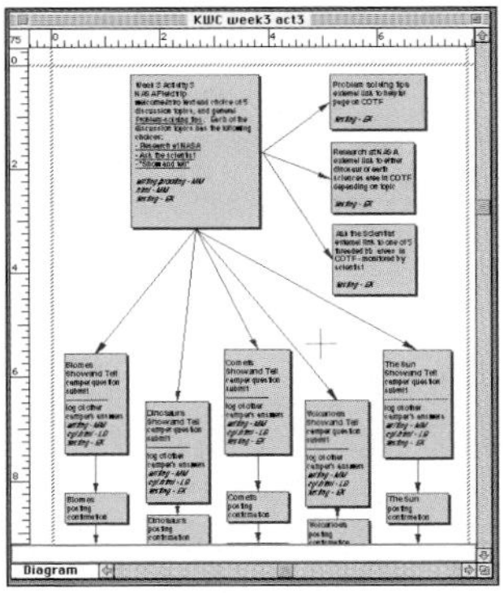

CREATING AN INFORMATION SITE MAP

For the same reasons you would not begin to build a house without a blueprint, you should not build a Web site without a site map. Site maps are not meant to imply visual directions; they are simply a means of communicating the flow of content throughout the site.

You can generate your site map in almost any graphics application; it helps if the program is vector-based, like Adobe Illustrator. Create your own language of symbols and a legend so that others can understand your map. Inspiration is a cross-platform application that allows simple, fast creation of a site map. The program automatically creates boxes of all shapes, generates text in the boxes, and understands levels of hierarchy and relationships.

The creation of a site map is an excellent process to share with the client so that they too can begin to see and understand the site. Once the client approves the site map, you are ready to explore visual design directions.

Session

A3 Visual Design

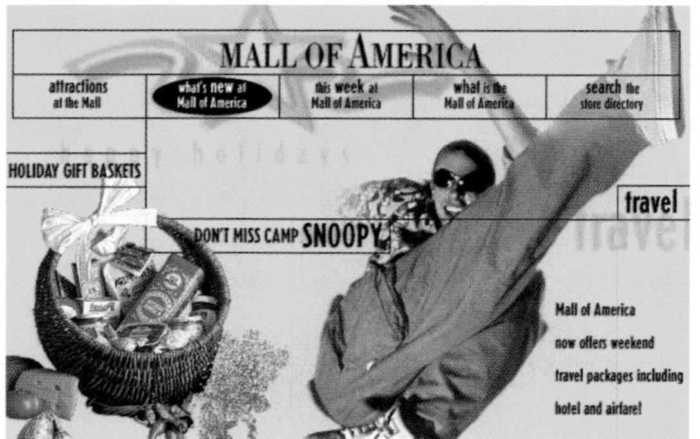

One of the four design directions presented to Mall of America included a colorful, modern look. Ultimately, the client chose a direction closer the client's brand identity.

After organizing and prioritizing the site information as a result of the various conversations you've had with your client, you can begin exploring design directions. Generally, it is best to present a series of design directions, perhaps three to four, so that clients can have a range of ideas from which to choose. As an inspiration for your visual directions, you may want to draw upon the company's branding or a unique theme or concept.

CREATING DESIGN DIRECTIONS

Create two or three different visual design directions for one or two key Web pages so that your client can choose from a range of ideas. Remember that these directions, while polished and professional looking, most likely will not be perfect. Often clients will mix and match elements from the various directions you present.

DESIGN IDEAS

Before you begin exploring design directions, consider the demographics of your audience in terms of stylistic preferences. Often it is useful to develop a list of adjectives like wired, illustrative, wacky, or organic to help guide your design.

Should you decide to use a metaphor (such as a room or a book) in one of your design directions, do not make the mistake of taking the metaphor too literally. It is difficult, if not impractical, to extend a metaphor down through multiple layers of a site.

Also, no matter what the design concept, keep in mind any technical limitations, such as bandwidth and user limitations. During this process, take inventory of the average user's computer and bandwidth configuration.

PRESENTING DESIGN DIRECTIONS

Presenting directions online is a good way to make sure the client is familiar with the context of the final project. In some cases, using printed screen shots—along the lines of a more traditional design presentation—is a good idea too. Just make sure that at some point early in production, your client sees the work in progress online, (see Session F9). You must position the client's expectations prior to the launch date. This process is iterative. Expect multiple rounds of feedback and revisions.

CARRYING THROUGH THE DESIGN

Once the visual design has been established and approved, it must be carried through the entire site consistently from home page design to its navigation graphics, area identifier graphics, and accessory graphics

In addition, at this stage of the process, you should finalize the font and color usage as well as the file format and palette decisions. This helps the team of production artists and designers keep a consistent feel throughout the site.

Session

A4 Web Production Roles

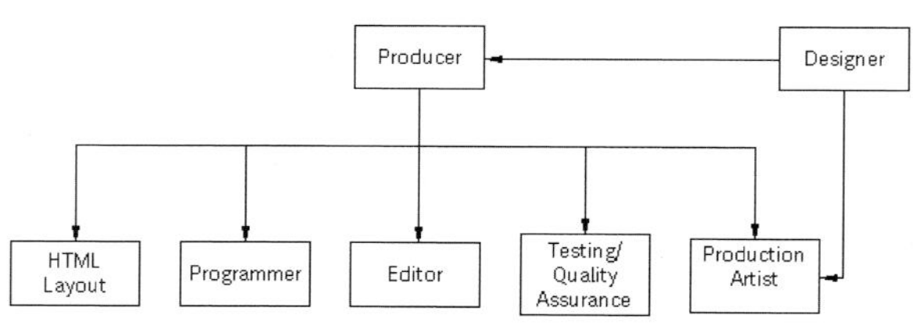

So, what exactly is the best mix and number of people to design and produce a Web site? The content, the scope, and the purpose of the Web site are elements that help determine a site production team. In this session, various roles are described, along with their responsibilities. Keep in mind, the number of people and roles required vary from project to project, but the following can serve as guide.

PRODUCER

The title of Producer brings with it a lot of responsibility. The Producer is the all-knowing, all-seeing, *owner* of the project. Ideally, this person has a background in project management or multimedia design and brings that experience to the project. The Producer manages all aspects of the project: schedule, budget, production, client contact, milestone deliverables, and client satisfaction. This person is the keeper of the assets and knows the project like the back of her hand.

The Producer manages all members of the team, and works closely with the Designer. Interactive experience is a bonus when choosing a Producer, as the Designer and Producer can then collaborate on issues of user interface, information design, and navigation.

DESIGNER

The Designer, sometimes carrying the title of Art Director, ideally should have a background in interactive media and understand the issues of information and user interface design. Because a Web site is more than just a series of independent pretty pictures, an understanding of the interactive experience is a necessity.

The Designer is responsible for the visual appearance of the Web site and, along with the Producer, determines the navigation and information design. Once the Designer establishes the visual design, generally by mocking it up in a graphics program such as Photoshop, he manages a Production Artist that carries the design consistently through the site.

PRODUCTION ARTIST

The Production Artist, managed by either the Producer or the Designer, produces all final graphics to be incorporated into the site. The Production Artist should have a background in design, and should be a Photoshop whiz. Generally, the Production Artist starts with the design established by the Designer and uses it to generate final graphics for the site in the correct file format and palette. In addition, depending on the skill level of the Production Artist, this role may include a limited amount of design.

To assist with final production of the Web site, the Production Artist should be familiar with the naming conventions of the site, and should name the files accordingly. The Production Artist can also supply pixel dimensions of the files to the person who incorporates them into the site.

HTML LAYOUT

In some cases, either the Producer or the Programmer is also responsible for the basic HTML of a project. If the project is large enough, you should consider hiring one or more people to focus on the HTML. This person, managed by the Producer, should have HTML experience, and be at least familiar with the more complex implementations of tables and frames.

If your design relies heavily on a table or frame structure, be sure to include the HTML layout person in overview design meetings. Keep in mind that some visual issues and challenges can be resolved in HTML.

PROGRAMMER

Your Programmer, managed by the Producer, works closely with the HTML layout person to build the framework of the site. The Programmer should have experience with CGI scripting, but knowledge of Java, JavaScript, VBScript, C++, and Dynamic HTML for Internet Explorer 4.0 is also helpful.

Involve your Programmer in early meetings regarding definition of the site. The Programmer can then make suggestions regarding programmatic answers to issues of user interface and information design, before the design begins.

EDITOR

To ensure consistency of writing style, you should have an experienced editor review a site that has a moderate to extensive amount of text. This also includes text that appears within graphics, as mistakes in graphics can be easily overlooked. The Editor works closely with the HTML layout person to correct errors and suggest re-writes. In some cases, the Editor has HTML experience and can make changes directly in the HTML.

Session

A5 Project Tracking

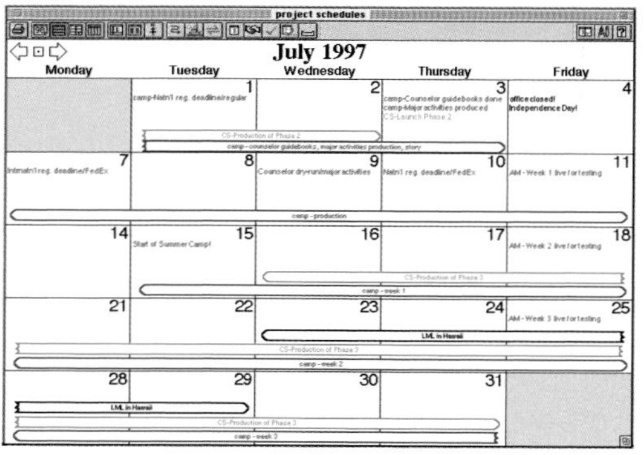

Companies commonly lose money on Web-based projects due to lack of schedule and budget management. And, no matter how beautiful and wonderful the finished site is, if a project loses money for anyone, it is generally not considered a success. This session covers the basics of schedule and budget management, with the intended outcome of maximing your profit margin.

PROJECT TRACKING

Before the project starts, create a detailed schedule that shows the *critical path*. The critical path refers to items on a schedule that are interdependent. For example, the visual design needs to be finalized before graphics based on the visual design can be created. As another example, the site should be nearing completion before testing and quality assurance starts. In these two cases, reversing the order of these tasks doesn't make sense.

Plotting the critical path of a project, as well as the ancillary tasks, helps you schedule resources, keeps you focused, and helps you stay within your budget. Everyone needs to understand that a delay or a problem in any one of the critical path items creates an adverse ripple effect down your overall timeline. The later critical path items often can be condensed in time to make up for the schedule slip, but don't count on this happening.

You can do this type of tracking with a regular desk or wall calendar or a calendar or project management application on the computer. There are even applications that enable you to track project management online, and can give your client access to the status of the project at their convenience.

WORKING WITH A LONG DISTANCE CLIENT

In these days of Internet access everywhere, it is no longer a handicap to work with a client who is out of town, across the country, or even on another continent. It can be, however, a challenge to carry on all communication via irregularly scheduled conference calls.

To ensure comfort and confidence, you should, at the very least, conduct weekly updates during the production of the site. After posting updates to the work-in-progress site, schedule a conference call with your client and walk them through the changes. These meetings also give you the opportunity to discuss any questions or issues that have presented themselves during the past week.

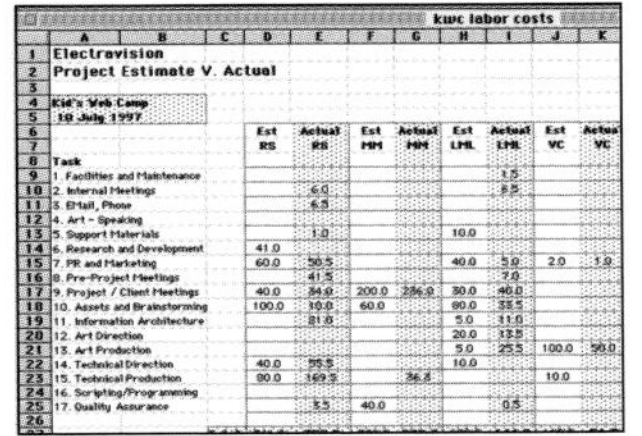

kwc labor costs

Electravision
Project Estimate V. Actual

Kid's Web Camp
10 July 1997

Task	Est RS	Actual RS	Est MM	Actual MM	Est LML	Actual LML	Est VC	Actual VC
1. Facilities and Maintenance						1.5		
2. Internal Meetings		6.0				8.5		
3. EMail, Phone		6.5						
4. Art - Speaking								
5. Support Materials		1.0			10.0			
6. Research and Development	41.0							
7. PR and Marketing	60.0	50.5			40.0	5.0	2.0	1.0
8. Pre-Project Meetings		41.5				7.0		
9. Project / Client Meetings	40.0	34.0	200.0	286.0	30.0	40.0		
10. Assets and Brainstorming	100.0	10.0	60.0		80.0	33.5		
11. Information Architecture		81.0			5.0	11.0		
12. Art Direction					20.0	13.5		
13. Art Production					5.0	25.5	100.0	50.0
14. Technical Direction	40.0	55.5			10.0			
15. Technical Production	80.0	169.5		36.8			10.0	
16. Scripting/Programming								
17. Quality Assurance		3.5	40.0			0.5		

SCHEDULING AND BUDGETING

The most difficult part of a Web site project is not always the design or the production, but the creation of a schedule and budget for a project. Once you've worked on a variety of projects, you'll get a sense of time and cost necessary for various types of tasks.

If you make a habit of recording the time your team spends on a project engaged in various tasks, you will be better prepared to estimate the schedule and budget of future projects.

In many cases, you may be forced to work backwards from one of these elements. For example, if a particular event is driving the launch date, that may impact the budget and scope; or, if the client has a limited budget for a project, make sure that this is reflected in the scope and timeframe.

PROFIT TRACKING

Time is money. Make sure that everyone on the team tracks each and every hour associated with the project. Most likely, your company's accounting system can generate reports automatically of each team member's time. Your accounting system should also generate a standard profit and loss report (or P&L) for an individual project. This information gives you a very good idea of how much the project is costing your company.

The only missing part of this equation is the addition of overhead, which is the cost of doing business generally not associated with an individual project. Overhead includes rent on a studio space, lights, phone charges, computers, furniture, and so forth. Make sure that your project costs reflect a certain percentage of overhead. The appropriate percentage can be determined over time, as you have more projects behind you.

Session

A6 Marketing Your Site

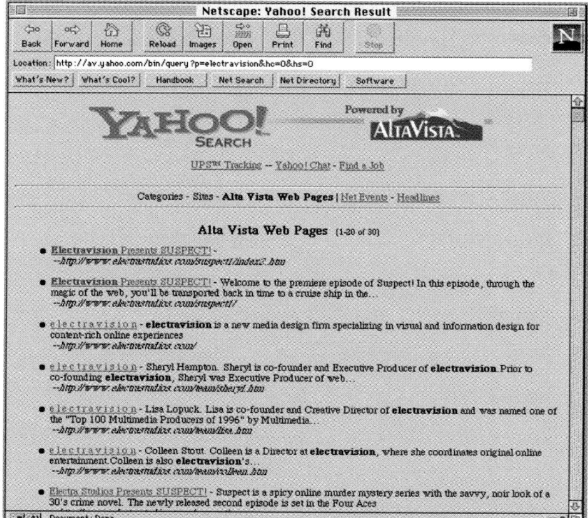

Once your information and visual design are finalized and approved, and all the HTML and CGI scripts are completed and tested, you are ready to launch your site. Now, you need to make sure that people know about your site. There are many ways to advertise and market your site—online as well as offline—through traditional advertising media. Be careful of companies who offer to perform this service for you, especially via unsolicited email. Although many of these companies are reputable and capable, you can save time, money, and grief performing these tasks yourself.

SITE PROFILE FOR ONLINE REGISTRATION

Before you register your site online, you should create a site profile. This includes the information you'll need when registering at various search engines and directories. Generate list of information about your site that includes the title of the Web site, URL of the Web site, name and email address of the key contact for the site, eight-to-ten keywords that describe the site, and 25-word, 50-word, and 70-word descriptions of the site. Creating this profile prior to starting the registration process allows you to focus on the big picture of the site offline, and then cut and paste portions into active registration forms.

SEARCH ENGINES AND DIRECTORY LISTINGS

Search engines and directory listings work a little differently. A search engine, like *Alta Vista*, actively searches the information developers have input describing their sites, as well as information outside the service on the Web. Search engines, in some cases, actively search individual pages within a Web site. Directory listings, like *Yahoo*, on the other hand, access only the information contained within *Yahoo* that a site developer has entered. What this means is that generally the results of a search within a search engine is more extensive than the results from a directory listing.

If you perform a search within *Alta Vista* for a site that you know well, you may notice that the results you get often include more than one reference to the site. These search results generally yield multiple pages that match the search criteria. And, the results offer not only the name of the site, but also the titles of the HTML pages and the first three lines of text on those pages.

Search engines sometimes find keywords that are embedded in a certain area of the page's HTML called *meta tags*. These are words that exist in an HTML page, but do not appear to the user. When a user performs a search on the word "motorcycle" from a search engine, the result lists sites that have used "motorcycle" in a meta tag, even if the site doesn't have the word motorcycle anywhere visibly on the screen. This sort of keyword tagging is often abused by sites trying to get attention from everyone, so it has become somewhat ineffective.

Directory resources include:

- *Yahoo, www.yahoo.com*
- *Excite, www.excite.com*

Search engine resources include:

- *Infoseek, www.infoseek.com*
- *Alta Vista, www.altavista.com*
- *Lycos, www.lycos.com*

MAILING LISTS AND NEWSGROUPS

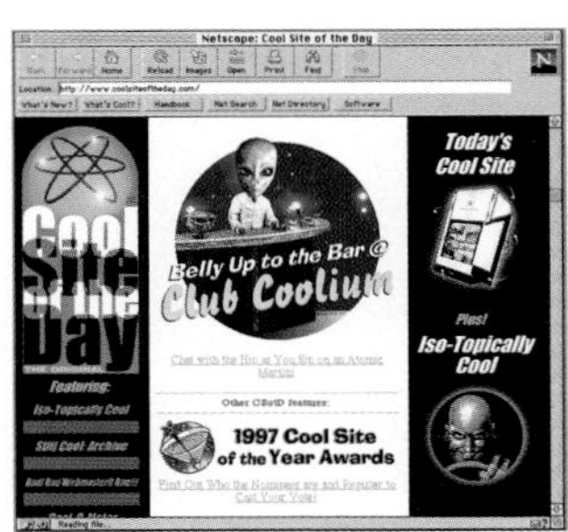

Posting to specific mailing lists and newsgroups is a great way to reach a target audience for your site, but not if the recipients think your message is junk mail. Make sure that your message is concise and appropriate for the audience.

Mailing list and newsgroup resources include:

- *www.nova.edu/Inter-Links/listserv.html*, for mailing lists and instructions
- *tile.net/listserv*, for mailing lists and instructions
- *comp.infosystems.www.announce*, a newsgroup for general announcements of general Web sites

Chapter B

INPUT AND ILLUSTRATION

Whether you are starting from a scan or starting from scratch, in this chapter you will learn basic Web graphic production techniques such as creating images and icons directly on the computer, how to integrate your company's logo into your Web graphics, and how to adjust colors to be Web-safe. You also will learn key production tips and techniques using two powerful graphic production tools, Photoshop and Illustrator, as well as how to use them together to generate professional-looking Web site graphics.

CHAPTER SESSIONS

B1 *Illustrating with Illustrator*

B2 *Illustrating with Photoshop*

B3 *"Indiana Jones" Text Effects*

B4 *Using Preserve Transparency for Color Correction*

B5 *From Grayscale Scan to Colorized Overlay*

B6 *Creating Channels for 3D Text Effects*

B7 *Applying 3D, Glossy Text Effects*

B8 *Applying Translucent Text Effects*

B9 *Creating Icons in Photoshop*

B10 *Making Web Banners with Layer Masks*

B11 *Creating Dither-Free Web Graphics*

B12 *Converting Pantone Colors to Web-Safe Colors*

CHAPTER TOOLBOX

Adobe Photoshop 4.0

Adobe Illustrator 7.0

IMAGES

Image Club, Studio Gear

Image Club, Photo Gear

Image Club, Object Gear

INPUT AND ILLUSTRATION 101

Before you begin creating graphics for the Web, you should become familiar with a number of important production details. For instance, how do you work with images of varying resolutions? What screen dimensions should your Web pages be so that users will not have to scroll to get important information? Below is a discussion of these issues as well as a handy top ten production list that you can use as a quick reference.

SCANNING FOR SUCCESS

Images for the Web should be 72 dpi screen resolution. Therefore, it is not necessary to scan images at very high resolutions. A good rule of thumb is to scan images at twice the resolution that you need them to be. So, if 72 dpi is your target, then you should scan at about 150 dpi. This is assumes that the image is the size (or larger) that you will be using on the screen. For instance, if you scan a tiny stamp and plan to use it at twice its size, you should double the scanning rule and scan the stamp at 300 dpi. Once you have scanned the image, save the original and use Photoshop to downsample a copy of the image to 72 dpi. Downsampling also helps sharpen any flaws in the scan.

WORKING WITH SCREEN RESOLUTION

Often when creating a collage of multiple photographs, you will deal with images that have different resolutions. This can pose problems when you start to combine images. For instance, regardless of an image's resolution, when it is dragged and dropped into another file, it will assume the other file's resolution.

So the best way to create a collage at the right resolution is to start with a new file in Photoshop that is set to 72 dpi. Then, drag the scanned images into the new file and use the Free Transform function in the Layers menu to scale them appropriately.

The first page of the *National Geographic Online* feature *Cats.*

DESIGNING AN INTERFACE WITH SCREEN SIZE IN MIND

One of the most overlooked Web design issues is designing Web pages that fit inside the user's browser window. Keep in mind that most people own 13-inch monitors. When you factor in the screen space that a browser interface takes, you are left with a space 600 x 350 pixels before users need to scroll. Therefore, try to design banners, navigational icons, and important information so that they fit within this space.

TOP TEN PRODUCTION TIPS

1. Always work in 72 dpi—the standard screen resolution of the Web.
2. When developing Web graphics, work in 24-bit, RGB mode.
3. Reducing images into a specific color palette is always the last production step before saving an image for the Web.
4. Save source files as layered Photoshop files. You never know when you will need to go back and make changes to your Web graphics.
5. Never flatten your Photoshop source files. Prepare them for the Web and then save over them. Always use the Save As feature.
6. Keep graphics as small as possible in terms of pixel dimension and file size. For example, if you are creating GIFs, never use right-to-left gradations, always make them top-to-bottom. This helps reduce file size.
7. Flat, solid areas of color reduce a file's size considerably.
8. Use the GIF file format for images featuring type, flat color, or crisp, well-defined images. Use the JEPG file format for organic, photographic-like images.
9. Keep important interface elements, text, and graphics of your Web page layout within the 600 x 350-pixel area. Most users have small monitors, and will have to scroll to see additional information
10. Use transparent GIFs whenever possible; the transparency helps to reduce file size. However, if you use transparency, be sure to prepare the files correctly (see Chapter D, *Creating Interface Elements*).

Session

B1 Illustrating with Illustrator

Rather than scanning images and then retouching them in Photoshop, you can create realistic Web illustrations by using Illustrator and Photoshop. Because Illustrator is vector-based, it is excellent for illustrating geometric objects such as cars, houses, and in this case, guns. In *Suspect, Murder on the High Seas*, an online murder mystery game, all of the clues started as illustrations in Illustrator before being rasterized—converted from vector-based art into bitmap-based images—in Photoshop for finishing touches.

ADOBE ILLUSTRATOR 7.0
ADOBE PHOTOSHOP 4.0

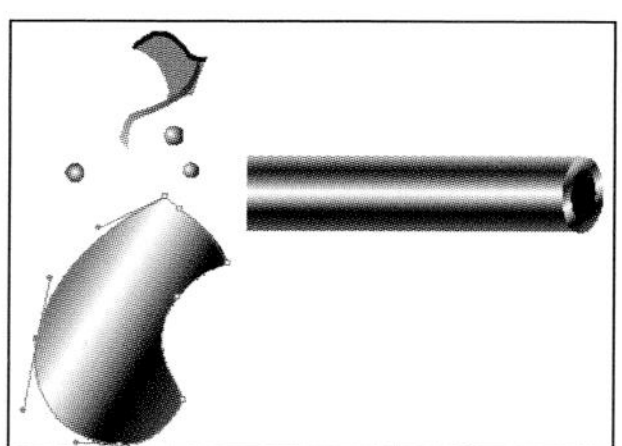

STEP 1: CREATING AN ILLUSTRATION IN ILLUSTRATOR

Open Illustrator and begin illustrating the various segments of the gun. For curved portions, such as the handle, use the Pen tool to outline the shape. When setting each point, click and hold to drag the handles that will define the arc of each curve. Beziér curves are little tricky, so you may want to try drawing curvy shapes using the Pencil tool. Use the Ellipse and Rectangle tools to draw the barrel of the gun and the barrel opening.

TIP: *You can combine two shapes by selecting both with the Selection tool, and then choosing Pathfinder > Unite from the Object menu. Likewise, you can use one shape to trim another by selecting both shapes and then choosing other filters from the Pathfinder menu.*

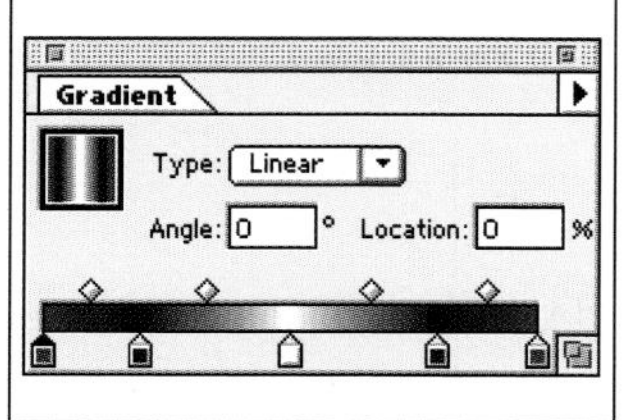

STEP 2: CREATING CUSTOM GRADIENTS

To create a custom gradient for the gun illustration, open the Gradient palette from the Window menu. Select the left-most triangle in color scale and set it to black by clicking on the black color swatch just below the color scale. Adjust the opacity of both end triangles to about 80% black. Add three more triangle points along the slider. Set the outer two trianngles to 100% black and the center triangle to 100% white as shown. Click the New button at the bottom of the Swatches palette to create a new gradient. You can double-click on the swatch to give is a name such as "Chrome."

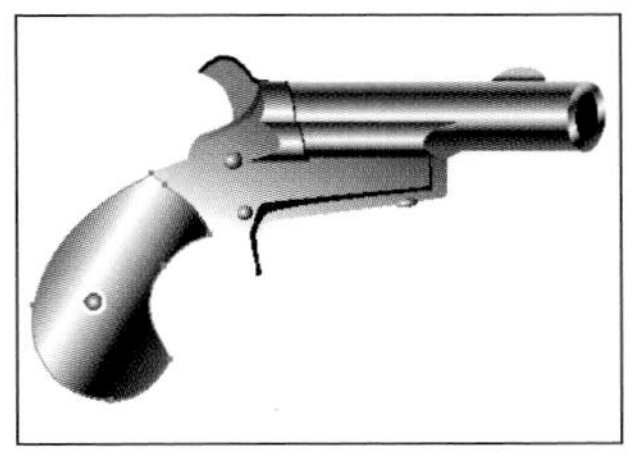

STEP 3: ASSIGNING GRADATIONS TO OBJECTS

Select individual shapes of your illustration and fill them by clicking on the Chrome gradient in the Swatches palette. You can direct the direction and length of the gradient by using the Gradient tool.

NOTE: *You do not need to be accurate about colorizing your Illustrator illustration. Simply apply the basic color scheme. For instance, the gun handle in this example will be heavily touched up later in Photoshop.*

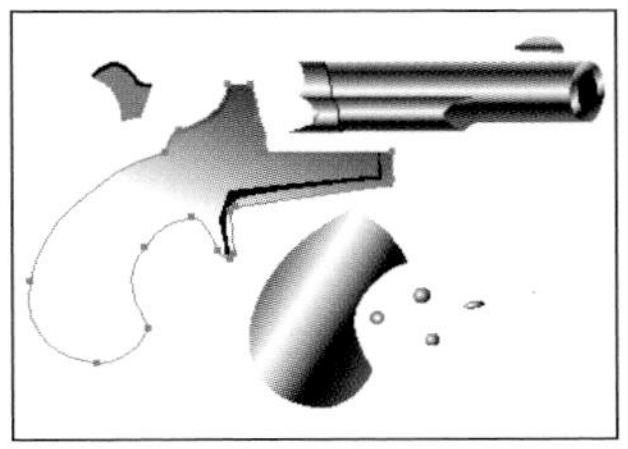

STEP 4: CREATING TWO COPIES OF THE ILLUSTRATION

Once the illustration is complete, save it, and then pull apart the component parts. Save the pulled-apart version under a different name. It is a good idea to pull apart an illustration because when Photoshop rasterizes graphics from Illustrator, it places them on a transparent layer. With all the component graphics separated on a transparent background, editing each one is easy.

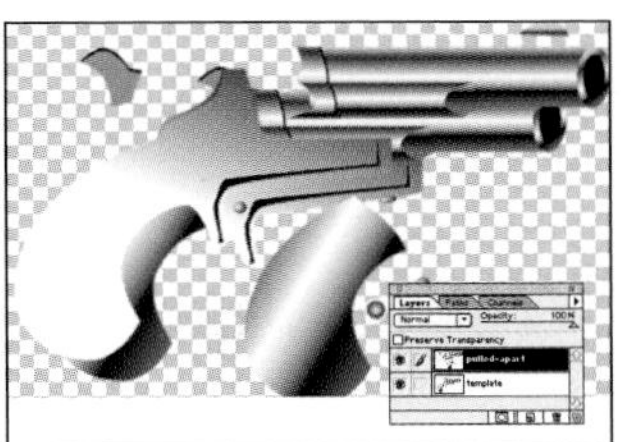

STEP 5: RASTERIZING IN PHOTOSHOP

Open both the intact and pulled-apart illustrations in Photoshop. In the Rasterize Generic EPS Format dialog box that appears, set the resolution to 72 dpi—the standard for Web graphics. Leave the height and width settings as they are and click OK.

Use the Move tool to drag the intact illustration to the pulled-apart illustration's window so that the two files are combined in one document on two layers. Position the intact layer underneath so that it can be used as a template to reassemble the component pieces in the pulled-apart version.

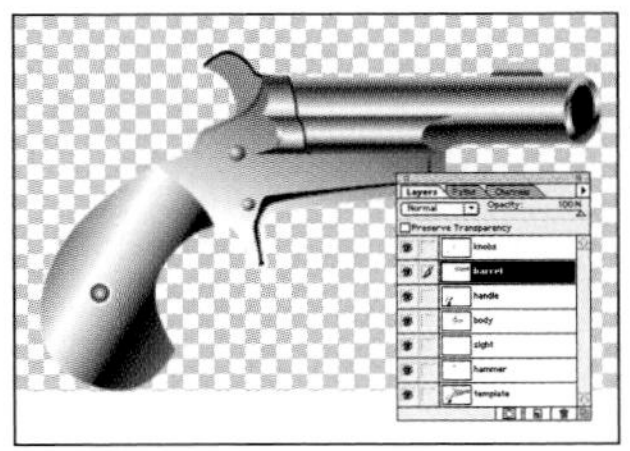

STEP 6: REASSEMBLING THE ILLUSTRATION

In order to reassemble the gun, you need to separate the component pieces into their own layer to enable you to use the Move tool to reposition them. To separate the component pieces into their own layer, use the Lasso tool and loosely select each piece. After selecting a piece, choose New > Layer Via Cut from the Layer menu. Once each piece is in its own layer, you can re-position it with the Move tool, using the intact illustration as a guide.

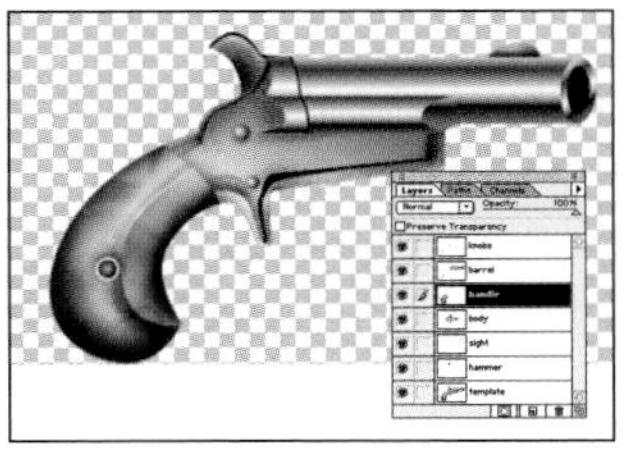

STEP 7: CREATING TWO COPIES OF THE ILLUSTRATION

Touch up each layer with a combination of painting tools and filters. Because each component piece is on its own layer, you can use Preserve Transparency (see Session B5) to assist in the editing process.

In this example, the gradation on the gun handle was fixed with the Airbrush tool, and then a filter was applied to achieve the pearled effect.

Session

B2 Illustrating with Photoshop

Puma by Lisa Lopuck for *National Geographic Online, Cats.*

Rather than scanning images into Photoshop and then touching them up, you can create illustrations from scratch directly in Photoshop. By using a variety of tools such as paths, multiple layers, preserve transparency, and custom brushes, traditional illustrators find Photoshop to be a powerful painting tool—especially when combined with the use of a pen digitizing tablet. This puma illustration for the *National Geographic Online,* Cats feature was created entirely in Photoshop starting with only a scan of a faxed sketch.

ADOBE PHOTOSHOP 4.0

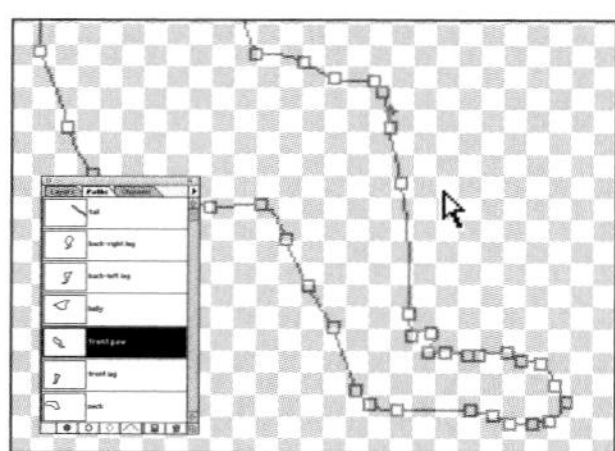

STEP 1: USING PATHS TO CREATE ACCURATE SELECTIONS

Start the illustration by creating a template sketch in one layer. This quickly maps out the proportions and lines of your illustration. In this case, a fax was scanned in and used as the template sketch.

Using the Path tool, draw an outline around just a portion of the illustration. You do not need to create the final illustration on one layer. In fact, it is simpler to concentrate on one portion at a time and keep each portion in a separate layer. Save each path by double-clicking on it in the Paths palette and giving it a name.

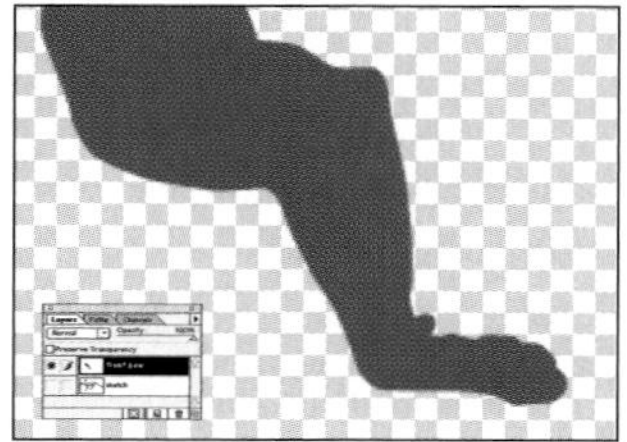

STEP 2: BUILDING AN IMAGE LAYER BY LAYER

Turn the path into an active selection by holding down the Command key (Mac), or the Control key (Windows), and then clicking on the path's icon in the Paths palette; or, you can choose Make Selection from the Path palette's pop-up menu. The selection settings should include a feather radius of zero with anti-aliasing turned on.

Create a new layer in the Layers palette and fill the selection with a solid, medium-value color.

Continue to outline each section of the illustration with the Path tool. Save each path as you create it, turn it into a selection, and then fill it with a medium-value color in each new layer.

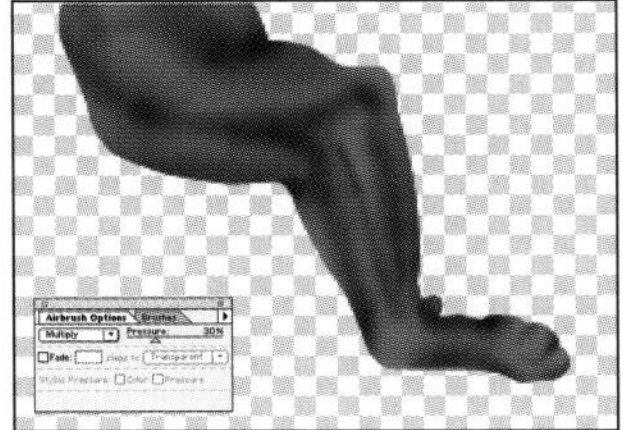

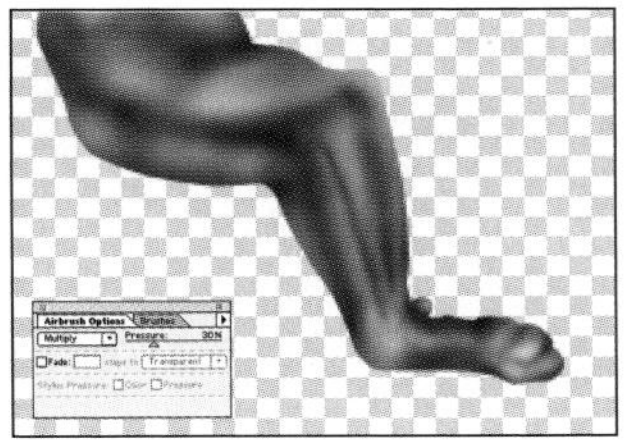

STEP 3: USING THE PAINT TOOLS TO ADD TONE

Once all portions of the illustration are in separate layers, you can begin to add initial lights and darks using the Airbrush and Paintbrush tools. Select the layer you want to paint first. Turn on the Preserve Transparency checkbox in the Layers palette so you do not over paint into the transparent background.

Paint the shadows first. For natural shadow effects, set the brush mode to Multiply in the Brush Options palette. Then, add the highlights by using either the Lighten Only or Overlay modes. Notice how quickly the image comes to life with just lights and darks!

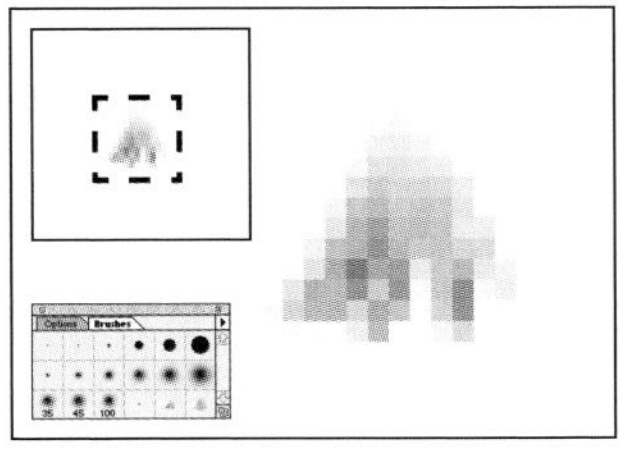

STEP 4: CREATING CUSTOM BRUSHES

To add realistic finishing effects, you can create a custom brush that has a specialized texture for your illustration. In this case, the puma needed a brush with a natural hair texture.

Using the Paintbrush tool with a small brush and black paint, illustrate a small texture as shown. Select the texture, and then choose Define Brush from the Brushes palette's pop-up menu. Your new custom brush now appears in the palette.

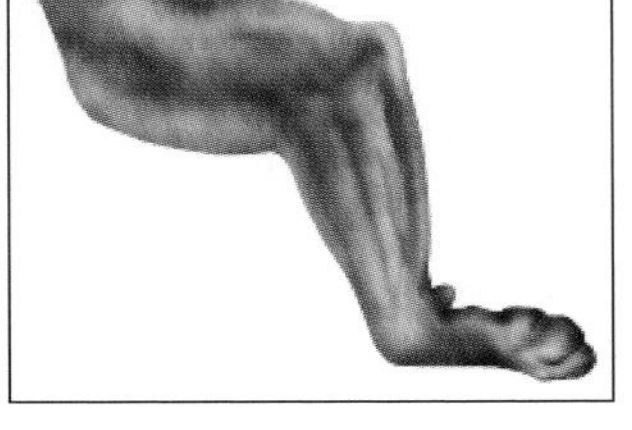

STEP 5: FINAL PAINTING DETAILS

Using the Multiply mode to create detail shadows and the Overlay mode to create detail highlights, use the custom brush to add texture, creating the final look.

NOTE: *For this illustration, Preserve Transparency was turned off during the final stage to get soft, hair-like edges.*

Session

B3 "Indiana Jones" Text Effects

In the navigation bar for *Suspect*, an online murder mystery, distorted *Indiana Jones*-like titles appear when the mouse rolls over each character's image. These names were first created in Illustrator, as demonstrated below, before using Photoshop for finishing touches. Distorted graphic text is a nice way to embellish a Web site's headlines or icon labels.

ADOBE PHOTOSHOP 4.0
ADOBE ILLUSTRATOR 7.0
Font: Bodega Sans

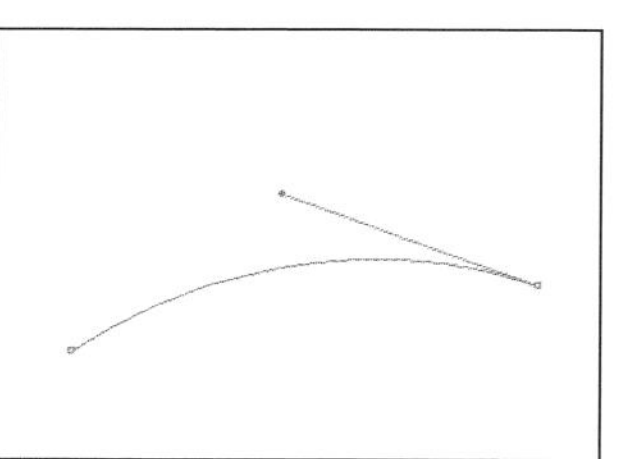

STEP 1: CREATING A PATH IN ILLUSTRATOR

Using the Pen tool in Illustrator, create a two-point arc. Click once to set the first point, and then click and hold on the second point, while dragging out a nice arc. This path becomes the baseline of your text.

STEP 2: TYPING TEXT ON A PATH

Select the Path Type tool. (To do this you need to click and hold the Type tool, and then select it from the pop-up list.) With the Path Type tool selected, click on the beginning of the arc you created in Step 1, a flashing text cursor should now appear. Type in a short phrase.

TIP: *For best results, select a medium to heavy weight font. Thin fonts may become unreadable when distorted.*

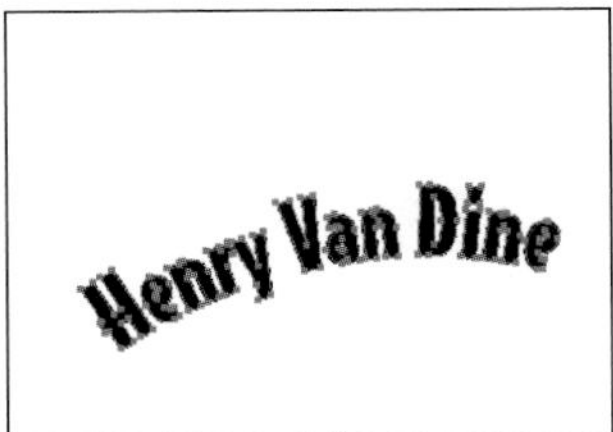

STEP 3: CREATE OUTLINES OF THE TEXT

Change to the Selection tool. If the text object is not already selected, click on it to make it active. From the Type menu, choose Create Outlines. This converts the text characters into path objects. Immediately group these objects by choosing Group from the Object menu.

NOTE: *The benefit of converting text to outline paths is that you no longer need the font installed on your machine to view it properly on the screen, and you can distort it freely. The drawback, however, is that once text is converted, it is no longer editable. For this reason you may want to save a copy of the file before converting any text to outlines.*

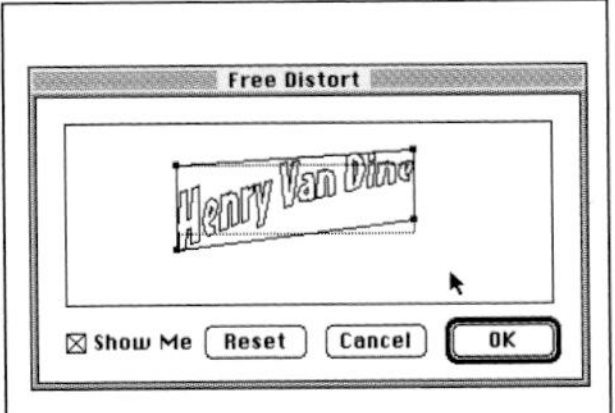

STEP 4: DISTORTING TEXT

Now you can distort the text with the Free Distort filter. First select the text grouping with the Selection tool, and then choose Free Distort from the Filter > Distort menu. A window appears the displays your text within a rectangular envelope with corner points. Pull on the corner points until you get the desired distortion, and then click OK.

STEP 5: PREPARING FOR PHOTOSHOP

Save the file. Open it from within Photoshop; or, if you have Photoshop open and can see a Photoshop window in the background behind your Illustrator window, you can drag and drop the text directly into the Photoshop window.

TIP: *Fill the text with black and be sure that there is no stroke. You can always colorize it later in Photoshop, see Session* B4.

Session

B4 Using Preserve Transparency for Color Correction

When creating Web graphics in Photoshop, you often will need to change the color scheme of both text and graphical elements—filling them with Web-safe colors (see Session F2) so they will not dither when viewed on the Web. By using the Preserve Transparency function in the Layers palette, in conjunction with the selection tools, you can quickly recolor images and text that are on a transparent layer. In this session, you will learn how to use the Preserve Transparency function to create a 3D "splat" button from scratch.

ADOBE PHOTOSHOP 4.0 Font: Fragile

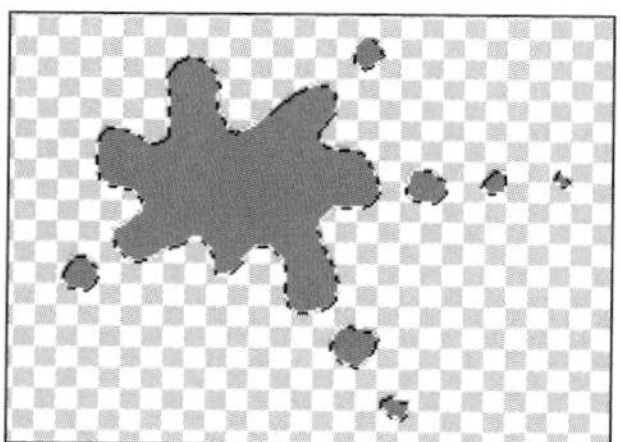

STEP 1: CREATE A SPLAT-SHAPED SELECTION

Make a new Photoshop file and using the Lasso tool, draw a splat-shaped selection on a transparent layer. Add splatter to the selection by holding down the Shift key and drawing in additional selections as shown.

Be sure the Preserve Transparency checkbox in the Layers palette is unchecked and fill the selected area with a medium-value color. Release the selection.

NOTE: *The Preserve Transparency checkbox applies only to the current selected layer.*

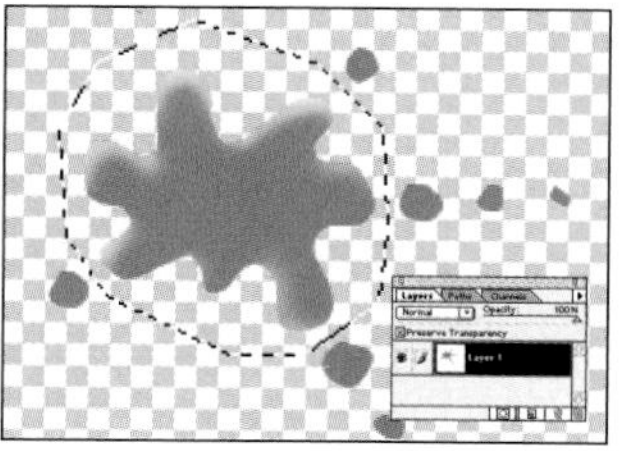

STEP 2: ISOLATING AREAS WITH SELECTIONS

Turn on Preserve Transparency in the Layers menu. Using the Airbrush tool, set on a medium-sized brush, paint a light color highlight on the upper left edges of the splat-shaped image. Notice that this action does not paint on the transparent background surrounding the splat.

To prevent painted color from being applied to other areas of an image, draw a loose selection around the area in which you want to work. The selection does not have to be accurate, it just needs to contain your work area.

STEP 3: PAINTING HIGHLIGHTS AND SHADOWS

Contain each area of the splat image with loose selections and Preserve Transparency. Within each area, use the Airbrush to add highlights to the upper left edges and shadows to the lower right edges until the splat looks three dimensional.

> **TIP:** *Try using the Gradation tool to apply a dark to light gradation on one of the splatter marks. Simply lasso the area containing the splatter and apply the gradation. If Preserve Transparency is turned on, only the splatter mark—not the area selected—will fill with the gradation.*

STEP 4: COLORIZING TYPE

Now that you have used Preserve Transparency in combination with selections to edit the splat button illustration, try using this technique to change the colorization of design elements.

Set the foreground color to black, and use the Type tool to create a text label for the splat button. Notice that after you create a text element, it becomes its own layer with Preserve Transparency automatically turned on.

Select a new foreground color (to select a Web-safe color see Session B11), and with no selection made, simply choose Fill from the Edit menu to replace the text color.

CAVEATS

Knowing when and when not to use Preserve Transparency comes with experience. However, the following situations highlight when Preserve Transparency should be turned off.

- Be sure to turn off Preserve Transparency before applying a filter such as Gaussian Blur. Preserve Transparency prevents any softening to bleed over into the transparent background surrounding an image, as shown in the drop shadow created for the splat.
- Preserve Transparency should be turned off if you intend to select and move a portion of an image. Photoshop creates a Floating Selection of the moved portion, which when dropped, becomes a second layer.

Session

B5 From Grayscale Scan to Colorized Overlay

Working from a black and white photo stat of the Torani logo, it was possible to seemlessly integrate it into their Web site design.

Often a company's logo, icons, or drawings exist only on paper in black and white. So how do you get these images onto the screen in dither-free, Web-safe color, superimposed on other images or colored backgrounds? The trick is to use Photoshop channels. In this example, the Torani logo existed as black-and-white line art that was first scanned, and then integrated into a home page design.

ADOBE PHOTOSHOP 4.0

STEP 1: SCANNING ART INTO PHOTOSHOP

Scan a logo or other art. It doesn't matter if the art is black and white—in fact black and white or grayscale is easier to work with. Open the scanned image in Photoshop. Depending on the type of image, you may want to adjust the contrast, using the Levels adjustment, until the image is pure white and pure black (as in this example). Select and copy the entire image.

STEP 2: GETTING THE LOGO ONTO A TRANSPARENT LAYER

In the Channels palette, create a new blank channel and paste the image in. Invert the image so that the text or logo is white on a black background by choosing Adjust > Invert from the Image menu. Load the channel as an active selection by choosing Load Channel from the Select menu. Once the channel is loaded as a selection, you may need to reselect the RGB channel at the top of the palette.

TIP: *To quickly load a channel as a selection, you can click the Load Channel as Selection button at the bottom left of the Channel palette.*

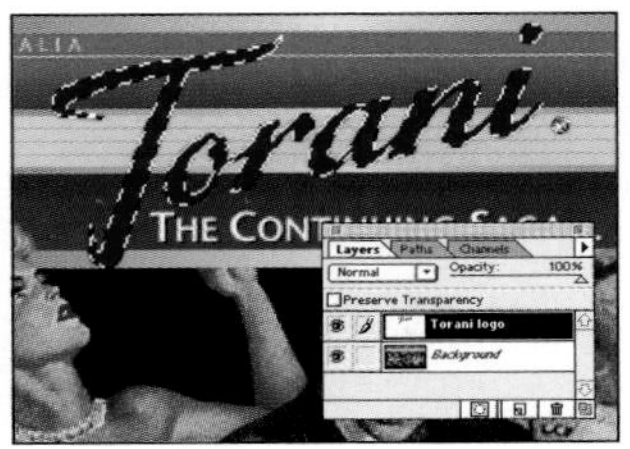

STEP 3: GETTING THE LOGO ONTO A TRANSPARENT LAYER

Switching to the Layers palette, create a new layer and fill the active selection with a Web-safe color. You now have the logo, filled with a color of your choice, on top of a transparent background under which you can insert any background.

TIP: *You can always change the color of an image on a transparent layer. With no selection whatsoever, simply check the Preserve Transparency checkbox at the top of the Layers palette, and choose fill from the Edit menu. To quickly fill with the foreground color, press Option+Delete keys (Mac), or Alt + Delete keys (Windows).*

STEP 4: CREATING A DROP SHADOW FOR THE LOGO

Now that the logo is in a transparent layer, it is easy to make an "instant" drop shadow for it (see Session B2). In this example, the drop shadow is not blurred, simply offset and filled with a new color.

Session

B6 Creating Channels for 3D Text Effects

Creating custom three-dimensional text elements for a Web site is as easy as mastering a few channel processing techniques. After you learn how to prepare channels for the two different effects described in this session, you can expand and refine them to create your own signature text effects, such as the high-gloss, wet-paint look in Session B7.

ADOBE PHOTOSHOP 4.0	Photogear, Underwater Life: Reef 1
ADOBE ILLUSTRATOR 7.0	Font: Adobe Garamond Condensed

STEP 1: CREATING BLACK-AND-WHITE TEXT IN A CHANNEL

Open a new Photoshop file and create a channel in the Channels palette. Set white as the foreground color and type a short phrase directly onto the new channel as shown. For best results, use a medium to heavy weight font. For reference, name the channel "Original Text."

TIP: *To expand your typographical capabilities, you can create text artwork in Illustrator and bring it into Photoshop. In Illustrator, create black text, turn it into outlines by choosing Create Outlines from the Type menu, and then save it as a normal Illustrator file. Open the text from within Photoshop, invert it so that the text is white on a black background, and finally copy and paste it into a new channel.*

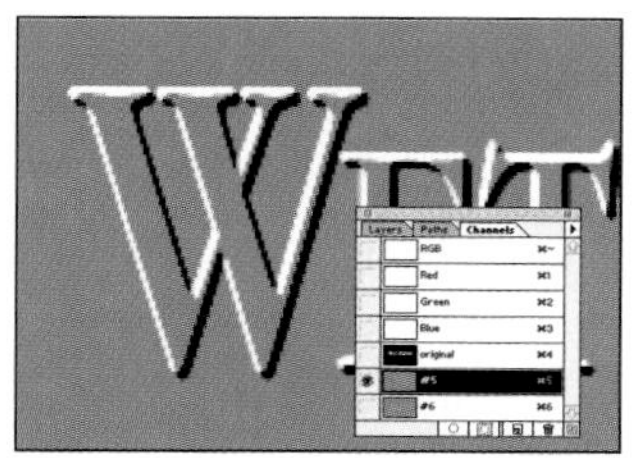

STEP 2: EMBOSSING TEXT IN A CHANNEL

Duplicate the original text channel and apply the Emboss filter from the Filter > Stylize menu. Depending on the size of your text, the Emboss settings shown may or may not work. Choose an Emboss height and angle that make your text appear evenly chiseled. Duplicate the embossed channel so that you now have a total of three channels: the original text, and two copies of the embossed channel. Name the two embossed channels "Highlights" and "Shadows" respectively.

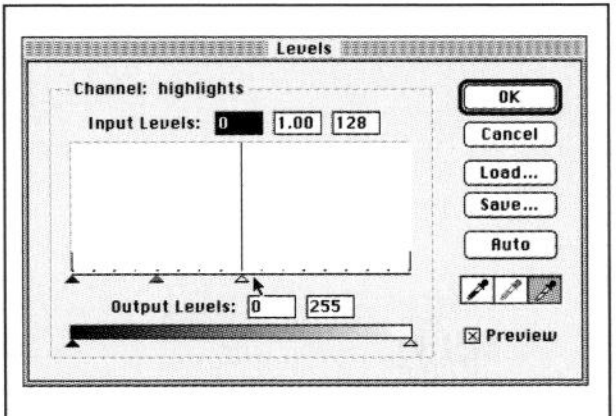

STEP 3: MAKING THE HIGHLIGHT CHANNEL

Select the Highlights channel in the palette and make sure no pixels of the image are selected. Using the Levels function found in the Image > Adjust menu, move the white triangle slider towards the center until all of the gray background lightens to pure white—leaving you with a black-and-white channel. Click OK. Now Invert the image so that the background is black with little white highlights around the edges of the letters.

TIP: *To quickly lighten the gray to white, choose the white Eyedropper tool in the Levels dialog box, and then click in the gray background of the embossed channel.*

STEP 4: MAKING THE SHADOW CHANNEL

Just as with the Highlights channel, select the Shadows channel and open the Levels function. This time, slide the left-most black triangle toward the center to darken the gray background until it becomes pure black—again leaving you with a black-and-white channel. You do not need to invert this channel because the white pixels become the active selection, selecting the shadow edges of the letters.

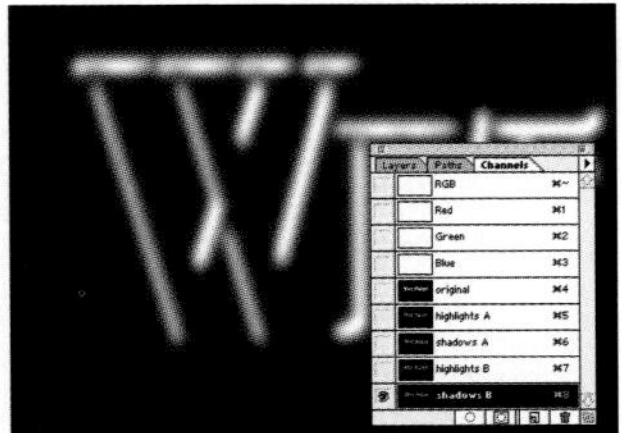

STEP 5: SOFTENING AND TRIMMING THE CHANNELS

Apply the Gaussian Blur filter, with a radius of two to three pixels, to both the Highlights and Shadows channels to soften them. Then make a duplicate set of the Highlights and Shadows channels so that you can apply two different trim options. Name the two sets "Highlight A" and "Shadow A," and "Highlight B" and "Shadow B."

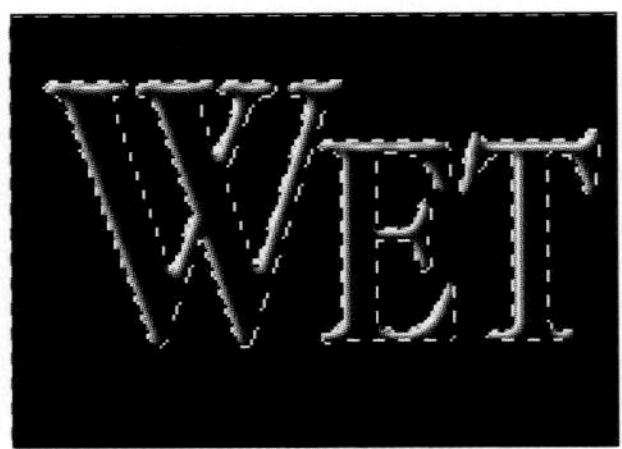

TRIM OPTION A: ROUNDED, 3D TEXT

Load the Original Text channel as a selection and invert it by choosing Invert from the Select menu. Select the Highlight A channel and fill the selection with black. This trims any blurring outside of the letter forms. With the selection still active, select the Shadow A channel and fill it with black to trim it as well.

TRIM OPTION B: TRANSLUCENT WATERMARK

Load the Original Text channel as a selection. Do not invert it. Select the Highlight B channel and fill the selection with black—filling in the letter forms. Select the Shadow B channel and fill with black as well.

You now have a series of channels that you can use to apply various three-dimensional text effects (see Sessions B7 and B8).

Session

B7 Applying 3D Glossy Text Effects

WET PAINT

You now can use the series of channels you created in Session B6 to apply custom 3D text elements to a Web page. Because you are working with channels, you can use the selections they generate to stamp out multiple text elements—each perhaps with a different color scheme; or, you can create an animation sequence of shimmering text by generating a series of channels with different highlight and shadow intensities. Note that while you can create instant 3D effects (see Session C3), using channels gives you greater control and flexibility over your effects.

ADOBE PHOTOSHOP 4.0 Font: Adobe Garamond Condensed

STEP 1: STARTING WITH THE ORIGINAL TEXT CHANNEL

Load the Original Text channel created in Session B6, and fill the selection it generates with a medium-value color on a new layer.

> **NOTE:** *Once you load a channel as a selection, you should always go through the following process in order to use it correctly on a layer:*
>
> 1. *In the Channels palette, click the top-most RBG icon so that a channel is not the active layer.*
> 2. *In the Layers palette, check which layer is active.*
> 3. *Either click on the layer where the selection will be used, or create a new layer.*

STEP 2: ADDING HIGHLIGHTS

Load the Highlight A channel as a selection. Navigate to the new text layer created in Step 1. Fill the selection with a lighter-value of the color you chose in Step 1.

STEP 3: ADDING SHADOWS

Load the Shadow A channel as a selection. Navigate to the new text layer and fill it with a darker-value of the color with which you have been working.

STEP 4: CREATING OPTIONAL HIGHLIGHTS

In this example, extra highlights were added by creating an extra channel. Open the Calculations function located in the Image menu. Set Source 1 as the Original Text channel and Source 2 as the Highlights A channel. Set Blending to Exclusion and click OK.

Invert the resulting new channel (with the Image > Adjust > Invert menu command) and name it "Gloss." Then, load the Original Text channel as a selection, Invert the selection (from the Select menu), and fill the background of the Gloss channel with black.

STEP 5: APPLYING THE OPTIONAL HIGHLIGHTS AND SHADOWS

Isolate each letter in the new channel with the Lasso tool and airbrush black over the letters, leaving the midsections and end points so that just the extreme highlights remain, as shown.

Load this edited channel as a selection. With the selection active, apply white with the airbrush to brighten just the extreme highlights of the channel for an added shine effect.

Load this modified channel as a selection, navigate to the Layers palette, and fill the selection with pure white.

Session

B8 Applying Translucent Text Effects

Following the directions in Session B6, you can create a series of channels that you can use to generate translucent text effects on top of any background. This technique is useful for embossing a logo, company name, or short text phrase on top of proprietary images as a watermark, or for simply creating interesting text banners for your Web site.

ADOBE PHOTOSHOP 4.0	Font: Overprint Photogear, Underwater Life: Reef 1

STEP 1: OPENING A BACKGROUND IMAGE

Open an image that will become the background of the translucent text. Copy it and paste it into the Photoshop document that contains either the channels you created in Session A6 or a new set of channels with different text. If you create a new set of channels, name them as you did in Session B6, Highlight A, Shadow A, and so forth.

STEP 2: LOADING THE HIGHLIGHT CHANNEL SELECTION

To create the translucent effect, you do not need to load the Original Text channel, only the Highlight A and Shadow A channels. Start by loading the Highlight A channel as a selection. Navigate to the Layers palette and create a new layer on top of the background image. Fill the selected area in the new layer with pure white.

STEP 3: LOADING THE SHADOW CHANNEL SELECTION

Load the Shadow A channel as a selection and navigate to the new layer created in Step 2. Fill the selected area with pure black.

Notice how the text immediately appears translucent. Also, because the 3D text is in a layer, you can insert any layer underneath and get the same effect, or you can move the text layer.

> **TIP:** *For an alternative effect, try loading Highlight B as a selection and filling it with white, and loading Shadow B and filling it with black. This produces an embossed, translucent effect.*

Session

B9 Creating Icons in Photoshop

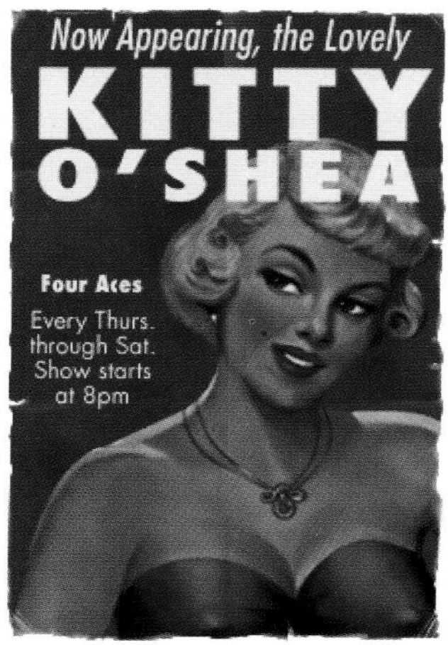

Creating interface elements for a Web site does not necessarily entail scanning existing artwork, or searching for the right clip art. You can create icons quickly in Photoshop without being an artist. This weathered poster graphic was created from scratch with selection tools, the paint brushes, and layers. You can insert a picture of anything you like, even your own photograph, to star in this poster.

ADOBE PHOTOSHOP 4.0 Font: Future Bold

STEP 1: STARTING WITH A SELECTION

Create a new layer. Using the Marquee selection tool, draw a rectangle the shape of your poster and fill it with a solid color.

To make the edges of the poster appear ragged, trim them using the Lasso tool. With the Lasso tool set to no feathering, and anti-aliasing on, draw a ragged edge around the poster. Invert the selection so that the background and a little bit of the poster's edge is selected as shown. Delete the contents of the selection.

STEP 2: WEATHERING THE EDGES

The Airbrush tool is used to create the look of old, weathered edges around the poster. Before you begin painting, check the Preserve Transparency checkbox in the Layers palette to prevent you from painting past the poster's edges.

Choose a light color that matches the poster color, and with a medium to small sized brush paint along the edges, just outside of the poster.

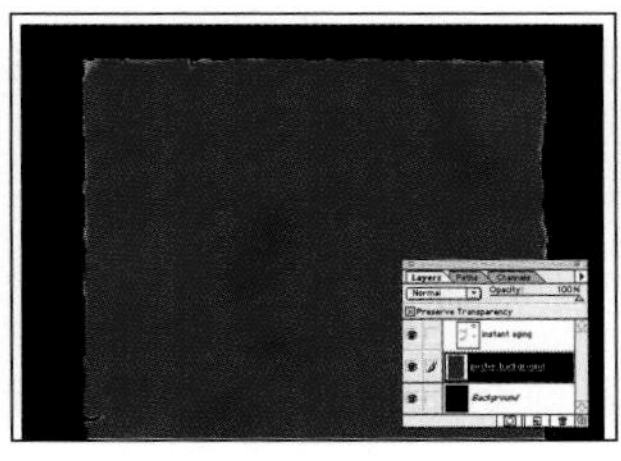

STEP 3: AGING THE POSTER

Create a new layer where you can add aging effects. With the Airbrush tool set on a large brush, select a darker color that matches the poster color and draw shadows onto the poster. You also can add highlights with a lighter color.

Don't worry if the shadows and highlights extend beyond the bounds of the poster. To trim them, create a clipping group with the underlying poster by holding down the Option key (Mac), or the Alt key (Windows) key while clicking on the line that separates the poster layer from the aging layer in the Layers palette.

TIP: *If the shadows and highlights that you create are too strong, you can adjust their intensities by selecting their layers and adjusting the Opacity slider in the Layers palette.*

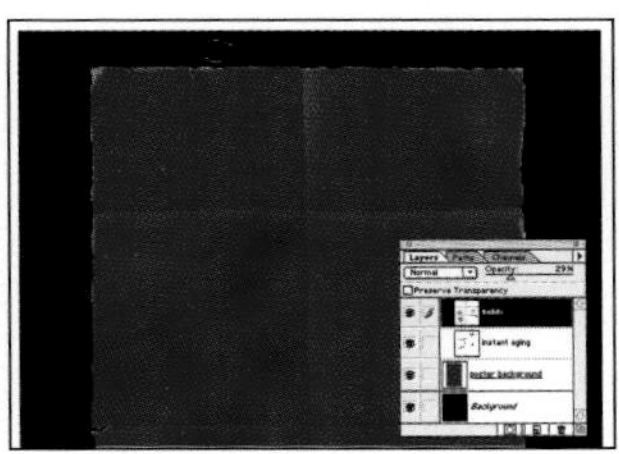

STEP 4: CREATING FOLDS IN THE POSTER

To create the illusion of folds in the poster, create a new layer. Make a hand-drawn, yet straight selection down the center of the poster with the Lasso tool. Use the Airbrush tool to spray a light color against the edge of the selection. Invert the selection, and use the Airbrush tool to spray a dark color against the opposite edge. Create the horizontal folds in the same manner. If the effect is too overpowering, adjust the opacity of the layer in the Layers palette.

Include the folds layer in the clipping group set by Option clicking (Mac), or Alt clicking (Windows) on the borderline that separates the fold layer from the layer below it.

STEP 5: ADDING TEXT AND IMAGES

Lastly, add text and images to the poster icon. To take advantage of the folds layer created in Step 4, reposition the image layer so that is below the folds layer in the Layers palette. Also, if the image extends beyond the bounds of the poster icon, include it in the clipping group as shown.

Session

B10 Making Web Banners with Layer Masks

Working with Photoshop layer masks enables you to create complex collages without actually cutting or erasing parts of your source imagery. Layer masks simply hide and show parts of an image. Using layer masks you have extensive creative control over your compositions, such as in this series of Web site banners. Each banner was created by using a variety of layer mask techniques. Then each banner shared the same layer mask to ensure a consistent gradated edge, fading to white.

ADOBE PHOTOSHOP 4.0
Photogear, Nature Collages: Green Leaves
Photogear, Mountainscapes: Mount 30
Photogear, Skyscapes: Skyscape 29
Photogear, Underwater Life: Coral 12
Object Gear, Travels: Shells On Sand
Font: Adobe Myriad Semi-bold Condensed

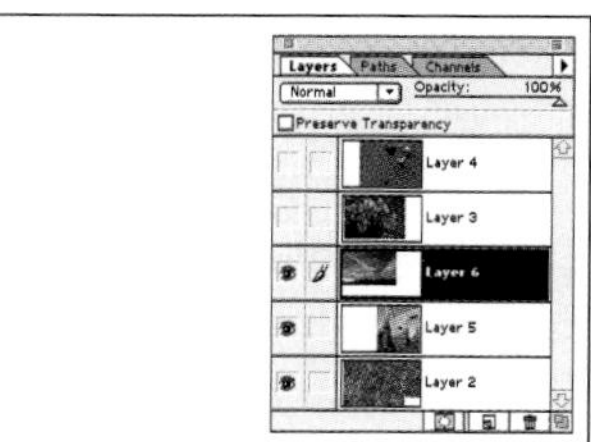

STEP 1: ASSEMBLING IMAGERY

Start by creating a new Photoshop file that is the width of your Web page, and the height of the banner space. Open all the source images that you will use in your collage. Using the Move tool, drag and drop all of the images into the new file's window so that each image is a new layer in the new Photoshop file. You may want to resize them as you go.

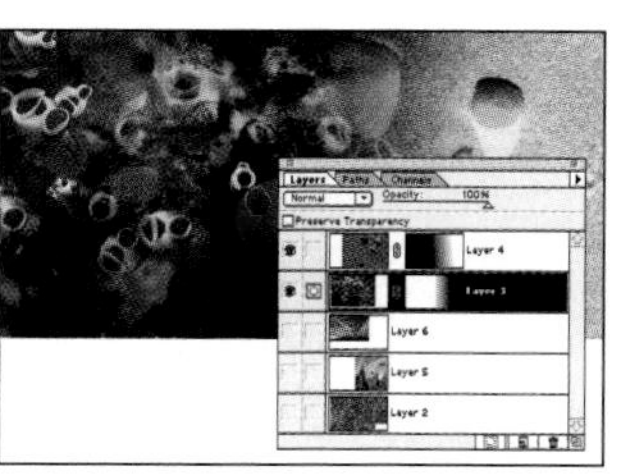

STEP 2: SETTING UP LAYER MASKS

Create a layer mask for the top-most layer by clicking once on the Add Layer Mask button at the bottom left of the Layers palette, or by choosing Add Layer Mask > Reveal All from the Layer menu. As we go, you will notice there are a variety of ways to generate layer masks.

NOTE: *A normal layer must be selected to create a layer mask. A background layer cannot have a layer mask.*

To edit the layer mask, be sure to click and highlight its icon in the Layers palette. Select the Airbrush tool, select a large brush, and set the foreground color to black. Begin painting on the layer mask. Notice that applying black paint is essentially applying transparency, while applying white paint brings the image back. Experiment by using the Gradation tool and other painting tools.

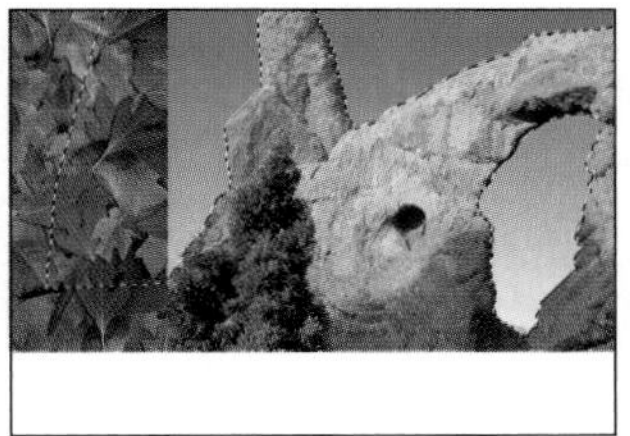

STEP 3: CREATING A LAYER MASK FROM A SELECTION

Another way to create a layer mask is to start with a selection. On one of the other layers, create a selection around a portion of the image you want to remain visible. Invert the selection, and then click the Add Layer Mask button in the Layers palette. The selection automatically becomes the masked area. For a soft-edged effect, feather the selection before creating the layer mask; or, if you have already created the layer mask, release the selection and apply a blur filter to the mask.

TIP: *To turn on and off the effects of a layer mask, hold down the Shift key and click the layer mask's icon in the Layers palette.*

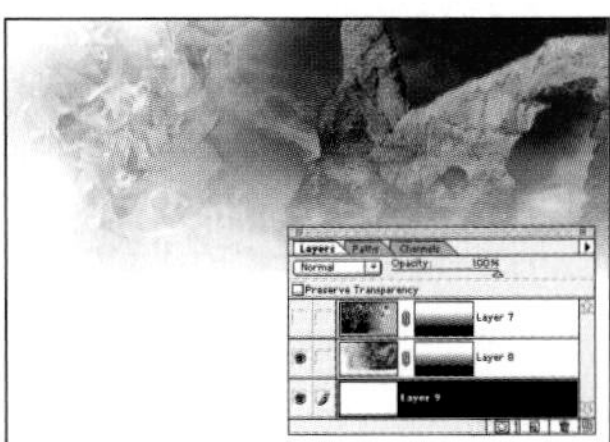

STEP 4: PASTING IMAGES INTO LAYER MASKS

Now that the a collage is complete, merge its layers together into a single layer. Then create another layer mask with a simple gradation. To copy this layer mask and use it on the other collage in the same document, first Option click (Mac), or Alt click (Windows) on the layer mask, this allows you to select and copy the contents of the layer mask and not the image. Then copy the layer mask and create a new blank layer mask on another merged collage layer. Option click on the blank layer mask and paste.

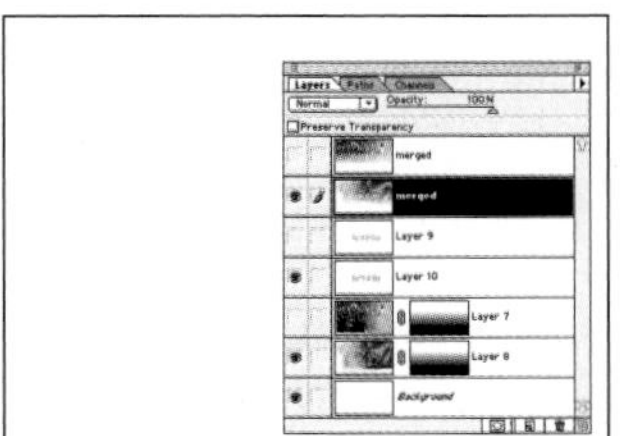

STEP 5: FINALIZING THE BANNER GRAPHICS

Once each collage banner shares the same layer mask, you can add a text headline. Finally, to process the banners for the Web, the collages need to be flattened Photoshop files. To save the layers and create a flattened version of the banner, first turn on the Eyeball icons of the layers to be merged, and then choose Copy Merged from the Edit menu.

NOTE: *An alternative to using the Copy Merge feature is the Option-Merge function that merges the selected layers onto a new layer in the same document (see Session C9). Option-Merge (merging layers while holding down the Option (Mac) or Alt (Windows) keys) is preferable when you have a series of merged layers that need to be cropped, such as an animation sequence.*

Session

B11 Creating Dither-Free Web Graphics

Spinner is the guide to the *Kid's Web Kit*, a book for kids interested in making their own Web pages.

To avoid dithering—the pointillism-like method of blending colors—in your Web graphics, you need to primarily use specific Internet Web-safe colors from a standardized 216-color table while you work in Photoshop. By loading these Web-safe colors into the Swatches palette in Photoshop, you can easily sample these colors and incorporate them into your graphics. This session demonstrates how to create a table of Web-safe colors and load them into your Swatches palette.

ADOBE PHOTOSHOP 4.0

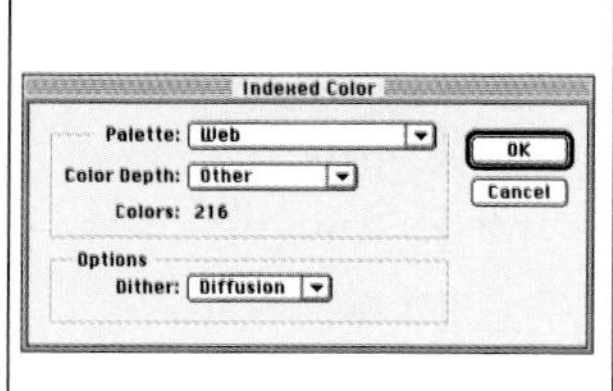

STEP 1: SWITCHING TO INDEX COLOR MODE

Before you can begin using the Web-safe colors in the Swatches palette, you need to create a Photoshop CLUT (color look-up table) file. This is done by saving the colors your used in an indexed image.

Open an image and change its mode to Indexed Color from the Image > Mode menu. In the Indexed Color dialog box, choose Web colors from the pop-up menu.

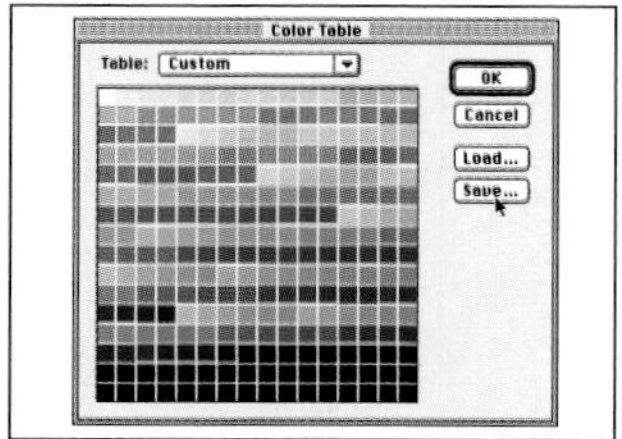

STEP 2: CREATING A WEB-SAFE COLOR TABLE

Now that the image has been indexed into Web colors, you can view and save them using the Color Table command found at the bottom of the Image > Mode menu. From here, click the Save button, name the color table "Web-safe," and put it some where easy to find. Close the image used to extract these colors now, without saving if you choose.

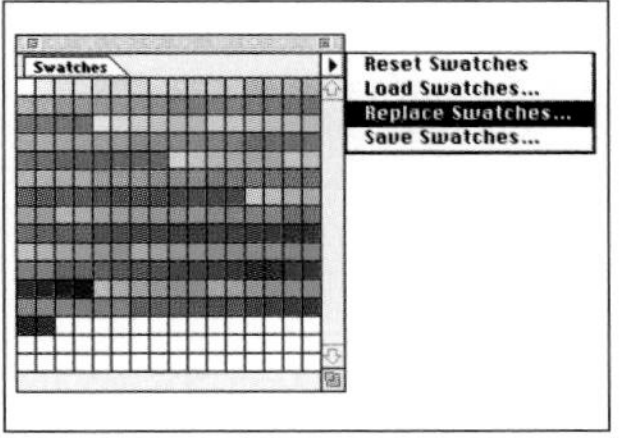

STEP 3: IMPORTING THE WEB-SAFE COLOR TABLE

To load the browser-safe color table into the Swatches palette, replacing the default colors, choose Replace Swatches from the Swatch palette's pop-up menu. Locate the browser-safe CLUT file and click OK.

STEP 4: SELECTING WEB-SAFE COLORS

With the browser colors loaded into the Swatches palette, choosing colors is easy. Regardless of what tool you have selected, when the cursor rolls over the Swatches palette, it temporarily turns into the Eye Dropper tool. Click a color to select it as your foreground color.

TIP: *If you have an image that is already colorized with flat, solid colors, it is easy to replace those colors with Web-safe colors. Select one of the colors in the image with the Magic Wand tool, set with a tolerance of zero and anti-aliasing turned off. Choose Similar from the Select menu. Choose a new Web-safe color from the Swatches palette and simply fill the selected area. To quickly fill with the foreground color, press Option + Delete (Mac), or Alt + Delete (Windows).*

Session

B12 Converting Pantone® Colors to Web-Safe Colors

The logo for Ejobs, Inc., an online job finding agency.

When a company wants to create a Web site, one of the first considerations is ensuring its brand is properly extended onto the Web. This includes proper representation of the company's logo, font usage, and company colors. Typically, a company's colors are described as PMS colors (Pantone Matching System). These colors are specified inks designed for the printing process, and not for display on a computer screen. Therefore, you may need to find Web-safe colors that closely match.

ADOBE PHOTOSHOP 4.0

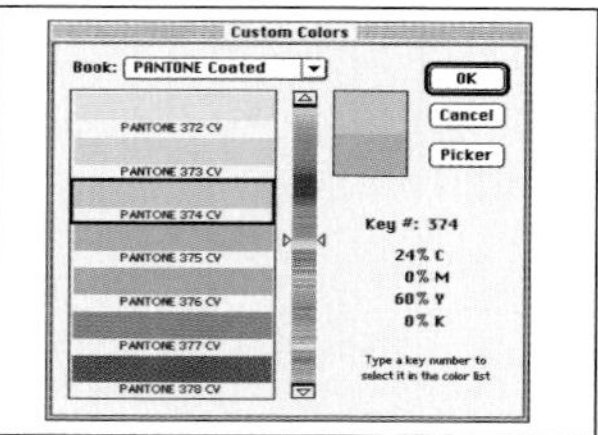

STEP 1: FINDING THE PANTONE COLOR IN PHOTOSHOP

You can use Photoshop to find a Pantone color using the Color Picker. Click on the foreground color swatch in the Tool palette to open the Color Picker dialog box. From there, click the Custom button. This displays a listing of custom color books to choose from, including a variety of Pantone color guides.

If you know the number of the Pantone ink color, you can type it in to quickly jump to it. Once you have selected a color, click OK.

NOTE: *Often times, the color appears different on screen from the printed version—depending on your individual monitor's display. These standardized computer color books tend to have the closest possible representation. You can always choose your own representation if you prefer.*

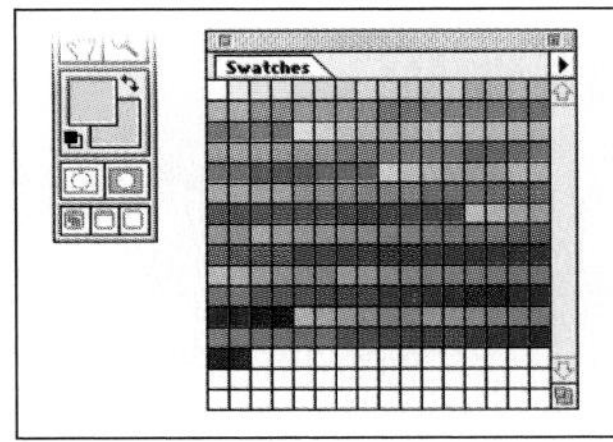

STEP 2: FINDING A SIMILAR WEB-SAFE COLOR

Switch the foreground and background color positions in the toolbar so that the selected Pantone color is the background color. (To do this, click on the bent double-headed arrow to the right of the color swatches in the Tool palette.)

Load the Web-safe color table into the Swatches palette following the directions in Session B11. With the Pantone color as the background color, choose a similar color from the Swatches palette. This color becomes the foreground color allowing you to compare it against the background Pantone color. Continue sampling colors from the Swatches menu until you find a close match.

STEP 3: CHANGING THE COLOR OF AN IMAGE

If the image, logo, or text element is on a transparent layer, changing its color to the new Web-safe color is simple. First make sure that the layer is selected in the Layers palette, then check the Preserve Transparency checkbox. Without any selection, choose Fill from the Edit menu, or use the keyboard combination Option + Delete (Mac), or Alt + Delete (Windows). This action fills the image with a solid Web-safe color.

NOTE: *If the image has multiple colors and exists on a single layer, you must first select the color region to be replaced. Use the Magic Wand tool or the Color Range command in the Select menu.*

Chapter C

Web Animation Techniques

Nothing adds more life to a Web site than animation. You can animate almost any part of a Web page including your entire interface, simple graphic headlines, or bullet points that introduce HTML text sections. From simple GIF animations to interactive Macromedia Flash and Macromedia Shockwave movies, this chapter teaches you how to design and prepare graphics for animation applications such as GifBuilder and Macromedia Director. Once you have created your animated graphics, look to Chapter I, "Adding Animation to Web Pages" and J, "Adding Audio and Video to your Site," to learn how to create Web-ready animation.

CHAPTER SESSIONS

C1 *The Option-Merge Technique*

C2 *Building an Animation in Photoshop*

C3 *Using Filters to Create a Simple Animation*

C4 *Creating Animated, Textured Type*

C5 *Not-So-Simple GIF Animation*

C6 *Avoiding Overlap in Animation*

C7 *Preparing Files for a QuickTime Movie*

C8 *Preparing Vector Graphics for Flash Animation*

C9 *Animating GIFs in a Table Structure*

CHAPTER TOOLBOX

Adobe Photoshop 4.0

Adobe Illustrator 7.0

IMAGES

Image Club, Photo Gear

Image Club, Object Gear

WEB ANIMATION 101

Animation on the Web takes many different forms—from Java to ActiveX to Flash. Fortunately, all of these forms require similar graphic production methods discussed at length in this chapter. For the most part, the differences in production are in the final output of animation frames; different animation forms require different color tables and file formats. By understanding the different animation forms currently available on the Web, and the type of graphics required by each, you can begin to efficiently integrate animation into the design of your Web sites.

ANIMATION TAKES MANY FORMS

With all the new technologies emerging everyday, it is difficult to stay up to speed with all of your animation options. The following is a short list of the current, more common, browsers supported forms of animation and the file formats that each require.

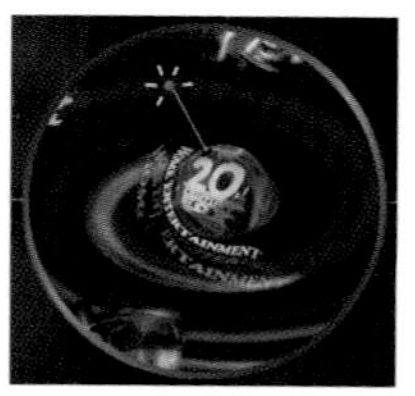

GIF ANIMATION

One of the simplest forms of animation is the GIF animation. GIF animation is built in to applications such as GifBuilder (see Session I 1), from separate GIF files prepared in a graphics application such as Photoshop.

NOTE: *While working with GIF files the term 8-bit occurs often. This refers to the color depth of an image having only 256 colors, as opposed to a 24-bit image that may contain over 16 million colors.*

SHOCKWAVE AND FLASH

Shockwave movies are exported from Macromedia Director files. Therefore, to create a Shockwave movie for the Web, you must first start with graphics that have been prepared for Director. Director requires either PICT (Macintosh) or Bitmap (Windows) files of any bit depth. To keep file size down, it is best to prepare 8-bit graphics.

Flash is a newer form of animation. It is created in a program available from Macromedia called Flash. Flash is unique in that it has the capability to utilize vector-based graphics generated in Illustrator and Freehand. Because vector graphics are significantly smaller in terms of file size than bitmap graphics, Flash animations are becoming increasingly popular. Prepare graphics for Flash as vector drawn illustrations saved as EPS files.

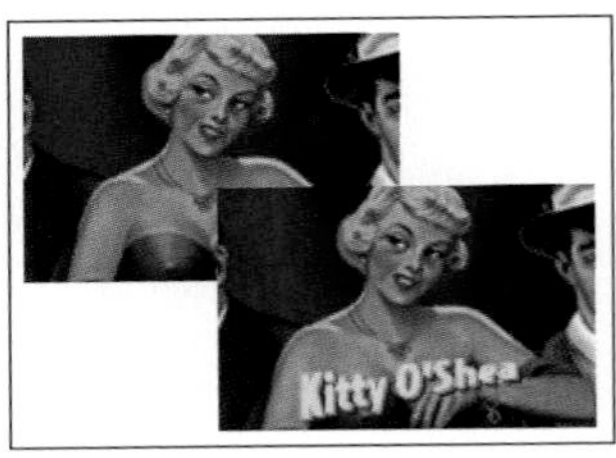

ACTIVEX

Microsoft's ActiveX controls come in a variety of shapes and sizes, and not all are geared towards animation. One that comes to mind, however, is the ActiveX HTML Layout control that allows you to create rollover and pop-up labels (see Session E6). Generally, ActiveX animation controls require either 8-bit Windows Bitmap files (.bmp) or GIF files (.gif).

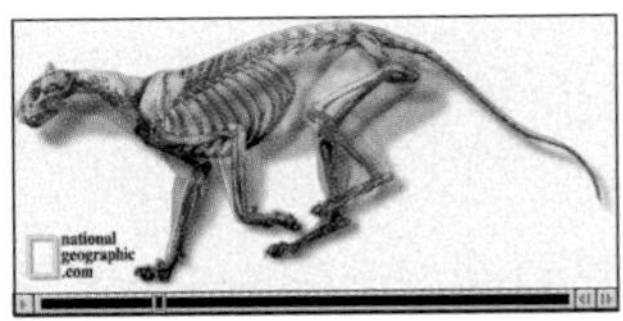

QUICKTIME MOVIES

One of the most overlooked forms of animation on the Web are inline and downloadable QuickTime movies. These movies can be prepared in both Adobe After Effects and Adobe Premiere. (See Chapter I, "Adding Animation to Web Pages," for hands-on sessions in using these programs to create movies ready for the Web.) Generally, graphics for QuickTime movies are prepared from 24-bit PICT or bitmap files (see Session C7).

QUICKTIME VR AND SURROUND VIDEO

Both Surround Video and QuickTime VR create two types of 3D image files: 360° panoramic vistas that you can pan around and look in any direction, and objects that you can rotate in a 3D space, viewing the object from any angle. Graphic files destined for Surround Video (an ActiveX control) should be saved as 24-bit bitmap files. Similarly, graphics for QuickTime VR should also be 24-bit, however, they should be saved in the PICT file (.pic) format and rotated 90° counterclockwise.

Session

C1 The Option-Merge Technique

The Photoshop Option-Merge technique is a way to merge layers into a new layer while keeping the original source layers intact. This technique is useful during Web graphic production because you can, from one Photoshop file, create source layers, merge them into different combinations, and then extract graphics to be processed for the Web. Generating animation frames into different layers of your Photoshop document is particularly useful. You can automate the Option-Merge process using the Photoshop Actions palette using a simple four-step process.

ADOBE PHOTOSHOP 4.0

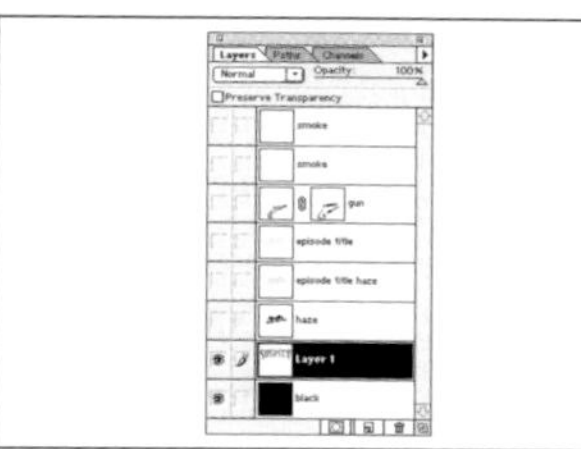

STEP 1: PREPARING LAYERS TO BE MERGED

Prepare layers for a normal merge by turning on only the Eyeball icons of the layers to be merged and making sure one of those layers is selected. Be sure that no layer's Eyeball icons are turned on if you do not want that layer merged.

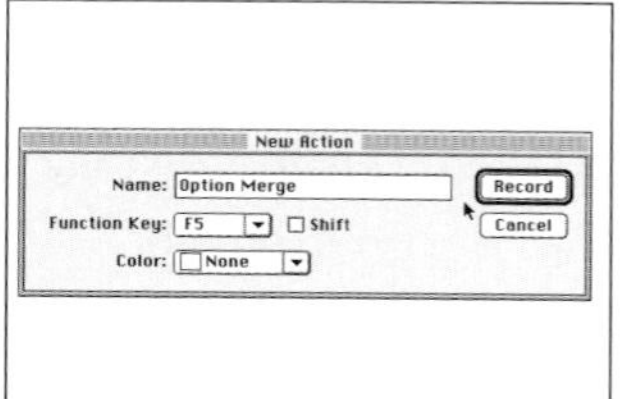

STEP 2: RECORDING THE NEW ACTION

Open the Actions palette from the Windows menu and choose New Action from the Actions palette's pop-up menu. In the dialog box, enter a new name for the action "Option-Merge," and assign a function key. Next click the Record button to begin recording the Option-Merge sequence.

NOTE: *There is no need to feel rushed to complete the sequence. The Actions palette does not record how long it takes you, simply the clicks and selections you make.*

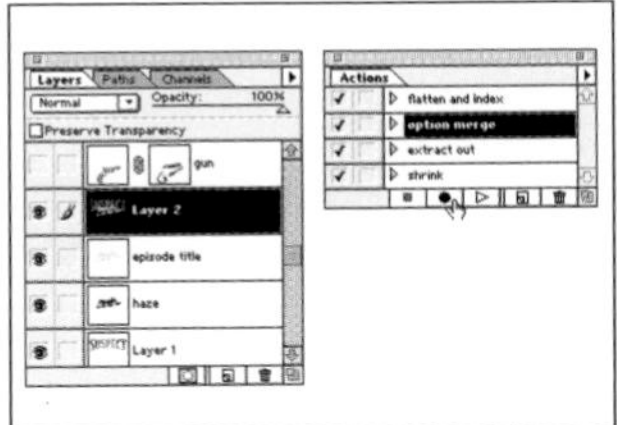

STEP 3: THE OPTION MERGE SEQUENCE

Now that the Actions palette is recording, go to the Layers palette and perform the following sequence:

1. Create a new layer. The new layer should automatically become the selected layer.
2. Hold down the Option key (Mac), or the Alt key (Windows), while you choose Merge Visible from the Layer palette's pop-up menu. Be sure to hold down the modifier key while choosing Merge Visible.
3. Click the Stop Recording button on the Actions palette to end recording the sequence.

STEP 4: TESTING THE OPTION-MERGE FUNCTION KEY

To test that you recorded the Option-Merge sequence correctly, first throw away the merged layer that resulted from recording the action in Step 3. Prepare the layers to be merged by turning on just the Eyeball icons of the layers to be included in the merge. Make sure one of these layers is actively selected, and then press the Function key that you assigned to the Option-Merge action. At the touch of the function key, the selected layers should merge into a new layer. If not, you may want to look at the action's recorded sequence in the Action palette to see that all the steps were recorded properly.

TIP: *The new, merged layer forms just above the layer that was active before you initiated the Option-Merge sequence. Therefore, to keep organized, it is a good idea to make sure the top-most layer to be merged is also the selected layer before you initiate the Option-Merge.*

Session

C2 Building an Animation in Photoshop

Suspect, the online murder mystery series, features an introductory Shockwave animtion, at *www.electravision.com*.

Most people don't think of Photoshop as an animation tool. However, Photoshop's layers provide a very effective way to create both the source files for an animation and the finished frames in the same document. The introductory animation for our *Suspect* site started out as one Photoshop document and with the help of Actions was quickly turned into a five-frame animation. Whether you are creating GIF animations, Flash or Shockwave movies, the following step-by-step process is the same.

ADOBE PHOTOSHOP 4.0

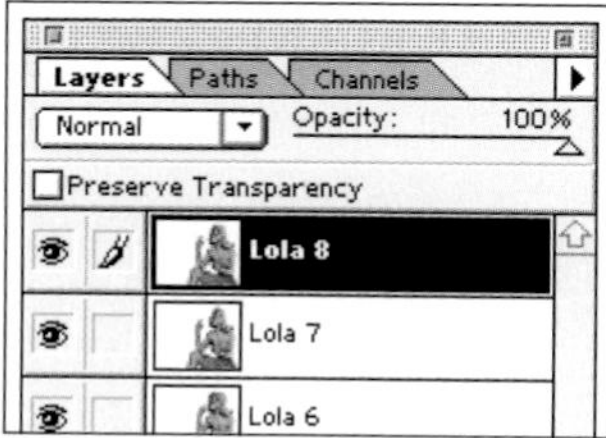

STEP 1: PREPARING LAYERS FOR A MERGE

Prepare a Photoshop file so that all the source images of your animation are in separate layers as shown.

Once all the source layers are prepared, merge the layers in different combinations to create the final animation frames. In the Layers palette, just as you would prepare a normal merge, turn on just the Eyeball icons of the source layers that comprise the first frame and make sure that you have selected one of those source layers.

STEP 2: MERGING LAYERS WITH THE OPTION-MERGE TECHNIQUE

If you merge the source layers, you loose the ability to recombine them to make other frames. Instead of merging these layers, do an Option-Merge (see Session C1). First create a new blank layer; it should be automatically selected. Then, hold down the Option (Mac) or Alt key (Windows), while choosing Merge Visible from the Layer palette's pop-up menu. Notice that the merge assembles on the blank layer, becoming frame 1 of your animation.

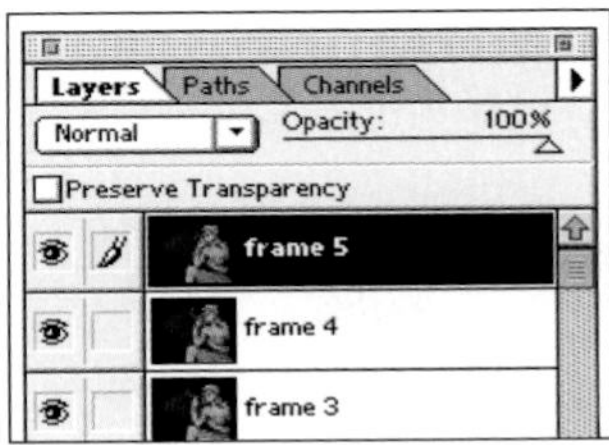

STEP 3: CREATING ANIMATION FRAMES IN LAYERS

Repeatedly using the Option-Merge technique, prepares all frames of your animation in different layers of the same Photoshop document. Be sure to turn off the Eyeball icon of each frame after creating it so that it does not become part of the next merge.

STEP 4: EXTRACTING ANIMATION FRAMES FROM LAYERS

After you have created all of the animation frames, select and copy each frame into its own new flattened file. In the end, you should have a separate Photoshop file for each frame of your animation. From here, you can process the files into a consistent color table (see Session F1), and save them in the correct file format. If your file's canvas size is larger than that required by the animation, make a rectangular selection and use it to copy the contents of each frame's layer.

NOTE: *If there is any transparency in the final frame layers, your animation's registration will be off. The selection tools ignore transparency and shrink to fit the contents of an image, thereby shifting registration. For tips on maintaining registration, see Session C9.*

Session

C3 Using Filters to Create a Simple Animation

Creating an animation sequence does not necessarily entail meticulously moving various aspects of each frame by hand. Nor does an animation need to be realistic, such as a moving car or a person waving. Often, simply distorting an icon or image is enough—especially where you just need to indicate that a button is clickable, or to provide feedback when a user clicks a button. In this session's simple four-step process, you can create a three-frame button animation using Photoshop's distortion filters.

ADOBE PHOTOSHOP 4.0	Object Gear: Culturals: Conch Shell Object Gear: Travels: Water Font: Adobe Chronos

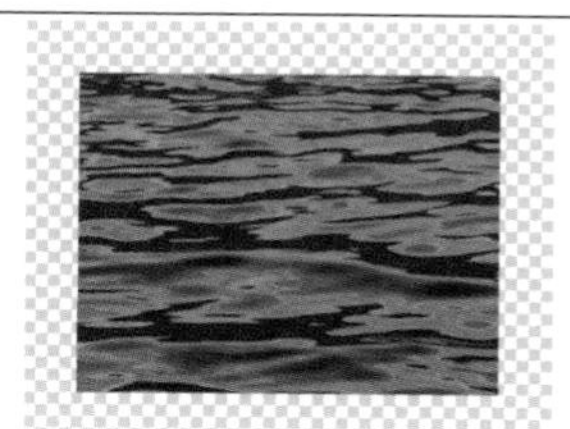

STEP 1: PREPARING GRAPHICS TO ANIMATE

When animating with the distortion filters, such as Twirl, Wave, Ripple, and Displacement, you can use just about any image and get great results. If, however, you are using a rectangular image, you may want to expand the canvas size to extend transparency all around the image. This gives the image room to distort cropping the edges of your workspace.

TIP: *Sometimes when you first open an image into Photoshop, it is flattened onto one opaque layer, indicated by the name* Background *in italics. To quickly transform a Background into a transparent layer, simply double-click on the layer's icon or its name in the Layers palette. Do this before you expand the canvas size.*

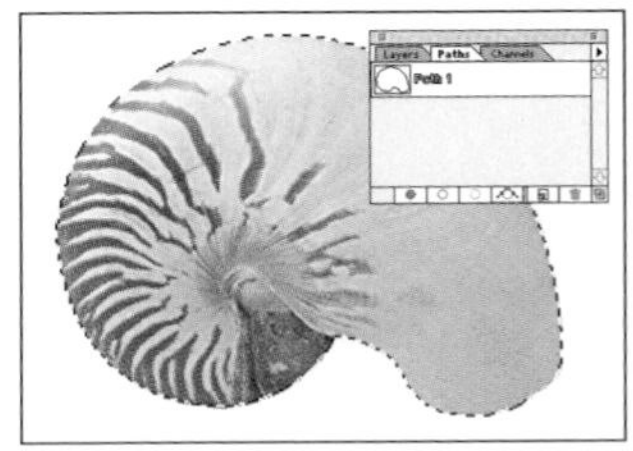

STEP 2: ERASING A BACKGROUND SURROUNDING AN IMAGE

Whether you are working with an irregular, shaped image or a rectangular image, you need to be sure that it is on a transparent layer. Even though you may have changed a background layer into a transparent layer, Photoshop does not automatically erase a solid background color surrounding an image. You must select the background color and delete it so that the object is surrounded by transparency.

When working with Image Club graphics, it is easy to float the image onto a transparent background. In the Paths palette, you'll find a perfect path selection. Turn the path into an active selection by Command (Mac) or Control (Windows) clicking it. Choose New > Layer Via Copy from the Layer menu, or simply use the keyboard shortcut Command + J (Mac), or Control + J (Windows). Once the image is copied safely to its own layer, you can throw away the original layer.

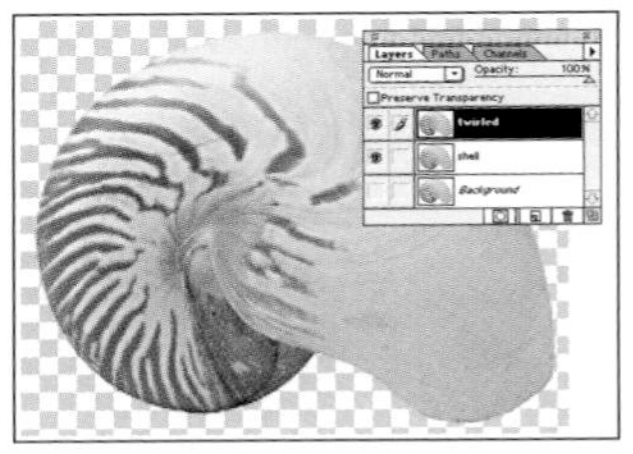

STEP 3: DUPLICATING THE LAYER

To create the first frame of your animation sequence, duplicate the layer that contains your image. Do not use the original layer; this way you can always go back to it and start again.

Select the duplicate layer, and be sure that Preserve Transparency is unchecked. Choose one of the distortion filters from the Filter menu and experiment with the settings until you get the desired effect.

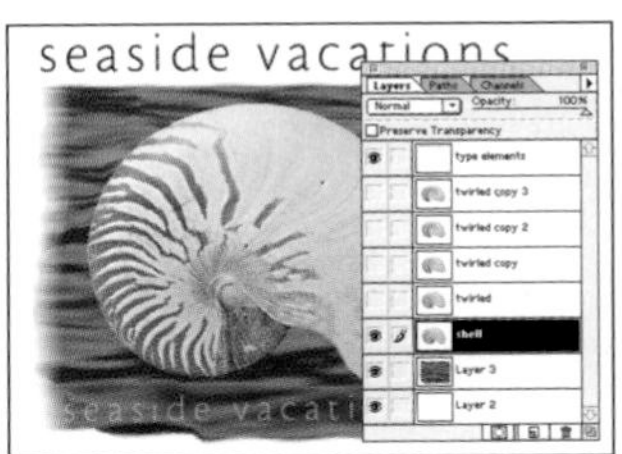

STEP 4: BUILDING UPON PREVIOUS DISTORTIONS

You may want to use just one filter (such as the Twirl filter) progressively. If you do, apply a minimal Twirl amount to the first frame. Duplicate the twirled first frame and apply the filter again. By duplicating and then twirling each frame successively, you can create a sequential twirl animation over four to six frames; or, you may want to apply a different distortion filter to each successive frame.

Once you have created all of your animation frames in separate layers, you can either export each frame as a GIF (see Session F3), or save each frame as a PICT or BMP file for use in a Shockwave or Flash animation (see Session F4).

Session

C4

Creating Animated, Textured Type

TRAVEL

To add life to an ordinary headline, you may want to consider creating a simple GIF animation where a texture or photograph appears to move through the letter forms. This technique is useful for both banner graphics at the top of your Web page, as well as for simple headlines sprinkled throughout the body of your page. By creating only three-to-five frames, you can keep the animation small in terms of file size, yet create an eye-catching animation effect.

ADOBE PHOTOSHOP 4.0	Font: Keplar Photogear: Skyscapes: Sunset 24.tif

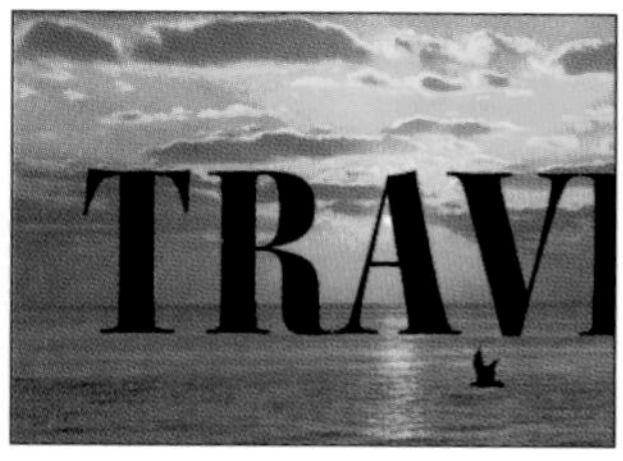

STEP 1: SETTING UP THE LAYERS

Open any photograph or texture that you would like to see animatied within the typed headline. Select the Type tool and click anywhere on top of the photograph to begin typing.

NOTE: *Before you begin typing, set the foreground color for the text. For this exercise, the color of the text does not matter because the photographic texture will cover it.*

STEP 2: SETTING UP THE LAYERS

In order to be mapped through the letter forms, the photograph or texture needs to be repositioned underneath the type layer. If the photograph is on the bottom and is titled "Background" in italics, you cannot reposition it. You must first convert the layer into a transparent layer by double-clicking it. (The photograph does not change in appearance, it is simply named Layer 0 as opposed to Background.)

Once turned into a transparent layer, reposition the photograph layer so that is on top of the text layer in the Layers palette. To do this, click on its thumbnail and drag it on top of the text layer's thumbnail.

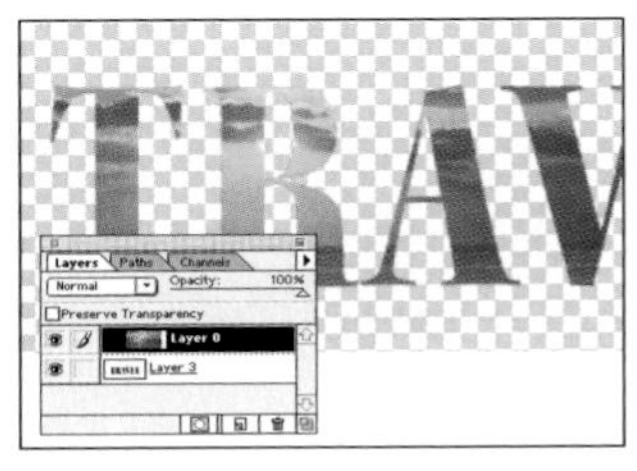

STEP 3: CREATING A CLIPPING GROUP

In this exercise, the animation shows the sunset moving from left to right through the text. To set up the first frame, use the Move tool to move the photograph over to the left side without revealing the text underneath.

To clip the photograph so that it only appears through the text, rather than covering it up, set up a Clipping Group. To do this, make sure the photograph layer is selected in the Layers palette. Then use the keyboard combination Command + G (Mac), or Control + G (Windows), which is the shortcut for choosing Group with Previous from the Layer menu.

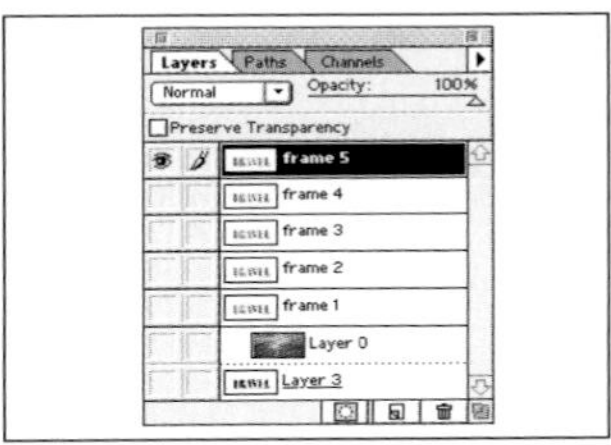

STEP 4: CREATING ANIMATION FRAMES

In order to extract an animation frame, you need to merge the text layer with the photograph layer. Doing so, however, prevents you from incrementally moving the photograph layer to create the remaining animation frames.

Therefore, you must create a merged new layer, leaving the source layers intact. To do this, use the Option-Merge technique described in Session C1.

Once you create the first animation frame with the Option-Merge technique, go back to the photograph layer and move it 10 to 20 pixels to the right with the Move tool. Again, use Option-Merge to create the second frame of your animation. Continue this process until you have four or five frames.

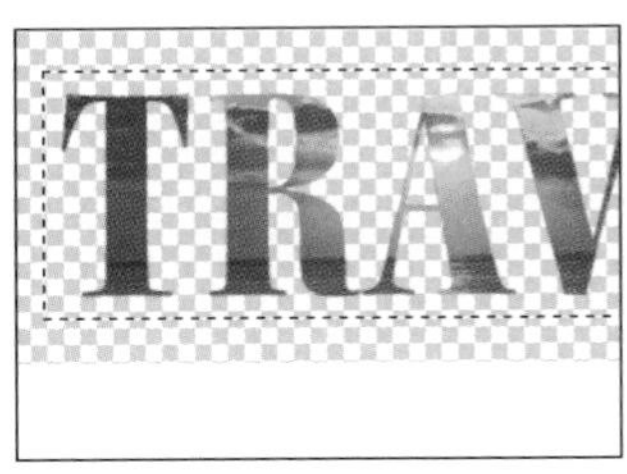

STEP 5: EXTRACTING ANIMATION FRAMES

When you have finished creating four or five animation frames, with each frame featuring the photograph moved about 10 pixels or more to the right—you are ready to extract frames for an animation.

In the Layers palette, select the layer that contains frame 1. Draw a selection around the headline. (The transparency will be ignored when you copy and paste later.) Copy frame 1 and paste it into its own new file. Come back to the layered file and navigate to frame 2. Continue copying each frame and pasting it into its own new file.

Prepare each animation frame for a GIF export following the steps in Session F1.

Session

C5 Not-So-Simple GIF Animation

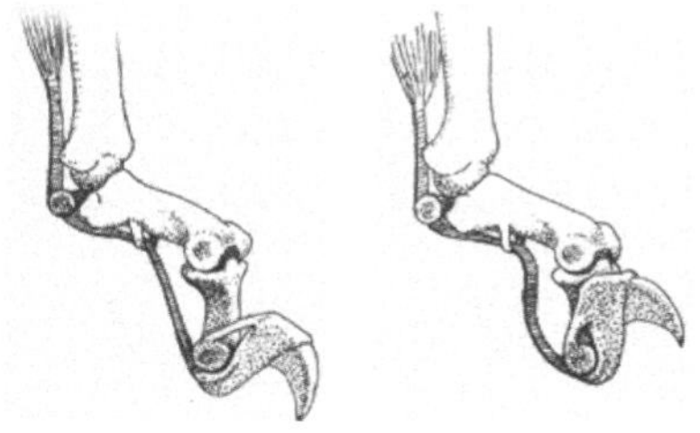

The *National Geographic Online, Cats* feature uses an animated GIF of a retractable claw.

ADOBE PHOTOSHOP 4.0

Although this two-frame GIF animation appears simple, it is actually rather complex in terms of the production techniques used to create it. The retractable claw animation used in the *National Geographic Online, Cats* feature, is created by first compositing each frame to the background tile texture, cutting out the frames so that they remain registered to one another, and then setting them onto a transparent background. The goal is to create an animation in which the frames remain registered to one another (by being the same width and height), and the file size is minimized by using transparency and the tightest possible cropping.

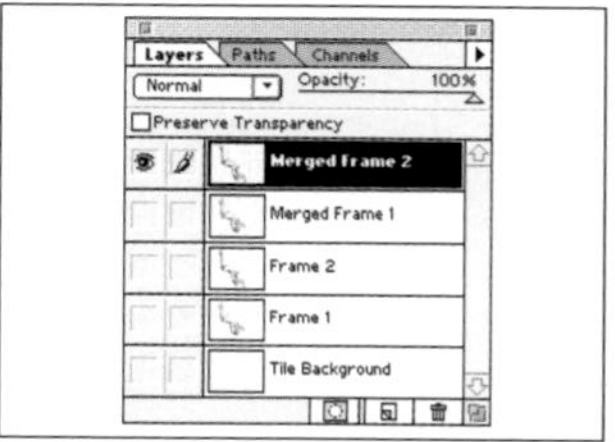

STEP 1: PREPARING MERGED ANIMATION FRAMES

Create a few animation frames in separate transparent layers, and then Option-Merge (see Session C1) the frames with the background tile texture so that they are ready to cut into separate GIF files. In this example, there are five layers: the background tile layer, two layers that are the original art on transparent backgrounds, and two layers that are the original art Option-Merged with the background tile texture.

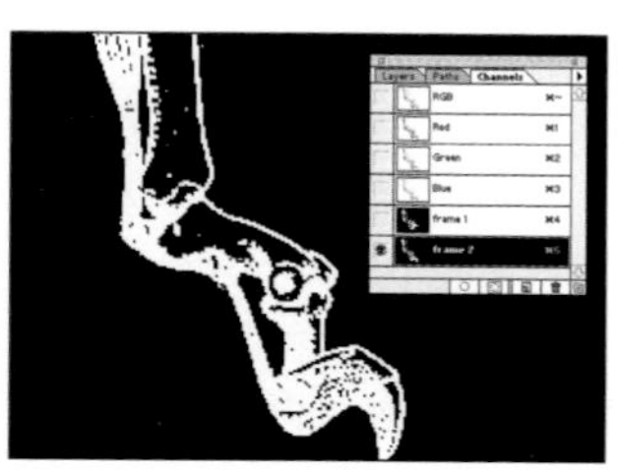

STEP 2: DETERMINING THE BOUNDARIES OF EACH FRAME

To determine the tightest possible cropping for each animation frame, first select one of the frames in the Layers palette. Using the Magic Wand set on a tolerance of zero and with anti-aliasing turned off, select the pure transparent background of the image. Choose Similar from the Select menu, and then Invert the selection. This selection shows you where the absolute edges of your image are—including the anti-aliasing—so that you do not accidentally crop any portion of your image. Save the selection as a channel.

Do the same procedure for the other frame and save it as a new channel as well. You should now have two channels, name them for reference "Frame One" and "Frame Two."

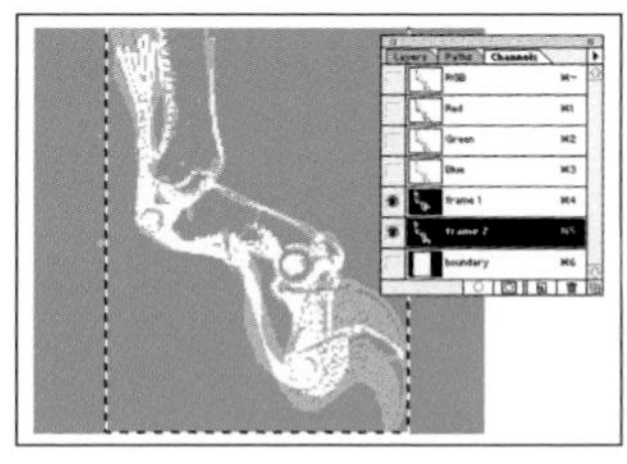

STEP 3: DETERMINING THE SMALLEST POSSIBLE COMMON DIMENSION

In the Channels palette, select either Frame One or Two and then turn on the eyeball icon for the other one. This allows you to see both channels at once so that you can see where the outer limits of both images are together. Create the smallest rectangular selection in which both frames will fit. Save this selection as a new channel perhaps "Boundary."

> **TIP:** *If you double-click on a channel, you will see a color swatch with a percentage next to it. When you look at two or more channels at a time, this is the color and percentage in which each channel is shown. If you are comparing three channels, then you need to set each channel's percentage to about 30%.*

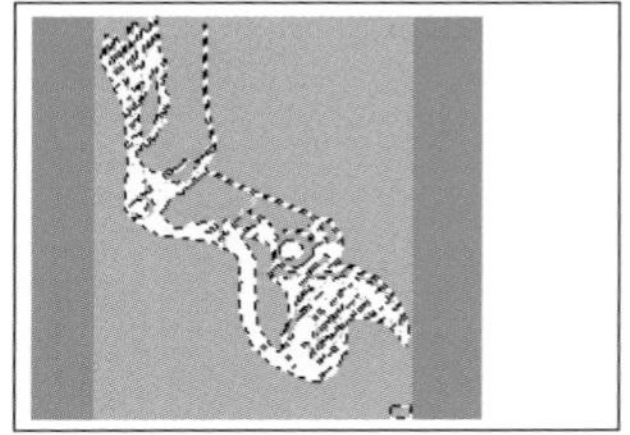

STEP 4: FANCY SELECTION WORK

Load the Frame One channel as a selection. You will use this selection to cut out the contents of the merged Frame One layer. However, we need to make sure that the cut out is the exact dimension as the Boundary channel. To ensure that the dimensions are the same, turn on the Eyeball icon of the Boundary channel. By holding down the Shift key, add a small square selection in the upper left and lower right corners as shown. These little selection additions ensure a consistent dimension when you copy the contents of each frame.

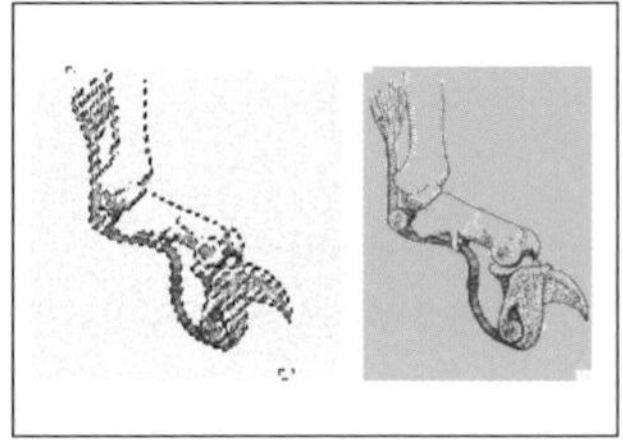

STEP 5: COPYING THE FRAMES INTO NEW FILES

Use this modified selection to copy the contents of the merged Frame One layer. Create a new Photoshop file and fill it with a bright, solid color from the Web-safe color table. This color serves as your transparent color. Paste the copied Frame One into the new file.

Go back to the layered file. Prepare another selection repeating Step 4, this time for Frame Two. Copy the contents of the merged Frame Two layer and paste it into a new Photoshop file on top of a bright color that will become transparent.

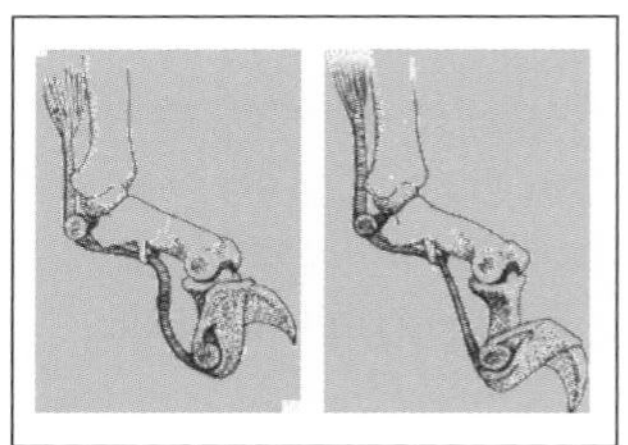

STEP 6: FINISHING TOUCHES

By now, you should have two new Photoshop files of the same dimension ready to be processed into a GIF animation. First, reduce each frame's colors (see Session F6), and then export each frame as a GIF (see Session F7).

> **NOTE:** *Before you export your frames as GIFs, clean up the upper left and lower right corners of your animation frames by filling the little squares with the transparent color.*

Session

C6 Avoiding Overlap in Animation

When preparing graphics for a complex, interactive animation that features independent moving icons and rollover labels, it is important to make sure that the graphic components do not overlap one another. Because each graphic piece is cut out, it cannot contain fractions of neighboring graphics. Therefore, in situations where your graphics sit close to one another, you need to cut them in specific ways to avoid overlap. This exercise is for more advanced users, prehaps preparing to create complex Shockwave animations.

ADOBE PHOTOSHOP 4.0

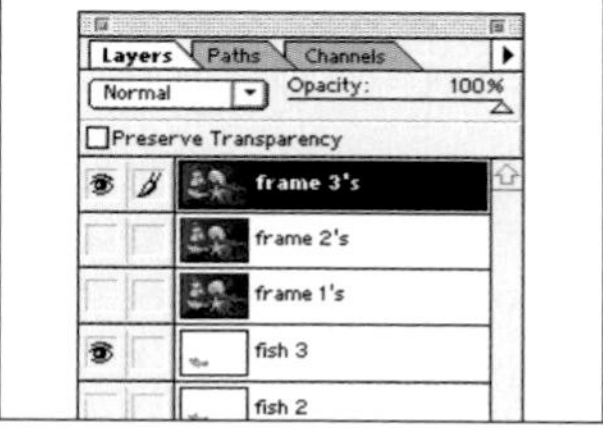

STEP 1: CREATING SOURCE LAYERS IN PHOTOSHOP

Following the steps in Session C3, create a series of three-frame animating icons on top of a background. Be sure that each animation frame is on its own layer. In this example, there are four icons with three animation frames for each, for a total of twelve layers. Without touching, position each icon fairly close to one another.

In addition to the source layers above, create three Option-Merged layers (see Session C1), that are ready to select—along with the channels you create in this session—and save as final animation frames. To do this, merge the first frames of all four icons with the background, then all the second frames, and then all the third frames.

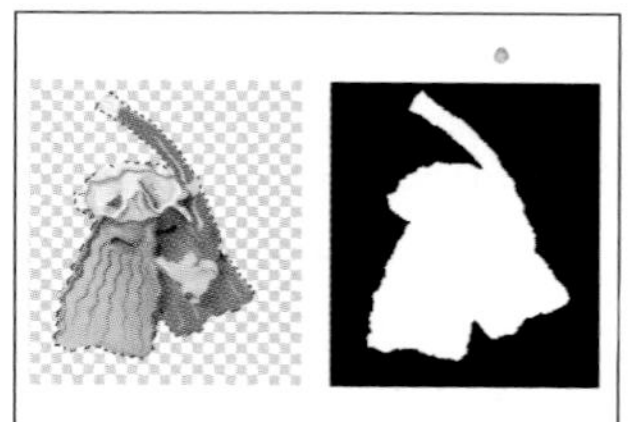

STEP 2: DETERMINING THE EDGES OF EACH ICON

As in Session C5, you need to determine the absolute outer boundaries of each icon series. The easiest way is to Option-Merge the three frames of each icon into a new layer. After you have merged all three frames of an icon, use the Magic Wand tool, set on a tolerance of zero and with anti-aliasing turned off, to select the transparent area around the icon. Select Similar to ensure all transparency is accounted for, invert the selection, and then save it as a channel.

Repeat this process for the remaining three icons, generating channels that show the silhouette of the icon's shape.

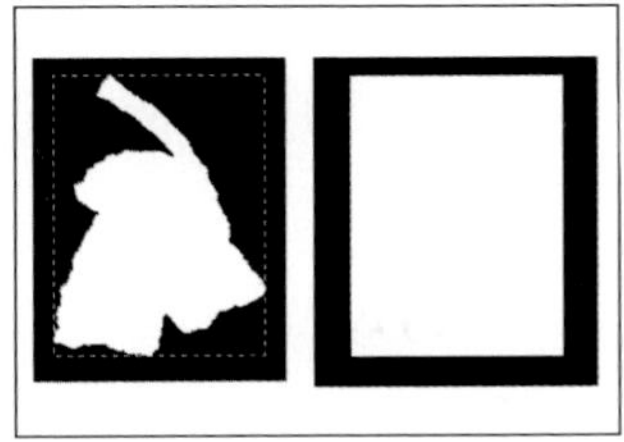

STEP 3: CREATING RECTANGULAR BOUNDARY CHANNELS

In the Channels palette, select one of the channels you created in Step 2. Draw a rectangular selection that fits tightly around the icon's shape and save the selection as another channel called "Boundary." Continue to draw a boundary selection around each of the other icon shape channels.

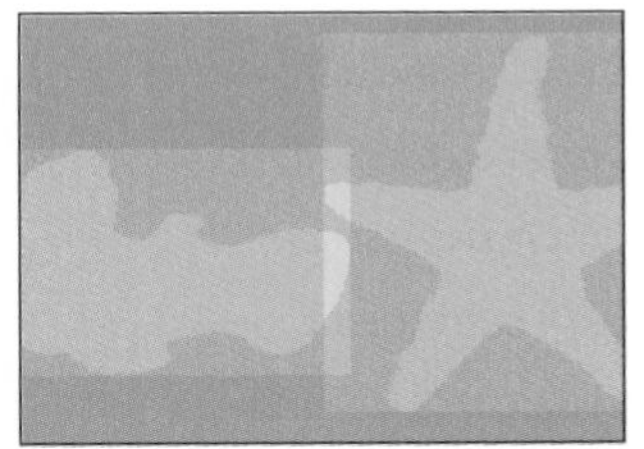

STEP 4: COMPARING BOUNDARY CHANNELS

Turn on the Eyeball icons for all four Boundary channels to see whether or not your cut-outs overlap. Use these boundary channels later as selections to copy and cut each animation frame from your layers.

For the boundaries that overlap, turn on the Eyeball icons of the icon shape channels. Comparing all these channels tells you how much you can shave off the boundary cut-out without excluding the icon itself.

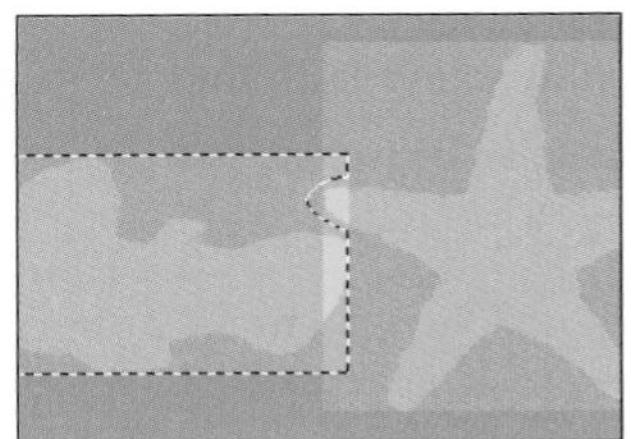

STEP 5: MODIFYING THE CUT-OUT BOUNDARY CHANNELS

While still comparing the channels, load one of the overlapping Boundary channels as a selection. With the Lasso tool, set on a feather of zero and the anti-aliasing turned off, subtract from the selection until it is no longer overlapping with another boundary. Make sure the icon shape is still contained within the cut-out.

Save the new modified boundary cut-out as a channel. Modify the remaining boundaries in the same way, starting with the boundary as a selection, and then subtracting from it so that it no longer overlaps. After you have a new, modified set of boundary channels for each icon, you can discard the original rectangular boundaries and the icon-shaped channels.

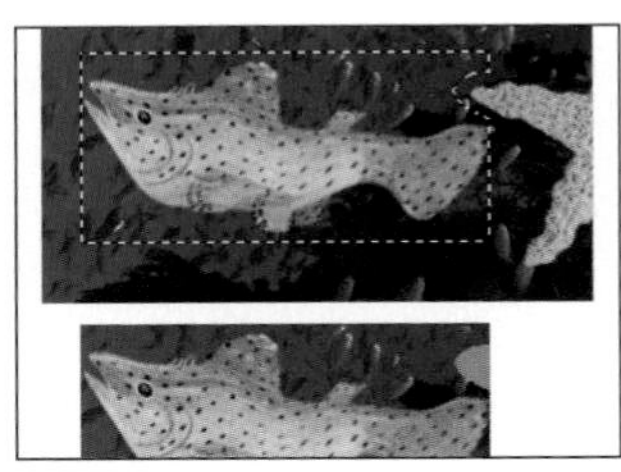

STEP 6: MODIFYING THE CUT-OUT BOUNDARY CHANNELS

Load one of the modified boundary channels as a selection. In the Layers palette, navigate to one of the merged layers and copy its contents.

Since the selection is not a perfect rectangle anymore, the area left out needs to become transparent. Create a new file (which will be the size of the copied icon) and before pasting, fill the file with a solid Web-safe color that becomes your transparent color. Select a color that is not used inside the icon. Paste the icon.

Go back to the layered file and copy the next frame of the icon using the same modified cut out. Again, paste frame of the icon on top of a transparent color. Continue copying each icon series.

Session

C7 Preparing Files for a QuickTime Movie

The *Cats* feature at *www.nationalgeographic.com* features a downloadable QuickTime movie.

ADOBE PHOTOSHOP 4.0

The *National Geographic Online, Cats* features a 170K downloadable QuickTime movie that shows a Puma being built from bones to fur. Such content is simple to create, fast to download, and highly effective at adding significant value to a Web site. In this Session, you'll learn how this movie was created using only three frames of the cat, plus an overlay frame containing the *National Geographic Online* logo.

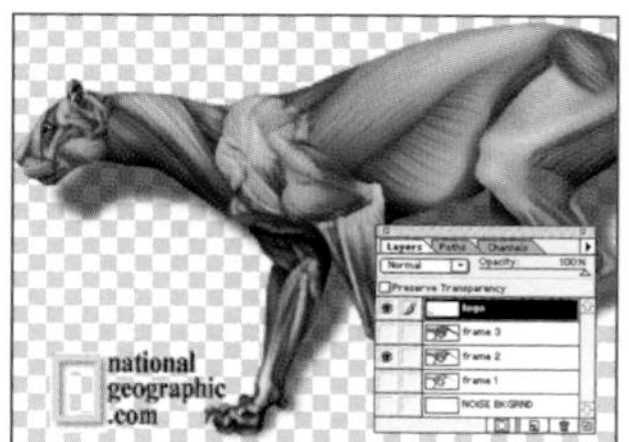

STEP 1: CREATING KEY FRAMES IN LAYERS

Create a new file that is the dimension of your QuickTime movie, and create a series of layers, each with its own key frame image. In one layer, also include your logo, or other graphic to be superimposed on top of the QuickTime movie.

TIP: *A key frame is one that is an important landmark of your animation. From just these three key frames: the skeleton, the muscles, and the coat, Adobe Premiere can blend the in-between steps creating an interesting layered effect.*

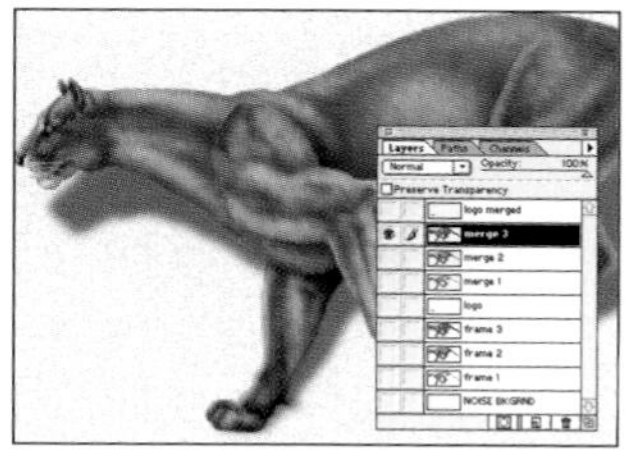

STEP 2: EXTRACTING KEY FRAMES

Option-Merge (see Session C7) the key frames with the background tile, excluding the logo overlay. Select All and copy the contents of each merged key frame layer and paste into a new Photoshop file. Save each key frame file as a 24-bit, RGB PICT (Mac) or BMP (Windows) file ready to import into Premiere.

STEP 3: OVERLAY FRAME PRE-PRODUCTION

Option-Merge just the logo (or graphic) overlay layer with the background layer. This composites the presumably anti-aliased logo with the background image. Set this merged layer aside and go back to the layer with the logo still on transparency.

Next, use the Magic Wand, set with a tolerance of zero and no anti-aliasing, to select the transparency surrounding the logo. Choose Similar from the Select menu to capture all pure transparent areas.

STEP 4: FILLING THE OVERLAY WITH A TRANSPARENT COLOR

Keep the selection active and go back to the logo merged with the background layer. Select a bright color, like blue or green, that will become your transparent color and fill the selected area on the merged logo layer. Though the image may look funny, it blends perfectly once in Premiere (see Session L6).

NOTE: *Be sure to select a transparent color that does not occur in your image. Otherwise, parts of your image become transparent as well.*

STEP 5: PREPARING THE OVERLAY FRAME

Select All and copy the contents of the merged logo layer, and then paste into a new file. Save the new file as a 24-bit, RGB PICT or BMP file ready to import into Premiere.

Session

C8 Preparing Vector Graphics for Flash Animation

One of the more popular forms of interactive animation that you can include on a Web page are Flash animations. Flash is popular because of its ability to integrate vector-based graphics as opposed to the more limiting, heavyweight bitmap graphics. Vector graphics are ones that are defined mathematically by points connected by curves, and are therefore much smaller in file size. You can import vector graphics into Flash, create an interactive interface, and end up with a file half the size of a similar Shockwave file.

ADOBE PHOTOSHOP 4.0 **ADOBE ILLUSTRATOR 7.0**	Object Gear: Design Elements: Duck

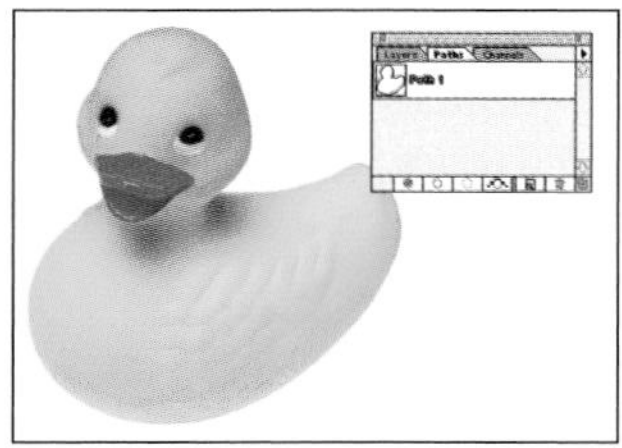

STEP 1: CONVERTING BITMAP GRAPHICS TO VECTOR GRAPHICS

Since vector graphics are created by points connected by curves, you cannot create vector-based photographs. Photographs are best left as bitmaps. The best bitmaps to convert into vector graphics are simple images like the duck used in this example, or flat, cartoon-like graphics.

If you are using Image Club graphics, you already have a perfect path ready to export. If not, use the Pen tool to create an outline around the graphic. Choose Export Paths to Illustrator from the File menu to save the path to a file. In addition, save the image as an EPS file so that you can place it in Illustrator for tracing.

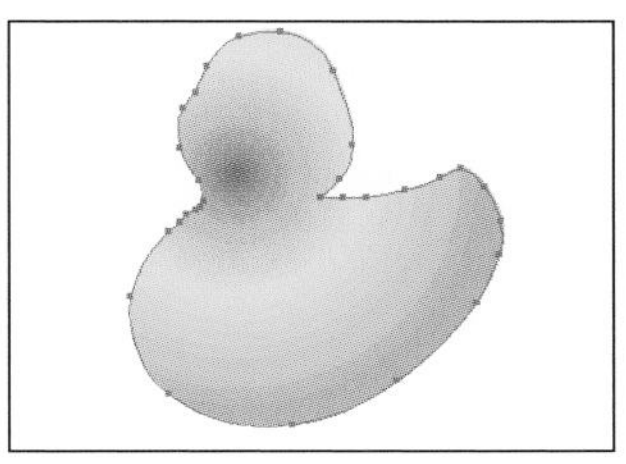

STEP 2: OPENING PATHS IN ILLUSTRATOR

In Illustrator, open the path you exported from Photoshop. When it opens, the path is invisible. To reveal the path, choose Select All from the Edit menu. Once selected, open the Paint palette and assign a fill or a custom gradient, in this case, to the outline.

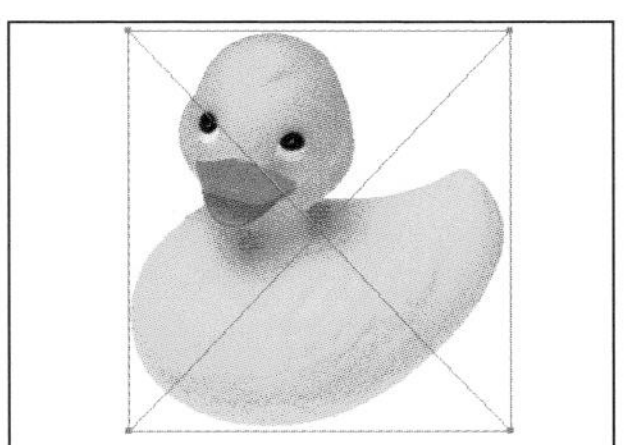

STEP 3: PLACING THE EPS FILE AS A TEMPLATE

At this point, only the silhouette of the object has been traced in Illustrator. To trace the internal detail of the object, use the EPS file saved from Step 1 as a template. From Illustrator's File menu, choose Place to bring in the EPS file. Do not use the Open command.

STEP 4: TRACING THE ILLUSTRATION

Using the Pen tool, trace the various elements of the illustration and fill each path with a fill or custom blend. Build each element separately. For example, trace the red beak, and then the shine portion. The paths are automatically layered in the order that you create them. Therefore, if you need to reorder one segment—bringing it into the foreground or sending it behind other segments—choose the appropriate command from the Arrange menu.

TIP: *You can create complex shapes using Illustrator Pathfinder filters such as Back Minus Front and Intersection. Simply create two separate shapes with the Pen tool, select both, and then apply one of the filters.*

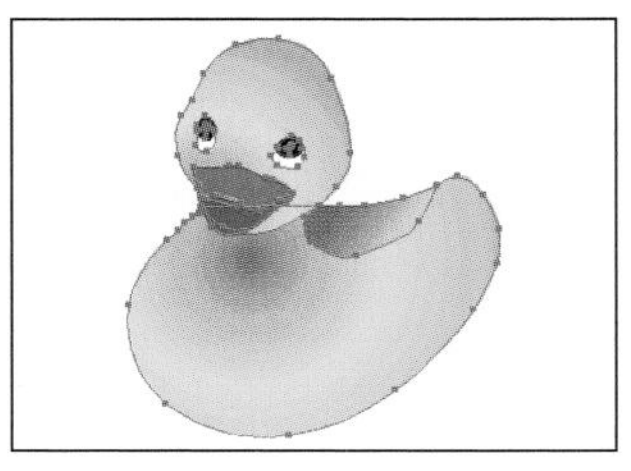

STEP 5: GROUPING THE ILLUSTRATION

Once you have completed tracing all the segments of the bitmap EPS image, you can delete it. Group all the traced segments together by choosing Select All from the Edit menu, and then Group from the Arrange menu.

Finally, save the completed vector-based illustration as an Illustrator EPS file ready to import into Flash.

Session

C9 Animating GIFs in a Table Structure

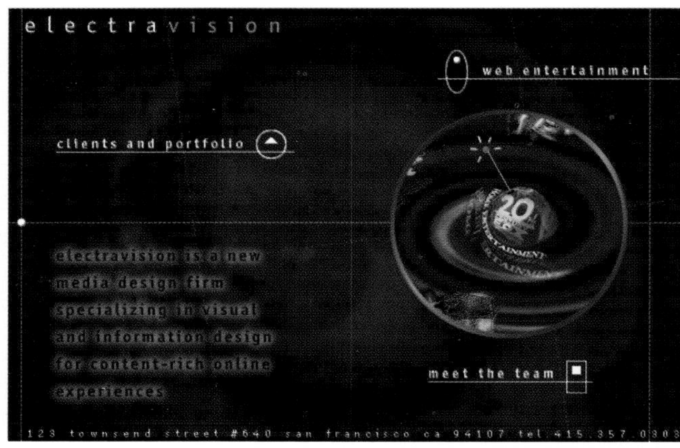

Because many animation technologies require that users download and install various plug-ins, an alternative is to design a complex table structure that features animating GIFs in the different table cells. All browsers support tables and animated GIFs, so you can add Shockwave-like animation (albeit without the interactive control) to your Web site without excluding any users. Keep in mind, however, that only one link can be associated with a GIF animation. Also, be forewarned that building such a seamless table structure that appears the same on different browsers, can be a lot of work and requires extensive cross-platform testing. For more information on building tables, see Session G2; or, view the source HTML of *www.electravision.com*.

ADOBE PHOTOSHOP 4.0

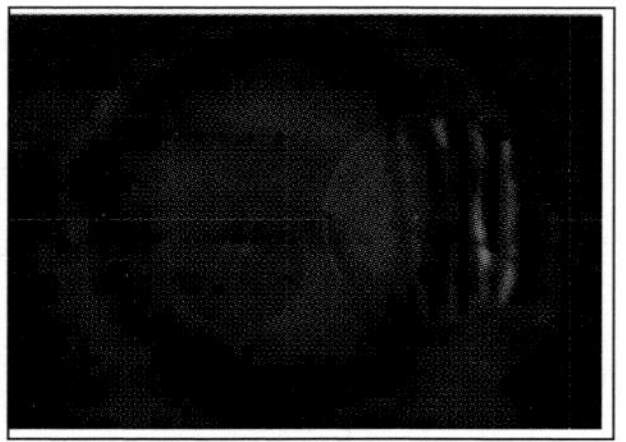

STEP 1: MOCK-UP A LAYOUT IN PHOTOSHOP

Create a new Photoshop file that is the same pixel dimension as the table structure you want to create. For usability reasons and to keep the download time to a minimum, it is best to keep the table size within 600 x 350 pixels.

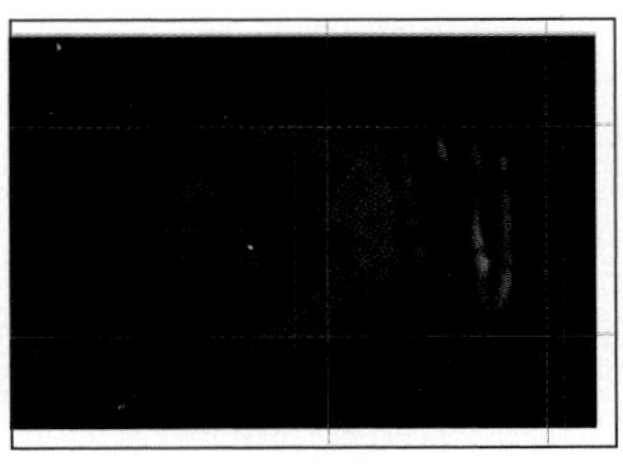

STEP 2: USE GUIDES TO MOCK-UP A TABLE STRUCTURE

Photoshop's guides provide an excellent way to mock-up a table structure. To set guides, first turn on the Rulers (located under the View menu), or use the keyboard combination Control +R (Windows), or Command +R (Mac). Simply click one of the Rulers and drag out a guide.

TIP: *To change the Rulers display from Inches to Pixels, open the Preferences > Units & Rulers option from the File menu.*

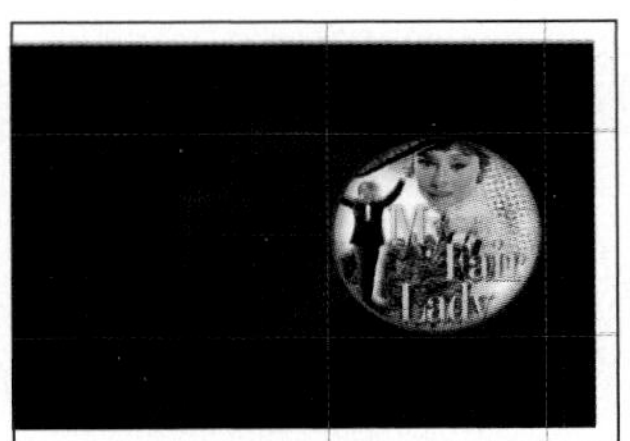

STEP 3: CREATE ANIMATIONS IN EACH CELL

Once each table cell is defined, begin creating graphics that animate only within each cell. Be sure that the animation frames of a cell do not bleed into neighboring cells. If they do, the animation appears cropped. In this example, graphics that do not change can be shared across the entire design.

As in Session G2, Option-Merge the source layers to create each frame of animation ready to be cut out.

STEP 4: CREATE CUT-OUT CHANNELS

Use the guides to draw rectangular selections for each table cell. Since you will use these selections over and over to cut out each animation frame for the given cell, save the selection as a channel. Once you have created cut-out selections for each table cell and have saved them as channels, compare the channels to make sure that they all line up next to each other perfectly. If the selections are perfectly juxtaposed, you should see a solid pink color with no lighter or darker pink lines.

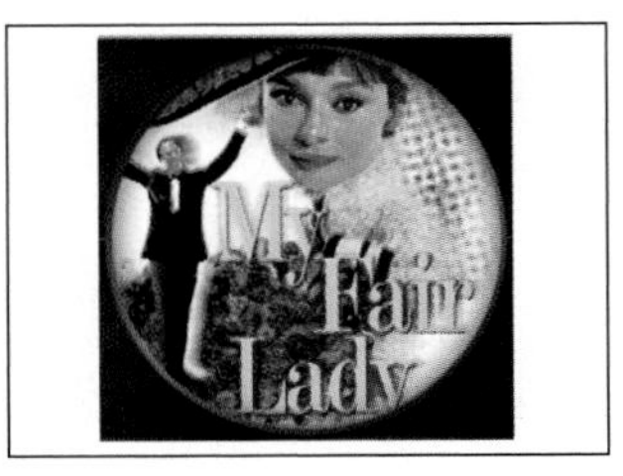

STEP 5: EXTRACT OUT ANIMATION FRAMES

Load one of the cut-out channels as a selection and use it to copy into a new file each frame of animation for the given table cell.

When creating a series of animated GIFs for a table structure, it is important that you record the pixel dimensions of each cell. You need to match the graphic's dimensions to the dimensions of its table cell so that you can ensure registration. In Photoshop, you can quickly get the dimensions of any image by holding down the Option (Mac), or Alt (Windows) key, and then clicking and holding down on the lower left border of the graphic's window where it displays document specifications.

Finally, process each individual file for a GIF animation (see Session F1).

Chapter D

CREATING INTERFACE ELEMENTS

From creating background tiles to making 3D buttons, mastering Web graphic production techniques is the key to producing professional-looking Web sites. In this Chapter, you'll learn basic, and not-so-basic, graphic production techniques using Photoshop 4.0 and Illustrator 7.0. For instance, how do you avoid the ugly white "halo" that often surrounds Web graphics? Or, how do you create interesting text effects including texturized text and text that wraps to the shape of an image? These step-by-step sessions cover production basics that you can build upon to create complex, professional Web graphics.

CHAPTER SESSIONS

D1 *Creating Instant Drop Shadows*

D2 *Creating Instant Cast Shadows*

D3 *Making Soft, 3D Buttons from Any Shape*

D4 *Trimming Graphics to the Smallest Possible Size*

D5 *Creating Seamless Background Tiles*

D6 *Converting Graphics from Anti-Aliased to Aliased*

D7 *Compositing Graphics to a Background Tile*

D8 *Creating Textured, 3D Text Elements*

D9 *Creating a Collage*

D10 *Wrapping Text to an Image*

D11 *Adding Natural Light and Shadows*

D12 *Creating Consistent Soft-Edged Buttons*

CHAPTER TOOLBOX

Adobe Photoshop 4.0

Adobe Illustrator 7.0

IMAGES

Image Club, Studio Gear

Image Club, Photo Gear

Image Club, Object Gear

INTERFACE ELEMENTS 101

There are a number graphic production terms and user interface design issues that you must learn in order to get the most out of this chapter and to become a more effective Web designer. These terms and design issues are the core of building professional Web site interface elements. For instance, understanding the difference between aliased and anti-aliased graphics and how they affect production decisions is a key concept to master. Learning how to solve the more abstract issues of interface design, through the use of conventions such as color coding and consistency will help your users navigate more effectively through your site.

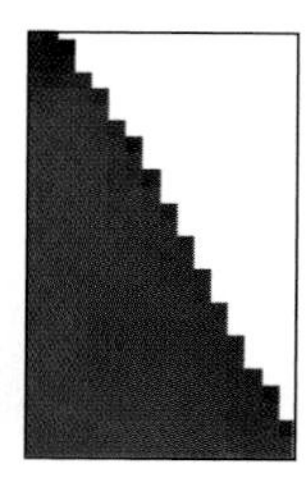

ANTI-ALIASED VERSUS ALIASED GRAPHICS

With exception of PDF files and emerging technologies that allow vector-based graphics to displaye on the Web, graphics produced for the Web are bitmapped graphics. This mean, that even objects with rounded shapes are invariably made up of tiny squares called pixels. Zooming into the edges of a bitmap graphic, you can see the inherent stair-stepped pattern of the pixels—especially apparent along the edges of a graphic. Long ago, software engineers came up with a way to soften the appearance of such jagged, "aliased" edges by slightly blending the edges of the graphic with its surroundings. This technique, anti-aliasing, accounts for the beautiful, organic imagery you see today on a computer screen.

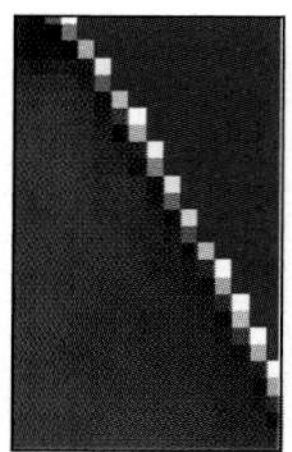

PRODUCTION ISSUES ASSOCIATED WITH ANTI-ALIASED GRAPHICS

While anti-aliased graphics look markedly better than aliased graphics, look out for are production land mines. Because the soft edge effect is achieved by blending the edges to a specific background image or color, the image will look strange when moved onto a different background. The most common mistake is to anti-alias a graphic to a white background, and then declare the white background as a transparent color. The semi-blended edges are off-white and so do not become transparent. Therefore, when you overlay the image is overlaid on top of a different background, a distinct rim appears around the image. Sessions D6 and D7 deal with ways to work with both aliased and anti-aliased graphics.

PRODUCTION ISSUES ASSOCIATED WITH ANTI-ALIASED GRAPHICS

When designing graphical interface elements for a Web site, such as navigation banners, buttons, and text, you must think how the user can interact efficiently. It is not enough to think of just one design element at a time, you must plan how pages of design elements can work together. The following list contains user interface design conventions to think about when designing Web pages:

- Try color coding each section of your Web site.
- Design "families" of icons or buttons that share the same look and feel.
- Create a consistent navigation bar that links to all of your Web site's pages. Make sure that the navigation bar is on each of your Web pages, and is always placed in the same location.
- Label icons and buttons clearly. Often it is difficult for users to guess what each one represents.
- Keep graphics small and concise. Larger graphics take too long to download and frustrate users.
- Design your Web pages so that important information fits within the screen space.

NOTE: *The most common monitors are the 13-inch, 640 x 480 pixels display models. When you consider that browser window interfaces take up a significant portion, the space you are left to design for is only 600 x 350.*

CACHING INTERFACE ELEMENTS

To maximize graphical interface elements, design them so you can reuse them on other pages of your Web site. Once a graphic is downloaded for use on a Web page, it is stored or "cached" in memory. Therefore, the next occurrence of that graphic on a second Web page eliminates the need to download the graphic again.

The *Mall of America Web* site, at *www.mallofamerica.com*, is an excellent example of efficient use of cached interface elements. The Web site is broken into five main sections, each of which is represented in a single navigation banner graphic that resides at the top of each Web page. Not only does this help cut down on the download time of each new page, users are able to quickly get from one main section to another.

When a user clicks on a main section, a tiny secondary banner appears just underneath the main banner as feedback, indicating where the user is in the Web site.

Session

D1 Creating Instant Drop Shadows

One of the simplest ways to add depth to a button, icon, photograph, or headline is to create a soft drop shadow. In Photoshop, you can create an "instant" drop shadow for any shape using a simple four-step process.

PHOTOSHOP 4.0	Object Gear, Gentleman's Study: Magnifying Glass Studio Gear Business Metaphors: SBM01

STEP 1: PREPARING LAYERS

Before you can create an instant drop shadow, the graphic must be on a transparent layer (as shown). Then duplicate the layer by choosing Duplicate from the Layer palette's pop-up menu. This copy becomes the drop shadow; so, in the Layers palette, position the copy layer so that it is underneath the original layer.

TIP: *To get an object off a background and onto transparency, first create a selection around the object. You can use the Magic Wand to select the background, and then invert the selection; or, if you are using Image Club graphics, each graphic comes with a path ready to turn into a selection. Once selected, float the object by using the Command + J (Mac), or Control + J (Windows). This puts a copy of the selected image into a transparent layer.*

STEP 2: OFFSET THE COPIED LAYER

In the Layers palette, be sure that the copied layer is selected. In the document window, use the Move tool to offset the image down and to the right. This gives the illusion of light shining from the upper left corner. (In this example, the center glass was selected and cut to a new layer so only the rim would cast a shadow.)

STEP 3: FILLING THE SHADOW WITH SOLID BLACK

The next step is to fill the copied layer with black. You do not need to make a selection around the image to do this. Simply check the Preserve Transparency checkbox on the Layers palette. This allows you to fill just the image with black without affecting the transparent background. To quickly fill the image with black, first make black the foreground color, and then hold down the Option (Mac) or Alt (Windows) key while pressing the Delete key.

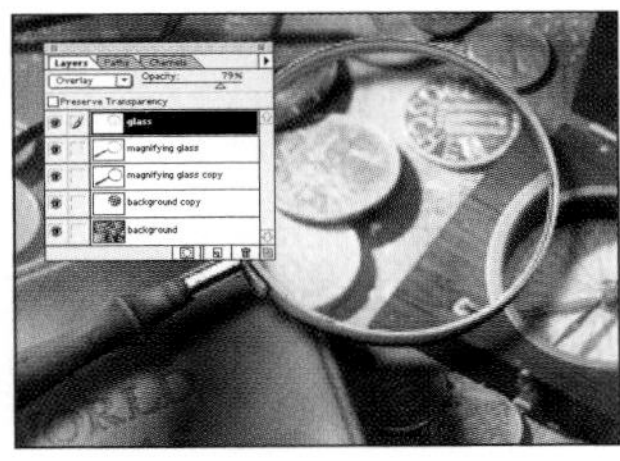

STEP 4: FINISHING TOUCHES

Uncheck the Preserve Transparency checkbox, and then choose Gaussian Blur from the Filter menu. Play with the setting amount until you get the desired softness. Finally, adjust the opacity slider on the Layers palette until you get the desired shadow effect. Create a new layer to go underneath and either fill it with a solid color or insert an image.

NOTE: *The reason you should fill the shadow layer with solid black, as opposed to gray, is because the layer opacity controls lend a naturally translucent gray effect.*

Session

D2 Creating Instant Cast Shadows

A variation on the instant drop shadow is a cast shadow that gives the illusion an image standing upright on a plane. This technique is an interesting alternative to the traditional drop shadow for buttons, icons, and photographs.

PHOTOSHOP 4.0 Object Gear, Culturals: Pinata

STEP 1: CREATING AN INSTANT DROP SHADOW

Following the directions in Session D1, and create an instant drop shadow for an image that is on a transparent layer. Do not, however, apply the Gaussian blur yet.

You will need to increase the size of your Canvas to allow for the cast shadow. Choose Canvas Size from the Image menu and expand your canvas size to the left or right of your image (whichever way you want to cast the shadow).

STEP 2: SKEWING THE SHADOW

It is best to cast the shadow back to either the left or right rather than casting into the foreground. To achieve the initial casting effect, choose Free Transform from the Layer menu.

To select the skew mode, press the Control key while you click and hold next to the image. This produces a pop-up menu from which you can choose the Skew mode (notice the other effects available to you. These same effects are also available from the Layer > Free Transform menu). With Free Transform set into Skew mode, drag the upper right or left handle to skew the image.

TIP: *To make both corners skew together, hold down the Option key (Mac), or Alt key (Windows), while you skew one corner.*

STEP 3: SCALING THE SHADOW

Next, you need to scale the skewed shadow. Press the Control key and click down next to the image to produce the Free Transform pop-up menu and select Scale; or, you can select Scale from the Layer > Free Transform menu. Now, when you move the corner handles, you scale the image as opposed to skewing it. You only need to scale it downward in a non-proportional scale to compress the shadow.

STEP 4: FINISHING TOUCHES

Now you are ready to "accept" the transformation by double-clicking inside the rectangular envelope or by pressing the Enter key on the keyboard. In this example, the legs need to be individually distorted to make them match. Each leg was individually selected and distorted with the Free Transform > Distort function.

Soften the shadow by appling the Gaussian blur filter and then adjust the shadow's opacity in the Layers palette.

Session

D3 Making Soft, 3D Buttons From Any Shape

To make a button look more "clickable," it's a good idea to give it dimension by creating a drop shadow for it (see Session D1), or by making it look three-dimensional. In this session, you'll learn how to turn any shape into an instant, soft 3D button.

PHOTOSHOP 4.0 Object Gear, Amusements: Smiley Face

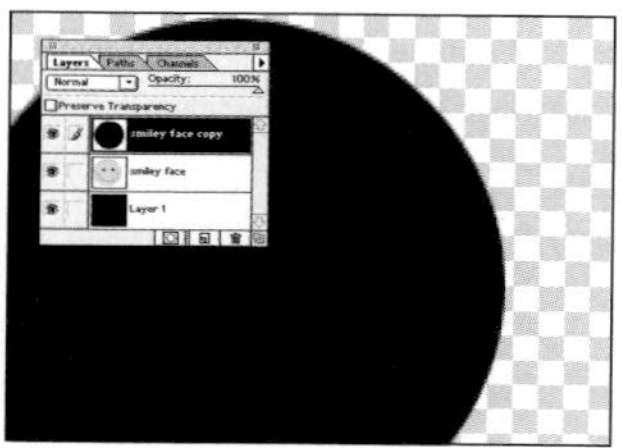

STEP 1: DUPLICATING THE BUTTON LAYER

Prepare your Photoshop file so that the button graphic is on a transparent background. Create a duplicate of the button layer and position the copy on top of the original.

Fill the button copy with black, creating a perfect silhouette. First set your foreground color to black and then check the Preserve Transparency checkbox in the Layers palette. Select Fill from the Edit menu. Uncheck Preserve Transparency.

TIP: *To get an object off a background and onto transparency, first create a selection around the object. You can use the Magic Wand to select the background, and then invert the selection. (If you are using Image Club graphics, each graphic comes with a path ready to turn into a selection.) Once selected, float the object by using Command + J (Mac), or Control + J (Windows) to put a copy of the selected image into a transparent layer.*

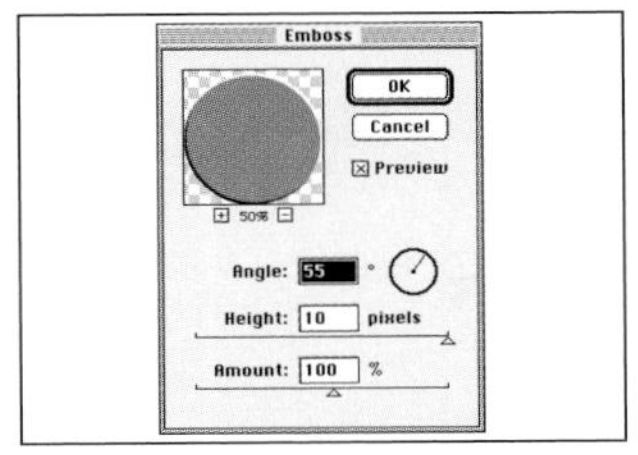

STEP 2: EMBOSSING THE BUTTON COPY

Be sure that the button copy layer (now filled with black) is selected. Choose the Emboss filter from the Filter > Stylize menu and enter the settings as shown. To have the light appear to be coming from the upper right corner, choose an emboss angle of 55°. The emboss height depends on your image; in this example, 10 pixels work best.

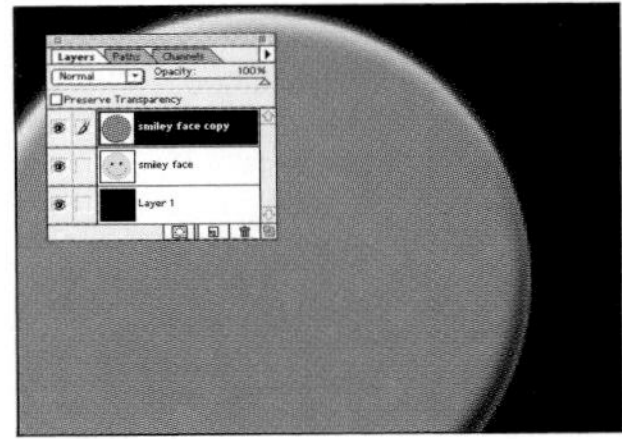

STEP 3: SOFTENING THE EMBOSSED EFFECT

Soften the embossed effect by choosing the Gaussian Blur filter from the Filter > Blur menu. Again, depending on your button size, you may need more or less blurring. For this button, a blurring radius of pixels was selected.

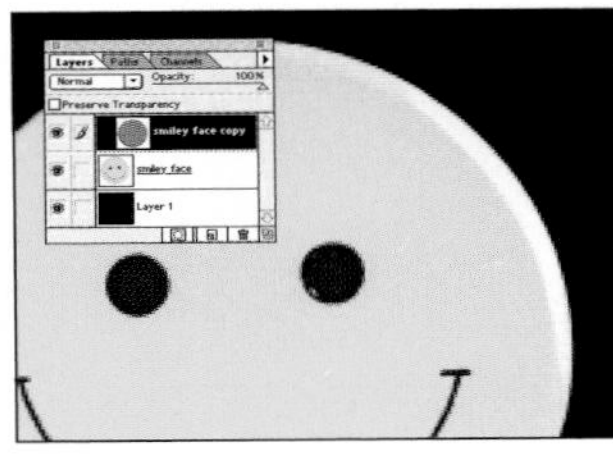

STEP 4: FINISHING TOUCHES

Now you are ready to apply the finishing touches. First, change the button copy's ink effect from Normal to Hard Light by selecting it from the pull-down menu on the Layers palette. You will notice instantly the 3D effect that this creates.

Next, because the button copy was blurred, it extends beyond the boundaries of the original button graphic. Create a clipping group between the button and the button copy by holding down the Option key (Mac), or Alt key (Windows), while clicking on the line that separates the two layers. This trims the button copy so that it fits within the button.

NOTE: *Although it seems counter-intuitive to have the grayscale button copy on top of the button, the positioning is necessary for the Hard Light ink effect to work.*

Session

D4 Trimming Graphics to the Smallest Possible Size

Web graphics always need to be made as small as possible in terms of file size. A few factors that contribute to making smaller files include reducing the color palette, using flat color whenever possible, avoiding horizontal gradients, and trimming your graphics to their smallest possible size. In this case, the image to be cut out has highly feathered edges. These types of graphics are difficult to cut out by simply "eye-balling" it. Often you end up cropping it too closely, and you see a hard edge once the image is on the Web (as shown).

PHOTOSHOP 4.0	Object Gear, Vol. 1 Design Elements: Skull Steer Object Gear, Travels: Road Sign Photo Gear, Skyscapes: Clouds#7 Font: Garage Gothic Black

STEP 1: MERGING LAYERS

If the image is in multiple layers, merge them. Use the Option-Merge technique discussed in Session C7 to keep the source layers intact.

TIP: *Instead of using Option-Merge, you can simply turn on all the Eyeball icons of the layers to be merged, and select Duplicate from the Image menu. Check the Merged Layers Only checkbox to create a new merged file apart from your source file.*

STEP 2: USING THE MAGIC WAND TO FIND THE EDGES

Using the Magic Wand tool, set on a tolerance of zero and with no anti-aliasing, select the transparent background surrounding the image. To ensure that you capture all the transparency, choose Similar from the Select menu. Invert the selection. This selection shows you the absolute outer edges of your image.

STEP 3: CREATING A RECTANGULAR SELECTION

To crop the image according to the selection created in Step 2, convert the selection into a rectangular selection. Hold down the Shift key to add to the current selection using the Marquee tool until you have a perfect rectangle.

Because you are adding to the selection, you do not have to do it all in one step; you can build it in stages. For example, start at the top-most point and draw to one of the side-most points.

If the Crop function is dimmed in the Image menu, your selection is not a perfect—there may be a tiny bulge somewhere. Crop the image with the Crop function once the selection is perfect.

NOTE: *The Crop tool does not work in this case because it erases your Magic Wand selection.*

Session

D5 Creating Seamless Background Tiles

You can create a seamless background tile in a number of complicated ways. However, using Layers, you can create a tile in just three simple steps. Any textured image can be used; however, it is recommended that you use an image that has a small pattern. Aesthetically, a smaller pattern is less obtrusive on your Web page, and looks less repetitive.

PHOTOSHOP 4.0 Photo Gear, Nature Collages: Dried Flowers

STEP 1: SELECT AND CUT OUT A TILE

In Photoshop, open any textured image or pattern. Select an area of the image to become the size and shape of your tile. Try to avoid large, landmark-like images within your selection as these make the tile too repetitive.

Copy the selected area into its own layer. For purposes of this exercise, this layer referred to as Layer 1.

STEP 2: DUPLICATE THE TILE LAYER

Create a duplicate of Layer 1. Using the Move tool, position Layer 1 and Layer 2 so that they are precisely side by side.

You will be working solely on Layer 2. Turn on Preserve Transparency so that you do not accidentally go beyond the bounds of the tile. Using both the Cloning tool and the Paint Brush, fix the edge of Layer 2 until it is seamless with Layer 1's edge beneath. Once the edge is perfect, you no longer need Layer 1. Throw the layer away.

STEP 3: CREATE A SECOND DUPLICATE OF THE LAYER

Now create a duplicate of Layer 2 and position both Layer 2 and Layer 2 copy such that, this time, they are precisely end-to-end as shown.

Work only on Layer 2 copy with Preserve Transparency turned on. This layer becomes your final background tile.

Edit the seam on Layer 2 copy until it blends perfectly with Layer 2 beneath. Once the edge is seamless, you no longer need Layer 2. Throw it away. You now have a perfect background tile.

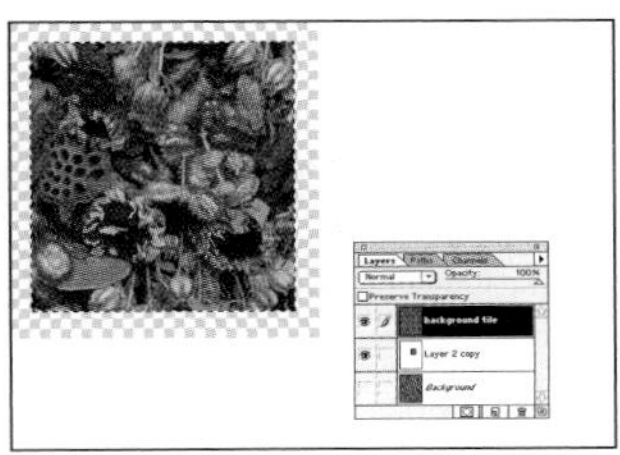

STEP 4: TESTING THE BACKGROUND TILE

To test your new tile, create a selection around Layer 2 copy. You can generate a shrink-to-fit selection quickly by Command (Mac), or Control (Windows) clicking on the tile's icon in the Layers palette.

Choose Define Pattern from the Edit menu. Drop the selection and make a new layer. Finally, fill the new layer with the tile pattern by choosing Fill from the Edit menu. Select Pattern from the Fill menu's pop-up menu.

STEP 5: EXPORT THE TILE AS A GIF

Copy the tile into its own new file, reduce its color palette to eight bits or less (see Session F1), and then export the tile as a GIF using Photoshop's GIF89a Export feature found in the File menu (see Session F3).

Session

D6 Converting Graphics from Anti-aliased to Aliased

For purposes of animation, or preparing graphics to sit on top of a background tile, you need to ensure that your graphics have aliased, or jagged edges. The problem, however, is that many graphics as you work on them are anti-aliased. Short of erasing the soft edges by hand, how can you quickly "un-anti-alias" graphics? This session shows you how to get rid of anti-aliased edges in a simple four-step process.

PHOTOSHOP 4.0	Object Gear Vol. 1 Design Elements: Fish Photo Gear Industrial Backgrounds: Electrical Wires Object Gear Amusements: Cowboy Hat

STEP 1: GENERATING A SELECTION

For best results, the image to be aliased, must be on a transparent layer. If the image has already been composited to a solid background (such as white), the process is similar, but not as accurate.

Generate a shrink-to-fit selection, also known as a "transparency mask," by pressing the Command key (Mac), or the Control key (Windows), while clicking the layer's icon in the Layer palette.

NOTE: *If your anti-aliased image has already been composited to a solid color, such as white, use the Magic Wand tool with a tolerance of at least 32 and the anti-aliasing on. Select the solid color, and then choose Similar from the Select menu to ensure you capture all of it. Invert the selection.*

STEP 2: SAVING THE SELECTION AS A CHANNEL

Once you have generated a shrink-to-fit selection around your image, save the selection as a channel (from the Select menu). Drop the selection.

Select the new channel in the Channels palette, and apply the Threshold function from the Image > Adjust menu. The default settings are OK. The Threshold function converts the channel into an aliased image which, in turn, yields an aliased selection.

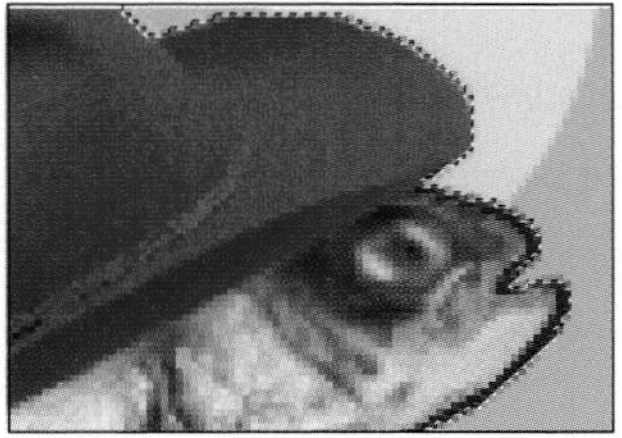

STEP 3: LOADING AND MODIFYING THE SELECTION

Load the channel as a selection and navigate back to the image layer. Once loaded, you will notice that the selection runs through the middle of the anti-aliasing and thus needs to be shrunk by one pixel all around. To shrink the selection, choose Modify > Contract from the Select menu.

STEP 4: TRIMMING THE IMAGE

To trim the image, invert the selection so that the transparent or solid-colored background, including the anti-aliased edging, is selected. Delete the contents of the selection. This should trim just the anti-aliased edges, leaving you with an aliased image.

NOTE: *This technique trims the edges of your image by about three pixels.*

Session

D7 Compositing Graphics to a Background Tile

To keep the download time to a minimum, while keeping a rich feel to a Web page, people often use a decorative background tile. The problem with background tiles, however, is correctly preparing graphics so they match when placed on top of the tile. Because you cannot predict where the tile will fall on the Web page, people often assume that they need to use rough-edged, aliased graphics. This exercise, however, shows how to prepare soft-edged, anti-aliased graphics that will match your tile.

PHOTOSHOP 4.0	Object Gear, Amusements: Dog Biscuits, Crocodile Font: Image Club Overprint

STEP 1: PREPARING A SINGLE MERGED LAYER

Prepare an anti-aliased, soft-edged image merged into a single transparent layer and set it aside.

STEP 2: FILLING A LAYER WITH A BACKGROUND TILE

Create a new layer and fill it with the background tile (To create a background tile, see Exercise D5.) To fill a layer with a background tile, first select the tile with the Marquee selection tool and then choose Define Pattern from the Edit menu. With the pattern defined, choose Fill from the Edit menu, and select Pattern from the Contents pop-up options.

STEP 3: CREATE AN ALIASED SELECTION

Leave the background tile layer and select the image layer. Using the Magic Wand, make an aliased selection around the image. To do this, set the Wand's tolerance to zero and uncheck the anti-aliased option. Click in the transparent area around the image, and then choose Similar from the Select menu to make sure that you capture all the transparent areas. Invert the selection so that the object is selected.

NOTE: *As opposed to generating a shrink-to-fit selection by Command-clicking on the layer icon, the Magic Wand works best in this case because you are creating an aliased selection that includes the soft anti-aliased edges.*

STEP 4: OPTION-MERGE

With the selection still active, merge the image layer with the background tile layer (or create an Option-Merge, see Session C7). Make sure the new merged layer is the active layer, and copy the selected portion. Although you have an aliased selection, you will grab the soft-edges that have been blended to the background tile pattern.

STEP 5: SELECTING A TRANSPARENT COLOR

Create a new file and fill it with a solid color from the Web palette (see Session F2 regarding the Web-safe color palette). This becomes your transparent color so be sure to select a color that is not in your image. (A bright color often works well.) Paste the copied image into this new file.

NOTE: *When you create a new file, its dimensions are automatically the size of the copied image.*

STEP 6: EXPORTING A GIF

Change the image mode from RGB to Index Color and select the Web colors or the Mac System palette. Next, export the image as a GIF using Photoshop's Gif89A export feature located in the File menu. When the Gif89A dialog displays, position the cursor over the color to be transparent and click once; the area should turn gray. Decide whether you want to be interlace or non-interlace the image and click OK.

TIP: *The Mac system palette includes all of the Web safe colors plus 40 extra colors. On 16- and 24-bit displays, you will not notice any change in quality. On 8-bit displays, the 40 extra colors will dither, but the effect is negligible.*

Session

D8 Creating Textured, 3D Text Elements

You can quickly create textured, 3D text elements by combining normal text with any texture or photograph. Using decorative text is an easy way to spice up a Web page design. For instance, if your Web site features long HTML text elements, adding nicely designed graphical text headlines add interest and break up an otherwise computer text-heavy design.

PHOTOSHOP 4.0	Photo Gear Vol. 1 Backgrounds and Textures: Marble #9 Font: Image Club Arquitectura

STEP 1: SETTING UP THE LAYERS

Open any image or photograph that you want to map inside of a text element. For best results, open an image that is larger than the text element.

Use the Type tool to create text directly on top of the textured image. The new text automatically ends up in its own layer as shown.

STEP 2: REARRANGING LAYERS

To map the texture inside of the text element, the texture layer needs to be on top of the text. If the texture layer is a background layer, indicated by the name "Background" in italics, you cannot reposition it. You must first convert it into a transparent layer by double-clicking its icon in the Layers palette. Once it is a transparent layer, drag it to the top of the text layer so that the texture covers the text.

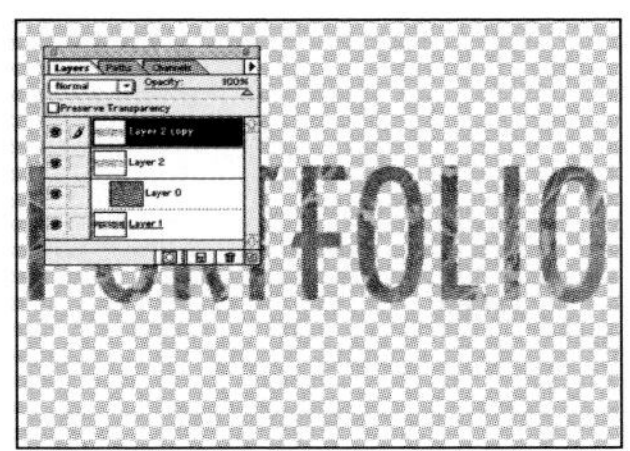

STEP 3: CREATE A CLIPPING GROUP

Create a clipping group between the underlying text and the texture layer by holding down the Option key (Mac), or Alt key (Windows), while clicking on the borderline that separates the two layers in the Layers palette. Notice how the marble texture is now mapped inside of the text.

Either merge the two layers together, or create an Option-Merge (see Session C7), so that the merge occurs in a new layer. Duplicate the merged layer. You will use these two copies to create the final effect.

STEP 4: APPLYING EFFECTS

To apply a beveled look to the text, follow the steps in Session D3. In this example, the Emboss filter settings were a height of five and an angle of 153°. To achieve the chiseled effect, rather than a soft effect, do not apply the Gaussian blur filter.

To make the text stand out, you can lighten the underlying copy using the Levels, Curves, or Brightness and Contrast controls.

To add a drop shadow to the text, follow the steps in Session D1.

Session

D9 Creating a Collage

One of the more common tasks in Photoshop is combining images to create a custom collage. In this exercise, you create a Web site banner, complete with text, that wraps to the image by combining multiple images in Photoshop, (see Session D10).

PHOTOSHOP 4.0	Object Gear Gentleman's Study: Personal Letter Object Gear Travels: Helm, Water Object Gear Amusements: Starfish 2 Font: Adobe Kepler

STEP 1: OPEN ALL IMAGES FOR THE COLLAGE

In Photoshop, open a few images that you would like to incorporate into your collage so that each image is open in a separate window. Create a new file with a white background that will be large enough to assemble your collage.

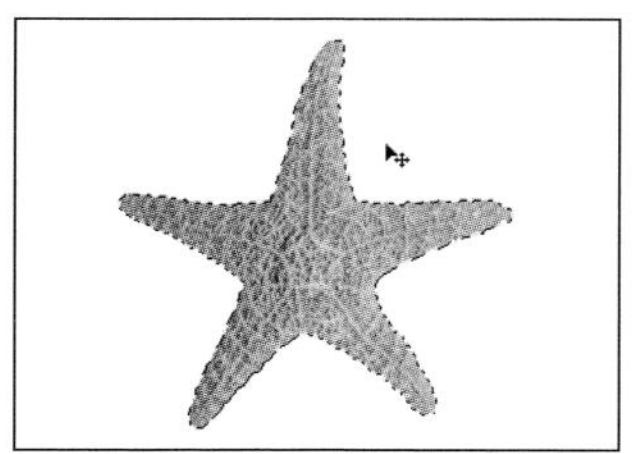

STEP 2: COMBINING IMAGES INTO ONE FILE

Using the Move tool, click one of the images and drag it into the new file. Drag the remaining images into the new file in the same way. If the image is on a solid background, the background comes with the image when it is dragged into the new file. To bring in just the image, select the background with the Magic Wand tool set on a tolerance of at least 32, with the anti-aliased checkbox selected. Invert the selection, and then drag the image into the new file using the Move tool.

TIP: *Image Club graphics have a perfect selection stored as a path. Simply go into the Paths palette, and load the path as a selection. To quickly convert the path to a selection, Hold down the Command key (Mac) or the Control key (Windows), and click the path's icon.*

STEP 3: RESIZING IMAGES

Resize each of the elements of your collage using the Free Transform function located in the Layer menu. To scale the image proportionately, hold down the Shift key while dragging one of the corner handles. To rotate the image, click and drag outside of the envelope.

TIP: *You can access other Free Transform functions by pressing the Control key while clicking and holding anywhere in the document. A pop-up menu appears with more Transform functions like Skew and Perspective.*

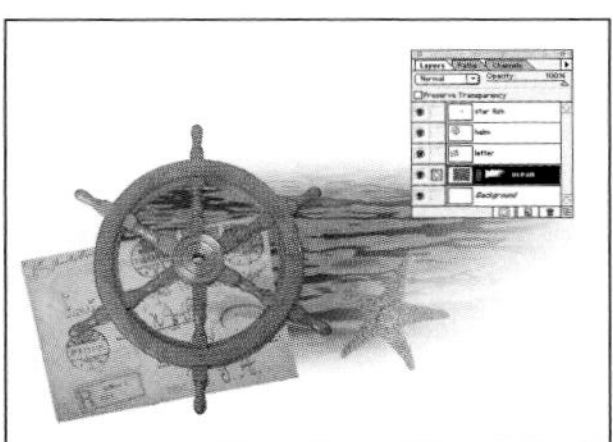

STEP 4: CREATING SOFT EFFECTS

To create the faded effect on the ocean image, create a layer mask for the ocean layer. Using the Paintbrush tool and a large brush, paint black into the layer mask. Painting with black is like painting with transparency. The advantage to using a layer mask is you can "erase" your image without really erasing your image. To turn on and off the effects of the layer mask, hold down the Shift key and click the Layer Mask icon.

STEP 5: FINISHING TOUCHES

Now that all the images are in place, you can add a few finishing touches to polish the look. Add an instant drop shadow (see Session D1) for the starfish, and create cast shadows (see Session D2) for both the helm and the letter. Enhance the color contrast of the helm using both the Curves and the Levels functions. Finally, you can add text that wraps to the shape of the helm by following the instructions in Session D10.

Session

D10 Wrapping Text to an Image

While Photoshop has extensive image editing features, Illustrator allows you to create interesting text effects like type that flows along on a wavy line or arcs around a circle. Using these two programs together, you can create text that wraps to the contour of an image, and then export the combination as a graphic ready for the Web.

PHOTOSHOP 4.0	Object Gear, Antiquities: Clown Bank
ILLUSTRATOR 7.0	Object Gear, Design Elements: Magnet
	Font: Image Club: Smile

STEP 1: FROM PHOTOSHOP TO ILLUSTRATOR

Create a merged layer that contains the image to which you want to wrap text. If you have enough RAM, open both Illustrator and Photoshop at the same time and position their windows so you can see the Illustrator window in the background. Using the Move tool, drag the flattened or merged layer from Photoshop directly into the Illustrator window in the background. If you do not have enough RAM, save a copy of your image as an EPS file. Then, place the image in Illustrator by choosing Place from the Illustrator File menu.

STEP 2: CREATING A TEXT PATH

Once the image is in Illustrator, you can lock it into position by choosing Lock from the Arrange menu.

In order to create text that wraps to your image, first define a path for the text. To create text that wraps around a circular path, as shown, select the Circle tool in the tool palette and draw a circle where you want the text. Keep in mind that the circle will become the baseline for the text. Once the circle is drawn, you may notice that it is filled with black—this will go away once you click it with the Text tool.

Choose the Text on Paths tool from the toolbar and click once in the circle where you want to begin typing.

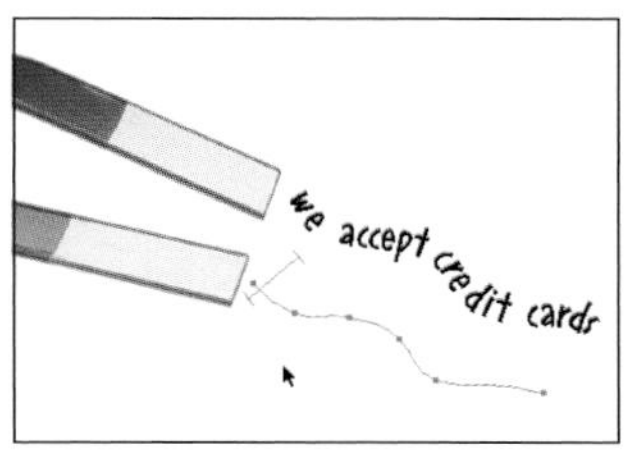

STEP 3: TEXT ON WAVY PATHS

To create wavy text, first define a wavy path with the Pen tool. As in Step 2, select the Text on Paths tool and click once on the wavy path where you want to begin typing.

TIP: *The text you create in Illustrator does not need to be in its final color. You can change the color of the text once it is in Photoshop using Preserve Transparency (see Session* *).*

STEP 4: FROM ILLUSTRATOR TO PHOTOSHOP

When you are through designing text in Illustrator, select it with the Selection tool, and drag it into the Photoshop window visible in the background; or, you can save the text in the normal Illustrator file format. You can open an Illustrator file from within Photoshop by simply choosing Open from the File menu.

TIP: *Sometimes text on paths does not render correctly in Photoshop. To get around this, convert your text to outlines in Illustrator by choosing Create Outlines from the Type menu.*

Session

D11 Adding Natural Light and Shadows

Often times images that you scan or illustrate need to be touched up—increasing or decreasing highlights and shadows until you have a perfect, natural image. In Photoshop, there are two painting techniques that enable you to paint with natural light and shadow. For example, you can add natural shines to hardwood floors, glows around light bulbs, or natural shadows to help add depth to an image.

PHOTOSHOP 4.0

STEP 1: PAINTING WITH LIGHT

In Photoshop, open an image that needs to be retouched. Create a new layer and set its mode to Overlay in the Layers palette. Using the Airbrush tool and a large brush, paint broad strokes of a light, off-white color. Notice how the image underneath appears to brighten as if natural light has been cast upon it. Change the layer's mode back to Normal and notice the large patches of solid color that, when in Overlay mode, create the lighting effect.

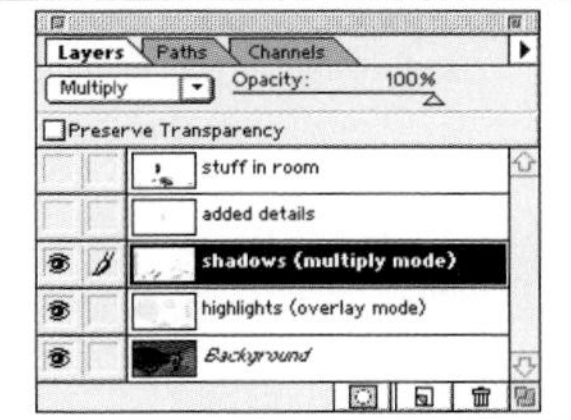

STEP 2: PAINTING WITH SHADOW

Adding shadow effects to an image is the same process as adding highlights. Create a new layer and set the layer's mode to Multiply as shown. Paint with a medium-dark color using the airbrush. Notice that, rather than covering over the underlying image, the medium-dark color enriches underlying colors while creating a shadowed effect.

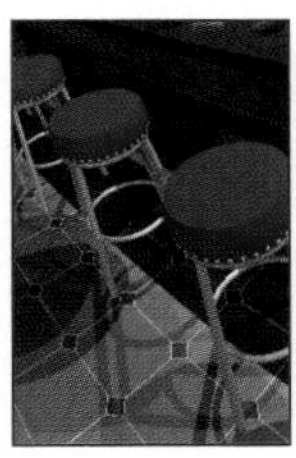

For *Suspect, Dead Birds Don't Sing*, an online murder mystery, the Surround Video room environments were first created and rendered in Strata 3D before placing them in Photoshop for finishing touches. These two images show how the rooms looked before and after Photoshop was used to enhance the highlights and shadows using the Overlay and Multiply modes.

Session

D12 Creating Consistent Soft-Edged Buttons

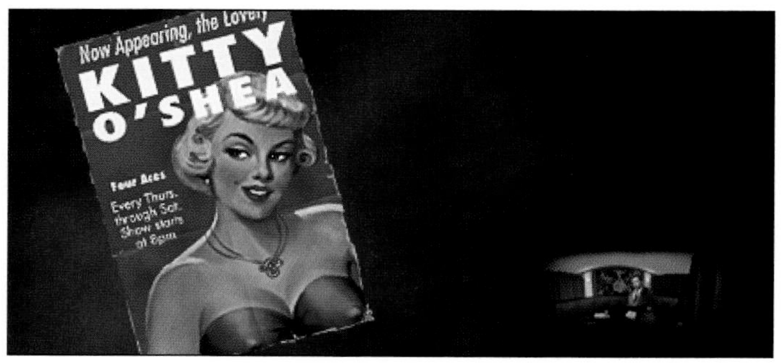

In *Suspect, Dead Birds Don't Sing,* an online murder mystery series, users wander through 3D rooms interviewing characters and searching for clues to crack the case. When users click on a clue, a detail screen appears, as shown, with a small icon in the lower right to take users back into the room. This button (one for each of the seven rooms), needed to have consistent soft-edges and be placed in the same location. This consistent treatment for seven different buttons was achieved using a single Photoshop layer mask shared through a large clipping group. Use this technique when you have a button that has multiple states, and needs to be trimmed and placed in the same location.

PHOTOSHOP 4.0

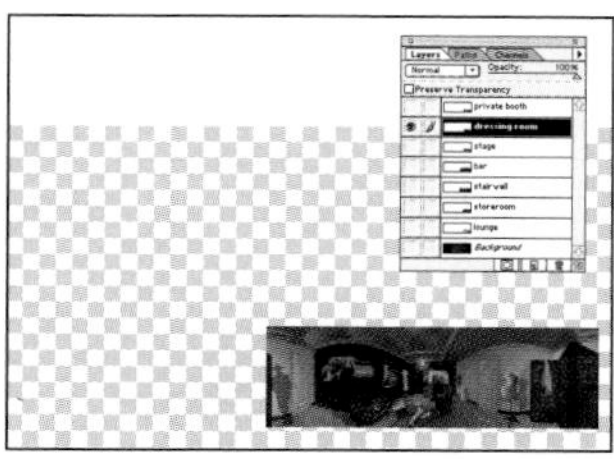

STEP 1: ASSEMBLING THE BUTTON STATES IN LAYERS

In Photoshop, assemble each state of the button in a different Photoshop layer. Because you will be trimming the button with one layer mask "cookie cutter," be sure that the button source art is larger than the trim.

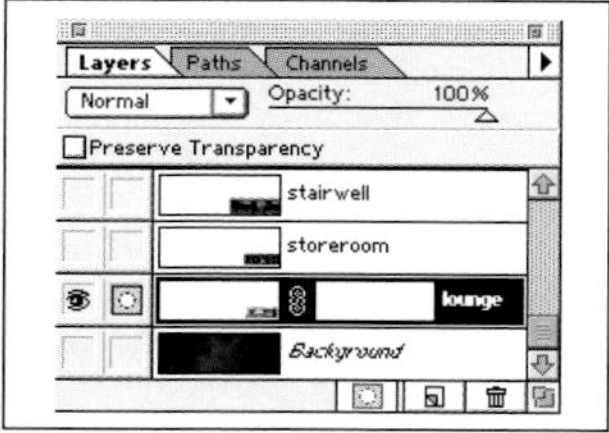

STEP 2: CREATING A LAYER MASK COOKIE CUTTER

In the bottom-most button layer, create a new layer mask. This layer mask will serve as the cookie cutter for all the other button layers. To ensure you are editing the layer mask, and not the layer, click the Layer Mask icon to select it.

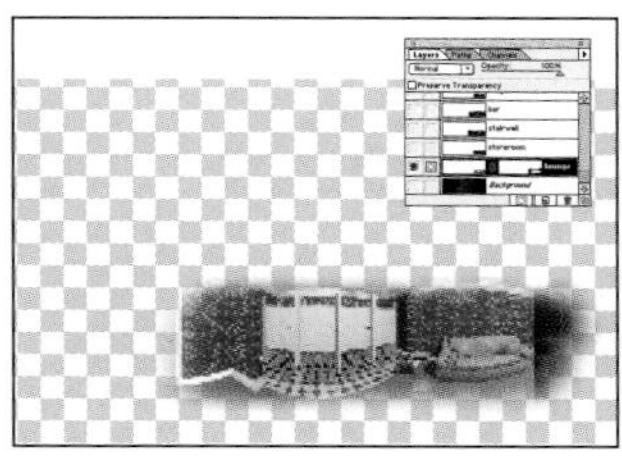

STEP 3: PAINTING WITH TRANSPARENCY

For an organic effect, select the Airbrush tool and a medium size brush. In the Tool palette, set the foreground color to black and begin airbrushing in the layer mask. Note that painting with black is like painting with transparency.

TIP: *Another way to create a soft-edged layer mask is to first create a rectangular selection around the image. Then, choose Feather from the Select menu and enter the desired softness. Select the inverse, and then click the Layer Mask icon in the Layers palette. Your inverted, feathered selection now becomes an instant layer mask.*

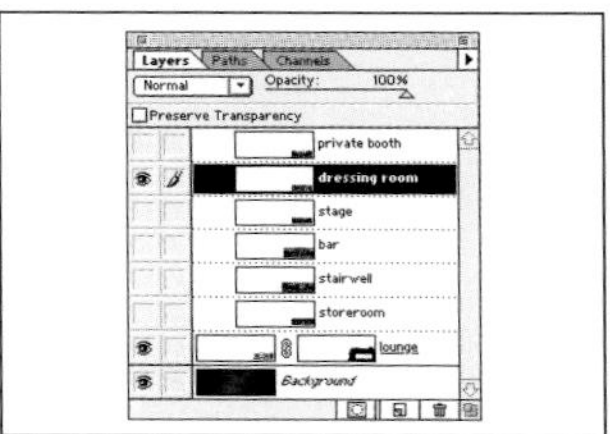

STEP 4: SETTING UP A CLIPPING GROUP

Now that you have created a layer mask, you need to share it with the buttons in the remaining layers. (This saves you the effort of duplicating the layer mask.) To do this, first set up a clipping group whereby the bottom layer with the layer mask defines the group. Create a clipping group by holding down the Option key (Mac), or the Alt key (Windows), while clicking on the border line between the two layers. Start with the bottom-most button layer and the layer directly above it.

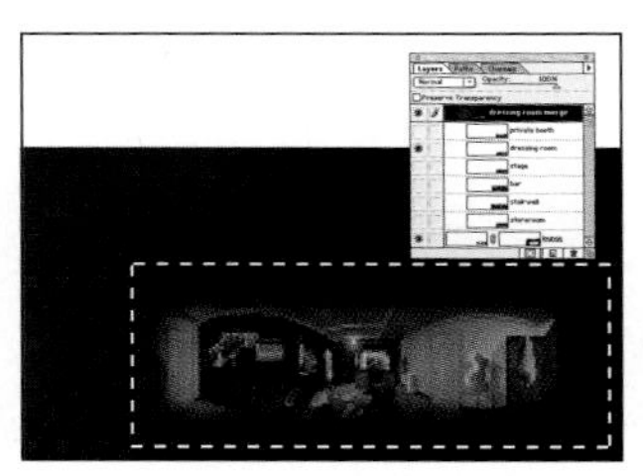

STEP 5: CUTTING OUT THE BUTTONS

Before you can cut out the buttons, you need to Option-Merge (see Session C7) them. Regardless of which button you are preparing for a merge, it needs to include the background layer and the bottom-most button layer that contains the layer mask as shown.

After you have Option-Merged all the button layer, create a single rectangular selection that you can use to cut them out.

TIP: *If you want to ensure that your rectangular selection is not cropping the buttons, and is the smallest size possible, see Session D4.*

Chapter E

Navigation and User Interface Ideas

Before you begin designing graphics for a Web page, you need design and plan the structure of the entire site. If the entire site is not planned ahead of time, the user interface cannot be consistent. Invariably, you will end up having to tack on interface elements for which there are no logical places. The Web site looks and feels unprofessional, and seems as though it is being held together with tape. We suggest that before you begin creating the interface elements contained within this chapter, you draw a blueprint, or site map, for your Web site so that you know which elements are required for each page. Doing this not only streamlines production, it helps you avoid design elements that look like an after-thought.

CHAPTER SESSIONS

E1 *Mocking Up Your Web Page Layout*

E2 *Creating Cross-Navigation Icons*

E3 *Finding Image Map Coordinates*

E4 *Making a Seamless, Three-Part Navigation Banner*

E5 *Creating Three-State Buttons*

E6 *Making Roll-Over Icon Labels*

E7 *Color-Coding an Interface*

E8 *Interfaces Beyond the Static Screen*

CHAPTER TOOLBOX

Adobe Photoshop 4.0

Adobe Illustrator 7.0

IMAGES

Image Club, Object Gear

Image Club, Festive Occasions

Image Club, Urban Colors

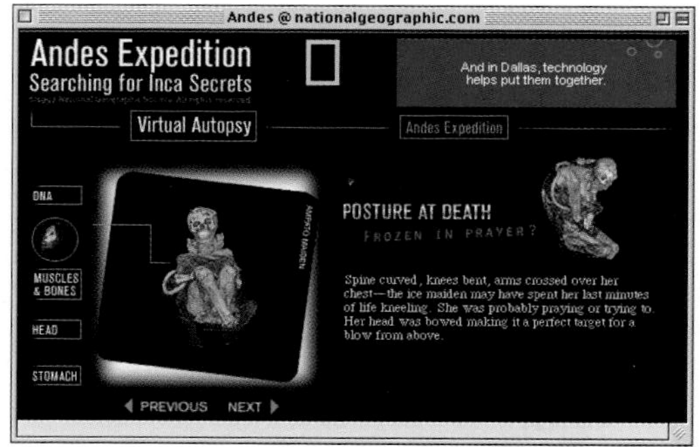

The *National Geographic Incan Mummies* Web site enables the user to toggle between the autopsy and expedition modes.

In designing and planning a Web site, deciding on the most appropriate design structure, or mix of structures, can be made simpler if you return to your initial content outline. Designing an interface with no more than seven main categories is a lot easier than designing an interface for ten or more categories! Therefore, it's best to edit your content outline with this in mind.

By categories, I mean major informational sections—not functions like search, email, and feedback. Grouping like-elements is a key part of designing an effective interface. In the case of the *National Geographic Incan Mummies* Web site, the user can toggle back and forth between the Autopsy and Expedition areas. These two buttons are grouped together, given the same visual treatment, and are located apart from other interface functions.

The Commscope We site features a color-coded navigational structure.

DESIGN AND NAVIGATION STRUCTURES

Design structures are the conceptual and physical models used to organize the content of a Web site. There are a number of common models to choose from including a basic hierarchy, a linear structure, and a flattened hierarchy. Hierarchies are just simple branching structures. The problem with hierarchies, however, is that users can easily get lost if the branching structure is too deep, breaking down into multiple sub-catagories, or too wide, offering too many categories at the top level. In addition, in a basic hierarchy, the user is forced to return to the home page to choose a different path. A flattened hierarchy solves this common user interface problem.

Rather than moving up and down different branches of a hierarchy, flattened hierarchies allow you to move laterally through a Web site's categories. This is achieved through a row of cross-navigational icons that represent all the main categories of a Web site(see Session E2). By placing a cross-navigational banner on each Web page, a user can quickly jump to other sections no matter where they are in your site.

This chapter explores a variety of ways to create cross-navigational systems. Also, don't miss Session E8 for an in-depth look at exciting alternatives to the common user interface design structures.

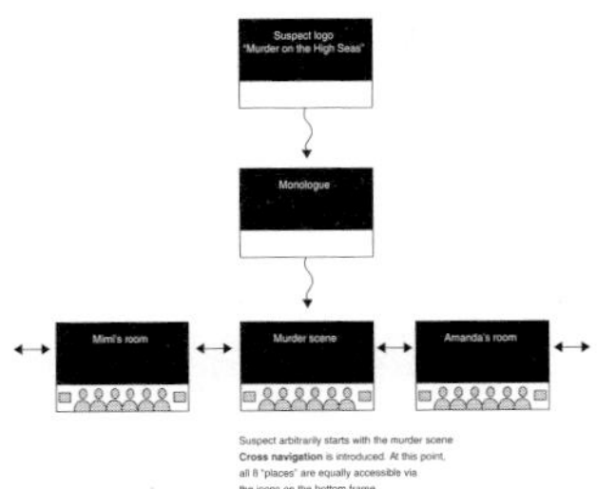

CREATING BLUEPRINTS, OR SITE MAPS, FOR A WEB SITE

The best place to work out a design structure and initial user interface issues is on paper. Once you have finalized a content outline—preferably with five-to-seven main categories—and a grouping of various other functions, you can begin to draw a flow chart that shows how all the categories and functions relate to one another.

The site map for *Suspect* series shows a linear introductory sequence indicated by the vertical arrangement of frames, which leads to the scene of the crime where cross-navigation is introduced. From the crime scene, users can navigate laterally—jumping from room to room—to solve the case. The lateral movement is indicated in the site map by a horizontal arrangement of frames interconnected by double-headed arrows.

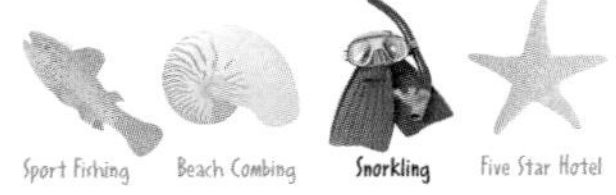

DETAILS, DETAILS

No user interface is complete without the little details that serve to enhance its usability. Things like user feedback, color coding, consistency, labeling, and placement on the screen go a long way to polish an interface, and are things you can integrate into almost any design.

Providing feedback for your users is simply letting them know where they are in a Web site and acknowledging their interaction. For instance, in a cross-navigational system, when a user clicks an icon to go to a section, you can highlight the icon to acknowledge their interaction and tell them where they are (see Sessions E4, E5, E6). Color-coding an interface is a form of user feedback. By associating a color with each main section of a Web site, users can quickly identify where they are (see Session E7).

Interface elements—especially navigational elements—should be treated consistently throughout a Web site. For instance, a row of navigational icons should always look the same and should be located in the same place on each Web page. They should not be arranged vertically on one page, then across the top on another page. In addition, buttons should not disappear from the navigation bar—even if they are representing a link to the page you are already on. Doing so changes the look and placement of navigational icons. More consistency means the user will be more comfortable with your site.

Lastly, no matter how self-evident you think your icons are, it is always a good idea to label their functionality. If the addition of text labels starts to clutter your interface, see Session E6 for ideas.

Session

E1 Mocking Up Your Web Page Layout

Mocking up your Web pages in Photoshop is a great way to visualize your Web page design and user interface decisions before you begin to write HTML code. By simply starting with a document the size of your Web page, you have a blank canvas on which to experiment. From Photoshop, you can decide the size and placement of all your interface elements as well as HTML text, tables, and frame structures.

ADOBE PHOTOSHOP 4.0

Icons from Session E2
Banner from Session B11
Graphic from Session D9
3D Text Headline from Session D8

STEP 1: CREATE A NEW PHOTOSHOP DOCUMENT

Start in Photoshop by creating a new document that is the same size as your intended Web page. Remember to keep the design of your Web page small enough that it fits within the browser window. Most users own the small, 640 x 480 pixels monitors. Once you consider that the browser interface cuts into that space considerably, there is not much screen real estate, only 600 x 350 pixels to work with.

TIP: *If you intend to have information scroll off screen, then create a longer Photoshop document and set guides at the 350-pixel cut-off point. This way, you can design an interface that works within the small browser window and leads your users to the information off screen.*

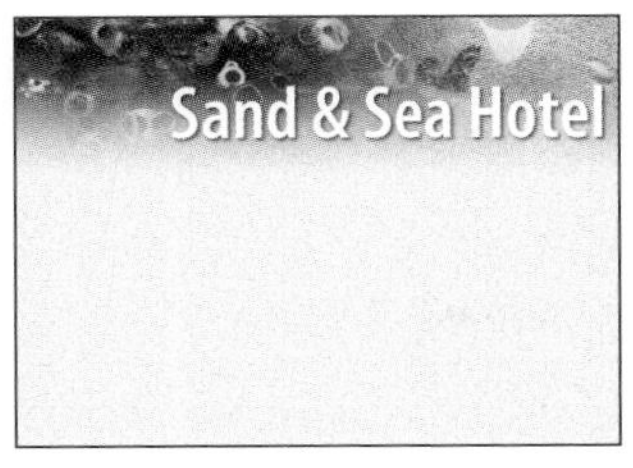

STEP 2: SET THE BACKGROUND HEXADECIMAL COLOR OR TILE

Select a color from the Web-safe color swatches for the background of your Web page (see Session B11). Use the Option + Delete (Mac), or Alt + Delete (Windows) keys to fill the entire background layer. This color is represented later in HTML as a hexadecimal number. To find the hexadecimal code for your RBG value, see the RBG to Hexadecimal Color Chart in Chapter F, "Preparing Graphics for the Web."

If you are going to use a background tile, then fill the background layer with the tile. To do this, open the tile graphic, select it, and then choose Define Pattern from the Edit menu. Choose Fill from the Edit menu and select Pattern from the pull-down menu.

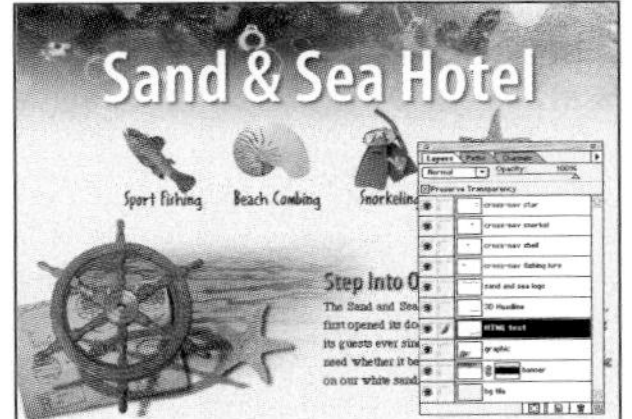

STEP 3: ASSEMBLE INTERFACE AND HTML ELEMENTS

In separate layers, assemble and position all of the interface elements with all of their highlighted and de-highlighted permutations. In addition, mock-up aliased, HTML text that you want to include in your real Web page.

STEP 4: PREPARE CUT-OUTS FOR FINAL GRAPHICS

Web page layouts are generally built from a variety of pieces that have been cropped to their smallest possible size to save on download time. Now that your Photoshop document looks like a complete Web page, its time to begin chopping up each of the elements and saving them in the proper format so you can recreate the layout in HTML.

Photoshop's guides allow you to determine multiple crop marks for your various interface elements. First, you must determine the smallest possible crop for each element or set of elements (such as row of icons).

TIP: *You can use the Magic Wand to find the smallest crop size for each element (see Session C5). Once you have generated a selection, you can drag out guides that will snap to the selection, creating an easy cropping guide.*

STEP 5: COPY OUT AND SAVE FINAL GRAPHICS

Because your interface elements are on transparent layers, you must composite them to the background color or tile before you cut them out. Use the Option-Merge technique from Session C1 to create composited layers without affecting your source layers.

Using the guides you set up in Step 4, create cut-out selections and copy all of the interface elements into new, separate files. If one of your interface elements contains multiple buttons in different highlight states (such as a row of icons), you must copy and cut out all of its permutations as a series of separate files (that are the same pixel dimension for easy registration).

Session

E2 Creating Cross-Navigation Icons

To quickly allow users to jump around from one important section of your Web site to another, you may want to consider designing a cross-navigational system to use throughout your site. This system can be as simple as a row of labeled icons consistently placed on each page throughout the site. For added usability, you may want to design a highlighting system for your icons. This helps create a "sense of place" for your users, letting them know where they are in your site.

ADOBE PHOTOSHOP 4.0	Object Gear: Culturals: Conch Shell Object Gear: Antiquities: Fishing Lure Object Gear: Amusements: Snorkel, Starfish 2 Font: Image Club Smile

STEP 1: SIZING ICONS

In this exercise, you will create a row of icons that represent the four major sections of a Web site. Open four graphics that you want to use as your icons and shrink them all until they are about 70 x 70 pixels each. You can use either the Free Transform function, located under the Layer menu, or the Image Size function located under the Image menu.

It is a good idea to float the graphics onto a transparent background before you shrink them. This helps reduce the amount of fringing around the edges.

TIP: *Once you float a graphic onto a transparent background, it may still retain some colored fringing around the edges. To quickly get rid of the "artifacts" choose Matting > Defringe with a one pixel radius from the Layer menu.*

STEP 2: ASSEMBLING ICONS INTO A BANNER

Once you have shrunk all graphics to an icon size, create a new Photoshop document that is large enough to arrange all of the iconsinto a banner. You can always crop later, so don't feel compelled to accurately anticipate the size of your banner. It is a good idea, however, to start with a new Photoshop file that is 600 x 350 pixels—the smallest common screen real estate. This way, you can judge how large your cross-navigational banner should be relative to the rest of your page.

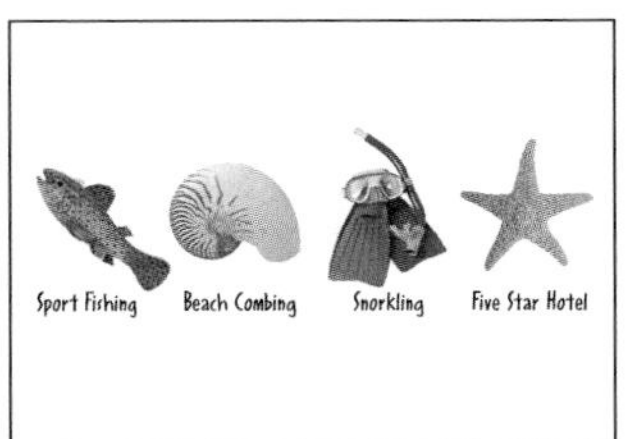

STEP 3: ADDING TEXT LABELS

Even if the graphics you choose for your icons seem self-evident in terms of what they represent, it is a good idea to label them. Add text labels for each of the four icons. After you have created each text label, merge it with its icon.

Rather than relying on Photoshop's limited text capabilities, you can use Illustrator to create curved text, or text that wraps to the shape of each icon (see Session B3).

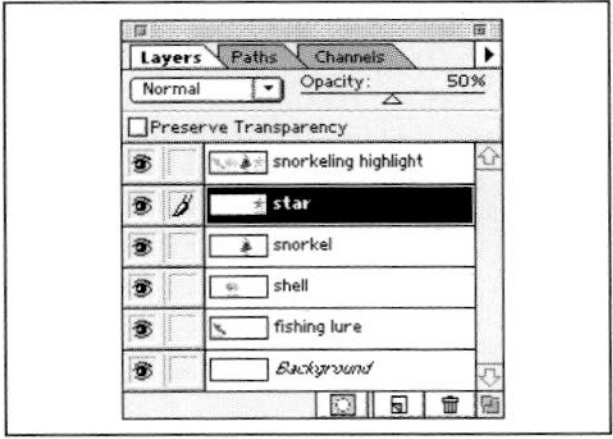

STEP 4: HIGHLIGHTING AND DE-HIGHLIGHTING ICONS

As long as each icon, with its label, is in a separate layer, you can easily create a series of navigational banners that each feature a different icon highlighted.

In the Layers palette, change each icon's opacity to 50%, except for the one you want to highlight. Option-Merge (see Session C1), all four icons with the background into a new layer ready to be cut out.

Change the opacities of each of the four icon layers again to highlight a different icon. Continue to change the opacities and then Option-Merge them to create a total of four new, merged layers—each with a different icon highlighted—ready to be cut out.

STEP 5: COPY EACH BANNER INTO A NEW FILE

Once you have created a series of merged layers, each with a different icon highlighted, create the smallest possible selection around the banner. Make sure that you do not accidentally clip any of the icons. (See Session D4 for instructions on how to determine the smallest size cut out that you can make.)

If you like, you can crop the file to the size of your selection by choosing Crop from the Image menu. Otherwise, save the selection as a channel to archive it. Use the selection to copy each of the four merged layers into their own files ready for final processing (see Sessions F1 and F3).

Session

E3 Finding Image Map Coordinates

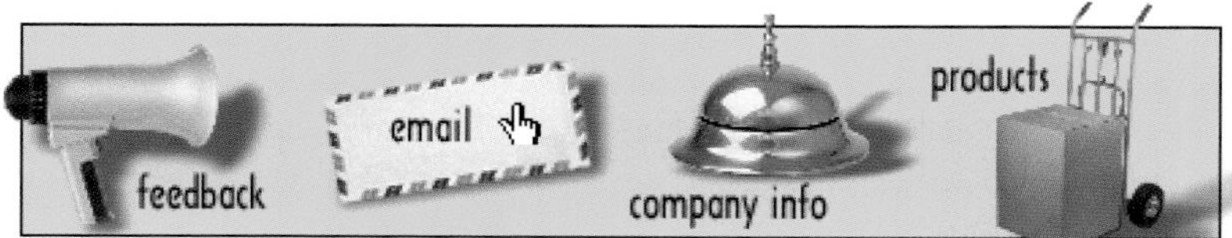

Rather than chopping up graphics into individual pieces so that each one can become a button, you can create one large image and define multiple hot spots, or buttons, using an image map. An image map works on a coordinate system. By knowing the pixel boundaries of each hot spot in relation to the size of the entire graphic in HTML code, you can assign links to each region. The Photoshop Info palette allows you to find the pixel dimensions that you need to enter into your HTML code to make an image map.

ADOBE PHOTOSHOP 4.0	Object Gear: Business Elements: Airmail, Object Gear: Business Elements: Handtruck Object Gear: Design Elements: Megaphone Object Gear: Antiquities: Hotel Desk Bell Font: Image Club Arquitectura

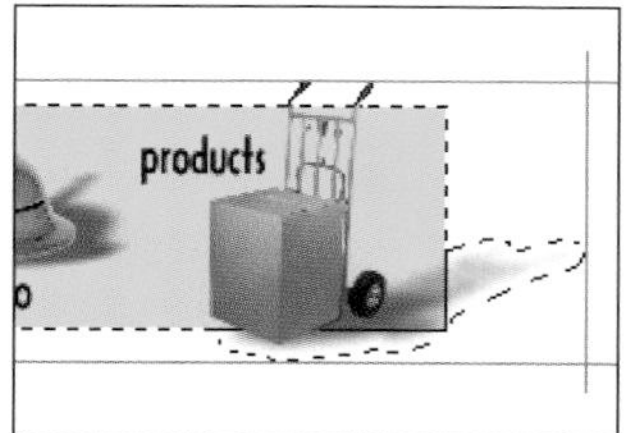

STEP 1: CROP THE BANNER TO THE SMALLEST SIZE

In this session, you will create an image map for a row of cross-navigational icons. The first step is to crop the banner of icons to its smallest possible size to save on download time. Use the Magic Wand tool to find the absolute edges of the banner, and then use the guides to create a rectangle around the banner (see Session D4 for more information on finding an image's smallest area). From the guides, create a rectangular selection and choose Crop from the Image menu.

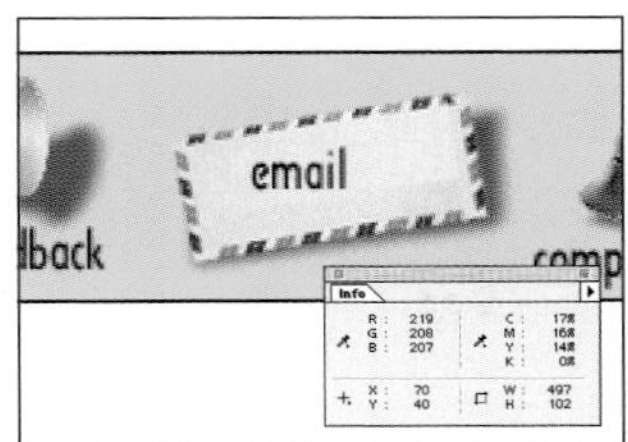

STEP 2: USING THE INFO WINDOW

Open the Info window located under the Window menu. Notice that if you move the cursor around in your image, numbers in the Info window change. Specifically, notice the X, Y coordinates; these indicate the exact pixel location of your cursor. Zero-zero starts in the upper left corner of an image and counts across for the X coordinate, and down for the Y coordinate.

You also need to know the entire dimensions of the banner so that you can add it into your image source tag in HTML. To quickly find the image's dimensions, Select All and note the dimensions shown in the Info window.

TIP: *If your X and Y coordinates are indicating inches instead of pixels, you can change the units in the Preferences menu.*

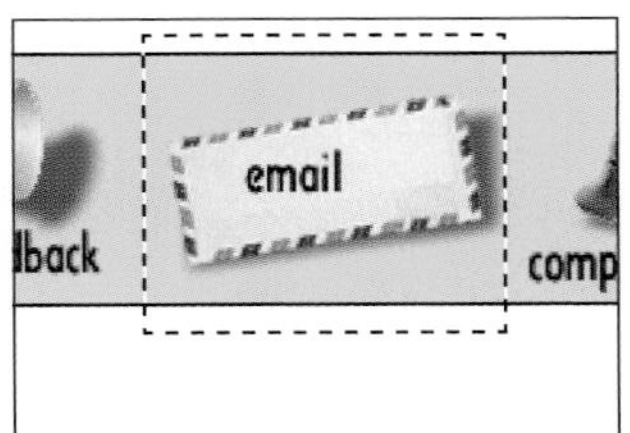

STEP 3: DRAW A SELECTION TO DEFINE A BUTTON

Using the Marquee tool, draw a rectangular selection around the icon. This selection defines the clickable area so make sure that the selection does not extend into the neighboring icons.

To draw all the hot spots at once, hold down the Shift key, which allows you add to a selection. Draw the remaining hot spots.

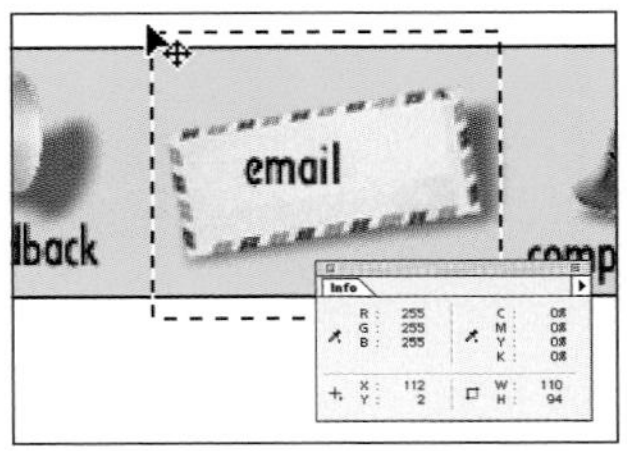

STEP 4: FINDING THE X, Y COORDINATES

Image maps are defined by the upper left corner X, Y coordinate first, followed by the lower right corner coordinate. To find the coordinates for each button, position the cursor at the upper left corner of the button selection and record the X, Y coordinates listed in the Info window. Next, position the cursor at the lower right corner and record those coordinates.

Write down the coordinates of both corners for each button.

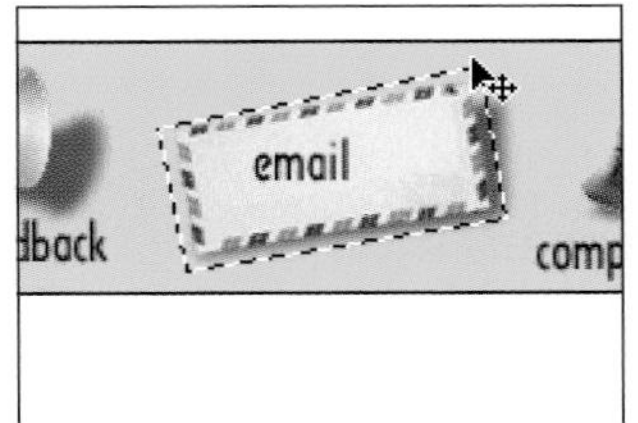

STEP 5: ENTER THE COORDINATES IN HTML

If, for example, the upper coordinates that you recorded for a button were X: 112 and Y: 2, and the lower coordinates were X: 229 and Y: 100, then you would enter them into HTML as follows: 112,2, 229,100

To create an irregular-shaped button, you need to define a polygon shape in Photoshop using the straight-edge Lasso tool. Record the X, Y coordinates for each point, starting with the left-most point. You should enter the coordinates in HTML for a polygon shaped button the same way you would a rectangular button. You simply will have a longer string of numbers. (See Session H7 for more information on creating image maps in HTML code.)

Session

E4 Making a Seamless, Three-Part Navigation Banner

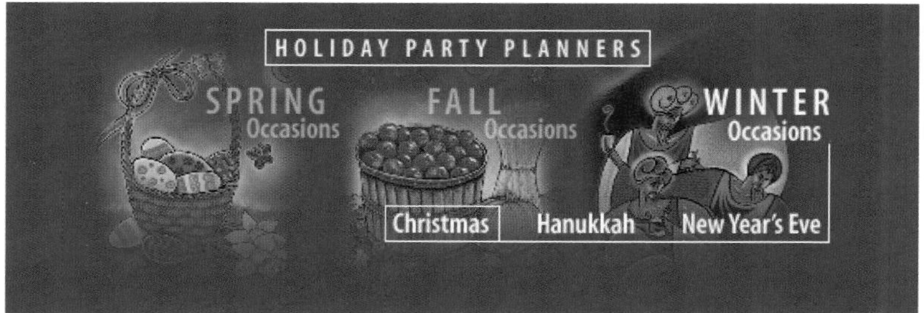

Because downloading graphics can take so much time (potentially driving away users), it makes sense to reuse graphics whenever possible—especially navigation graphics that should be on each Web page anyway. Once a graphic downloads, it is "cached" into memory. Therefore, when the graphic is reused on a different Web page, it does not need to download again; it is simply redrawn from the memory cache. Reusing the same graphic over and over, however, can be monotonous. To avoid the monotony, you can create a seamless multiple-part navigational system. By simply changing one of the parts, you can take advantage of caching, yet create the illusion that the entire banner has changed.

ADOBE PHOTOSHOP 4.0	Festive Occasions: Easter basket Festive Occasions: Fall Harvest Festive Occasions: Three Wisemen Font: Myriad Semi-Bold Condensed

STEP 1: USE GUIDES TO DEFINE AREAS

Create a new Photoshop document that is 600 x 350 pixels and set the background color or pattern to match your Web page (see Session E1).

One of the best ways to approach designing a three-part navigational system that you will chop into three separate pieces, is to set up a grid. Photoshop's guides provide an excellent way to define three areas. As you work, you can visually see where you can make your cut marks. Drag out guides from the rulers to mark off three sections.

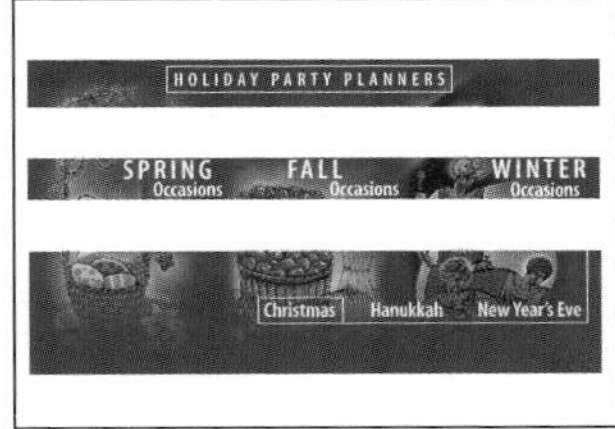

STEP 2: DESIGN A THREE-PART NAVIGATIONAL SYSTEM

Design a cross-navigational banner that consists of three labeled icons that, when selected, display a secondary navigational system below. For instance, in this example, three sub-choices are displayed when one of the main choices is selected.

The three sections of this example are the top section with the title, the mid-section with the three main choices, and the bottom section that features the sub-choices. Notice that each section is independent from the other. For example, the line connecting the bottom section choices does not extend into the mid-section. The illustrations, however, remain constant and therefore can be shared among all three sections.

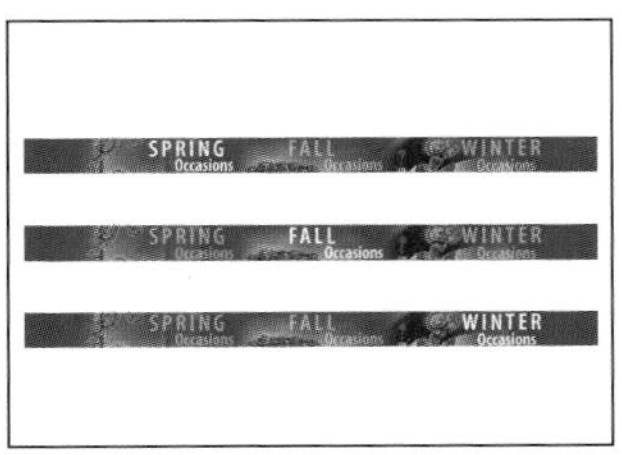

STEP 3: HIGHLIGHTING THE ICONS

There are three editions of the mid-section depending upon which icon is selected. In this case, the text of the chosen icon highlights, while the text of the unchosen icons dim to 50% opacity. Because the icon illustrations are shared among all three sections, it is better to change only the text to indicate a highlight—leaving the illustration unchanged.

Adjust the opacity of the labels so that the unchosen labels are set to 50% while the selected label remains at 100%. Option-Merge (see Session C1) the labels with the background and icon illustrations so that you create a series of layers ready to be cut out along the guide marks you set up in Step 2.

STEP 4: HIGHLIGHTING THE SUB-CATAGORIES

The sub-catagories for each of the three main choices are similarly highlighted and de-highlighted. Prepare all the sub-choices in their highlighted and de-highlighted states in the same way as in Step 3. Option-Merge them together with the icon illustration and background color so that you have a series of layers ready to cut out.

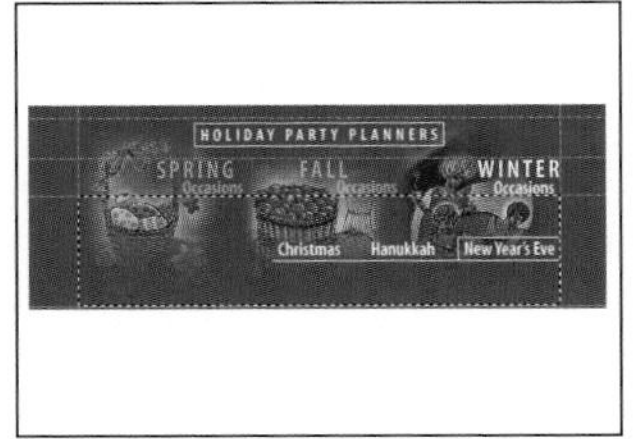

STEP 5: SELECT AND CUT OUT EACH SECTION

Following the guides you set up in Step 2, create a cut-out selection for each of the three sections. You may want to save each selection as a channel for archival purposes.

Use the selection to cut out all the permutations of each section. In the case of the top section, there is only one graphic that will not change. The mid-section has three variations, and the bottom section has nine variations.

After removing the graphics prepare them for the Web following the steps in Sessions F1 and F3.

Session

E5 Creating Three-State Buttons

Step 1: Choosing a Web Template

Step 2: Choosing a Graphic Theme

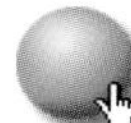
Step 3: Customizing Graphics

Step 4: Adding Text and Links

One of the key components to good user interface design is providing feedback to your users—letting them know where they are, what buttons are clickable, and whether or not the computer acknowledged their click. These issues can be addressed with a simple three-state button. A three-state button is one that changes its look based on the user's interaction. The first state is the resting, unselected state. In order to let the user know the button is clickable, however, the button changes slightly when the cursor rolls over or near it. When the user clicks the button, the button switches to its highlighted, selected state. Because of its dynamic nature, a three-state button cannot be implemented in normal HTML. It must be implemented using Java, ActiveX, Shockwave, Flash, or other application.

ADOBE PHOTOSHOP 4.0 Font: Adobe Myriad Semi-Bold Condensed

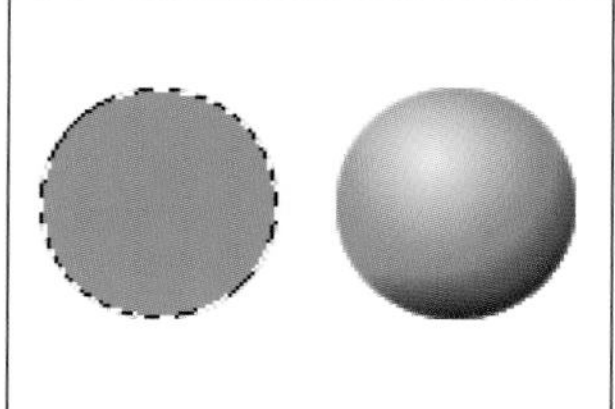

STEP 1: CREATING A PATH IN ILLUSTRATOR

In a transparent Photoshop layer, use the circular Selection tool to draw a perfect circle. While holding down the Option key (Mac), or Alt key (Windows), begin drawing a circle selection. This allows you to draw the circle from the center out. Use the Shift key as you draw to constrain your selection to a perfect circle.

Choose the Gradient tool and in its Options palette, set the blend from a light color to a dark color, and choose a radial gradation. Begin your blend where you wish the highlight and finish it where you want the shaded area. This graphic will serve as the selected state of your button.

TIP: *If you have Kai's Power Tools, you can quickly create a spherical button using the Glass Lens Bright function. First fill a circular selection with a flat color, then reselect the circle, including a little more than the circle. Choose the Glass Lens Bright filter from the Filter menu and voila!*

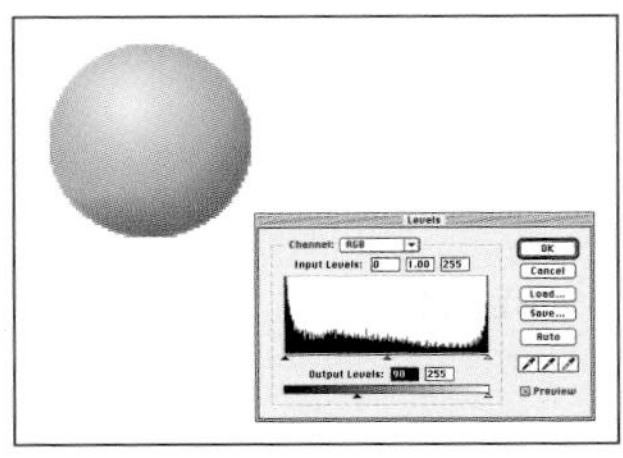

STEP 2: THE NON-SELECTED STATE

To create the non-selected state of the button, first duplicate the layer containing the button you prepared in Step 1. Generally, unselected buttons should darker, duller, or more faded than their selected counterparts. In this exercise, fade the button copy using the Levels function found in the Image > Adjust menu. Slide the lower left Output Levels to 90 and click OK.

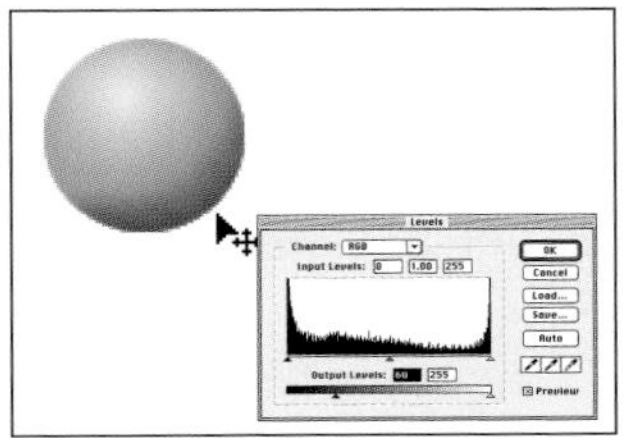

STEP 3: THE ROLL-OVER STATE

To indicate that a button is clickable, the unselected state should change when the mouse rolls over it. Depending on the treatment of the unselected state, simply changing the lighting or fading of the button may not be enough. You may want to consider moving the button, or animating it.

For this session, you will both brighten and move the button. Create a duplicate of the original, selected-state button. Choose the Move tool, and use the arrow keys on the keyboard to move the button down two pixels and over two pixels. Next, use the Levels again to fade the button. This time, set the Output Levels to 60.

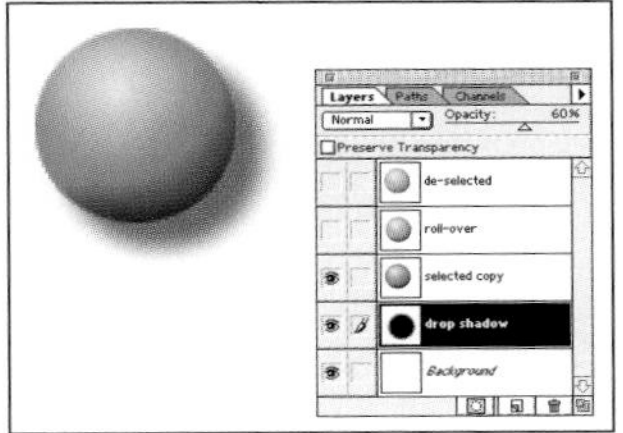

STEP 4: ADD AN INSTANT DROP SHADOW

Create an instant drop shadow for each of state of the button (see Session D1). You can create just one drop shadow for all three buttons, just keep in mind that you will need to move it slightly for the rollover state.

Option-Merge each state with the background (see Session C1), so that all three are ready for final processing.

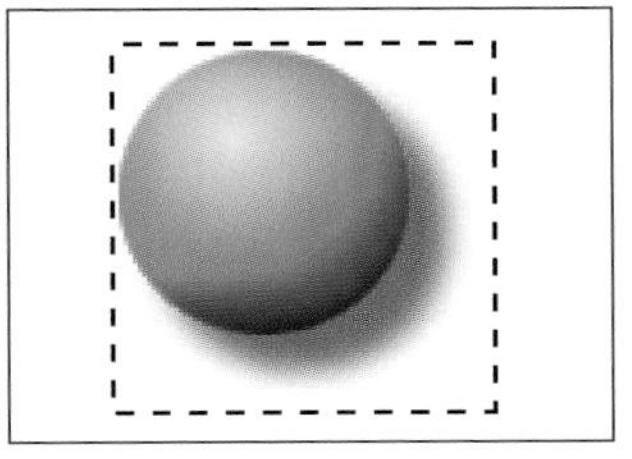

STEP 5: CUT OUT EACH STATE

Make a rectangular selection around the buttons, making sure not to accidentally clip out the shadow. (To trim graphics to their smallest size, see Session D4.) You should use this same selection to cut out each of the three buttons to ensure registration.

Once each button is cut out, final preparation of the files (i.e. palettes and file format), depends on the software you use to assemble the button, see Chapter C, "Web Animation Techniques."

Session

E6 Making Roll-Over Icon Labels

A variation on the three-state button is the two-state button that features a roll-over, or pop-up label. Not only does this type of button incorporate important labeling, it also helps indicate to a user that a button is clickable. This technique is especially useful when extensive text starts to clutter the screen. For an added flair, you can use Adobe Illustrator to create decorative text that wraps to the contours of each icon.

ADOBE PHOTOSHOP 4.0	Urban Colors: Aerobics, Scale, Breakfast
ADOBE ILLUSTRATOR 7.0	Font: Image Club Stanton

STEP 1: ASSEMBLE ICONS IN LAYERS

Create a new Photoshop document and assemble all the icons in separate layers. In order to create the decorative rollover labels that wrap to the shape of the icons, you need to prepare a template that you can import into Illustrator. Option-Merge the icons together into a new layer (see Session C1).

If you have enough memory, open Illustrator and position the Illustrator window such that you can see it in the background behind Photoshop. Using the Move tool, drag the merged layer from Photoshop directly into the Illustrator window in the background.

> **TIP:** *If you do not have enough memory to drag and drop files back and forth from Photoshop to Illustrator, copy and save the merged layer as an EPS file from Photoshop. Quit Photoshop, open Illustrator and choose Place from the File menu. Locate your EPS file and place it into the Illustrator window.*

STEP 2: CREATING LABELS IN ILLUSTRATOR

With the icons placed into Illustrator as a template, you can begin to create decorative text elements. Its best to lock the icons in place so that you do not accidentally move them while creating the text. To lock the icons, first select them and then choose Lock from the Arrange menu.

Using the Pen or Pencil tool in Illustrator, create paths for the text to follow. Select the Type tool and click once on the beginning of a path to start typing.

STEP 3: IMPORTING THE LABELS INTO PHOTOSHOP

Bring the text labels back into Photoshop by selecting them and dragging them into an open Photoshop window visible in the background. Position the text correctly on top of the icons.

If you do not have both applications open, simply save the text as a normal Illustrator document, not as an EPS file. You can then open the Illustrator file from within Photoshop.

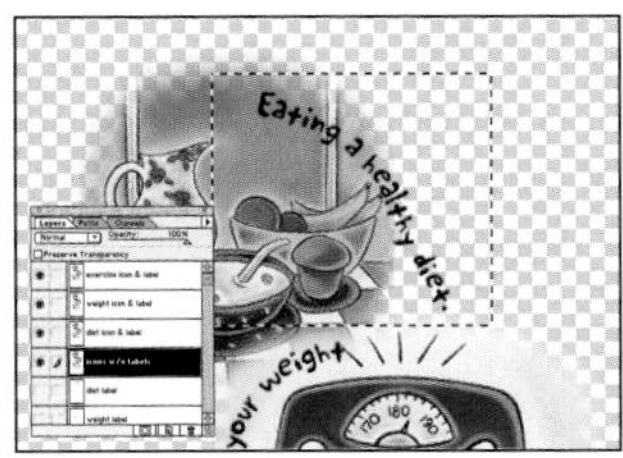

STEP 4: SEPARATE EACH LABEL

Because each label will appear and disappear independently, depending on the user's interaction, you need to separate each label onto its own layer. The easiest way to split apart images on one layer is to select each part, and then choose New > Layer Via Cut from the Layer menu.

Split the three text labels onto their own layers so that you have both the icons and the labels on separate layers ready for a series of merges. First Option-Merge the icons against the background without the labels, and then each individual icon with its label.

STEP 5: CUT OUT THE ROLLOVER LABELS

In this case the text labels overlap into neighboring icons. Therefore rather than using the same size cut out for both states of the button (with and without the label), it is best to cut out both according to their smallest size (see Session D4). In addition, the text should be anti-aliased to the icon illustration first, and then cut out onto a transparent background as shown. See Session D7 for step-by-step instructions on preparing this type of graphic.

Session

E7 Color-Coding an Interface

In addition to designing a cross-navigational system for a Web site, it often makes sense to color-code each section. By associating a color with one of the categories, users can quickly identify where they are in a site, even if they are a few levels down within a section. Color-coding should only be used to brand only the five to seven top-level categories of a Web site, excluding simple buttons like feedback and email. These colors should follow through each section—especially if you introduce sub-choices once a user selects a category. One of the largest mistakes people make is overusing color; doing so defeats the advantages that color coding affords.

ADOBE PHOTOSHOP 4.0

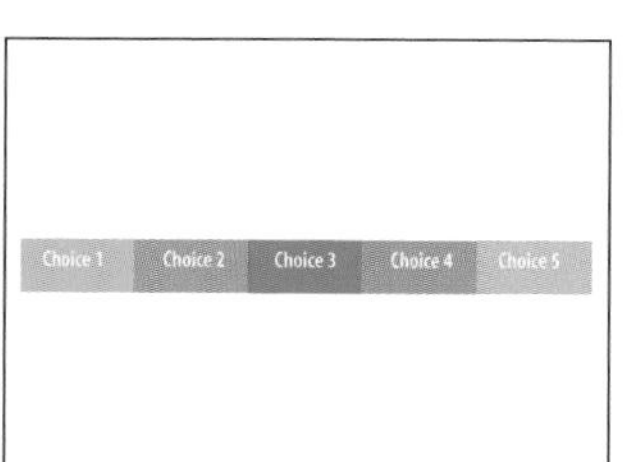

STEP 1: COLOR CHOICES

The most important step in designing a color-coded interface is choosing the colors themselves. A rule of thumb is to choose a set of colors that, together, make a family. For instance, if you select a series of light, pastel colors, do not include one bright, saturated color. Secondly, it is important to choose colors that are easily distinguished from one another. Reds and oranges, for example, often can be too close in value and hue.

If you are labeling sections, make sure that the text treatment you are planning is readable on all the colors. The last thing you want is to have a series of black labels and one white one because the underlying color was too dark for a dark label.

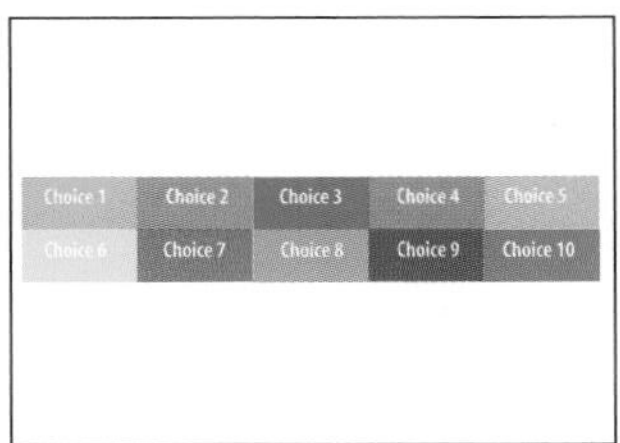

STEP 2: NUMBER OF COLORS

Color-coding breaks down if there are too many colors. A set of any more than five, perhaps six, colors becomes difficult to differentiate. In addition, too many colors are difficult to organize into a family—especially when choosing colors from the Web-safe color palette. There is also the added problem of finding a large set of colors that work well the the same text treatment as shown.

Therefore, color-coding is only recommended for Web sites that feature less than seven categories.

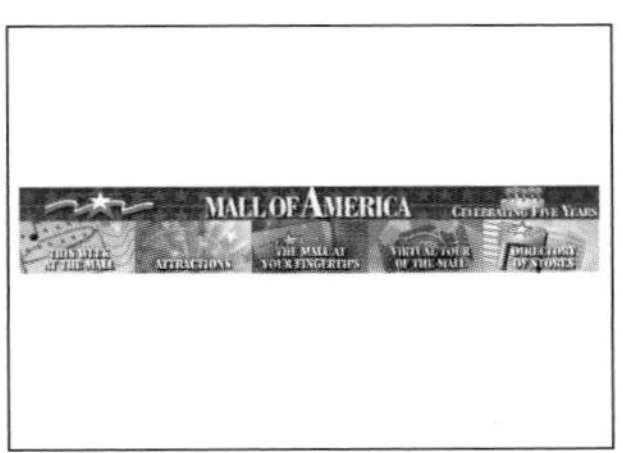

STEP 3: DETERMINE THE MAIN CATEGORIES

Color-coding should be reserved for only the important, meta-categories of a Web site. Things like feedback, links, credits, and email buttons are generally not major sections unto themselves. These types of buttons should not only be left plain, but probably left out of the cross navigation.

Color coded interfaces are particularly effective when coupled with a cross-navigational system. This way, the user is constantly reminded, by the ever-present set cross-navigational buttons, as to which colors go with which categories.

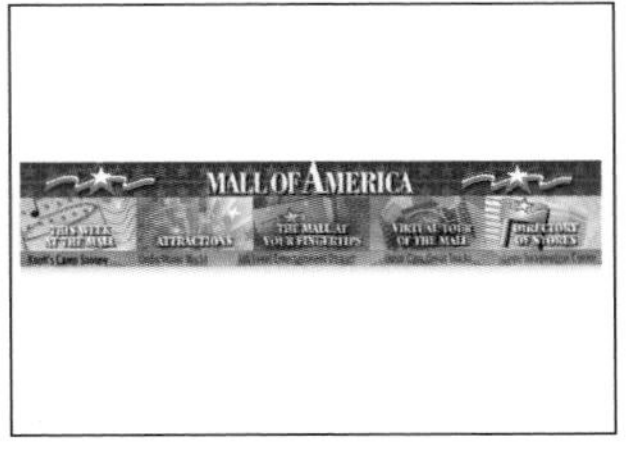

STEP 4: EXTENDING A COLOR THROUGHOUT A SECTION

If you plan to introduce a secondary cross-navigation system for sub-choices, the sub-choices should not introduce a new color-coding system. Rather, the color of the parent category should extend into the sub-choices, as demonstrated in the *Mall of America* Web site.

You may even go so far as to set the background color of each Web page to match its section. The *Torani* site at *www.torani.com*, designed by both SF Interactive and Electravision, uses this user interface convention.

Session

E8 Interfaces Beyond the Static Screen

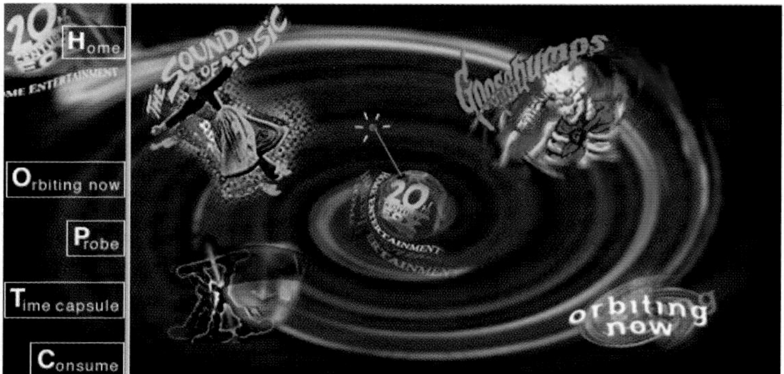

The *1996–97 Twentieth Century Fox Home Entertainment* Web site at *www.foxhome.com*, designed by Electravision, used time to cycle through a variety of movie choices.

www.foxhome.com
www.monkey.com
www.nationalgeographic.com
www.nintendo.com

Most of this chapter has stressed keeping the number of categories and choices on the screen to a minimum. Specifically, try and keep the number of categories between five and seven. But what about situations where there are more than seven choices, and all of them are equally important? In such cases, you need to think about time and space as a means to organize content. The following Web sites are excellent examples of strategic use of time and space in user interface design.

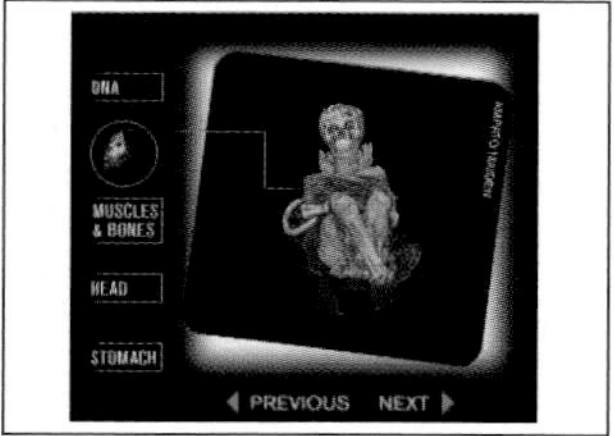

The *National Geographic Online, Incan Mummies* feature, designed by Electravision, converted actual CAT scans of the mummy into the interface for a virtual autopsy.

DYNAMIC TECHNOLOGIES

As technologies for the Internet progress, essentially what we are seeing is the same dynamic, interactive capabilities that the CD-ROM industry has enjoyed for years. Multimedia is slowly moving to the Web. The problem at this point, however, is such dynamic media generally requires plug-ins.

Even so, many people still think of the Web as a static page that has more in common with a magazine layout than a multimedia CD-ROM. As bandwidth increases and new dynamic technologies emerge, there will be an increasing trend towards more dynamic ways to present information.

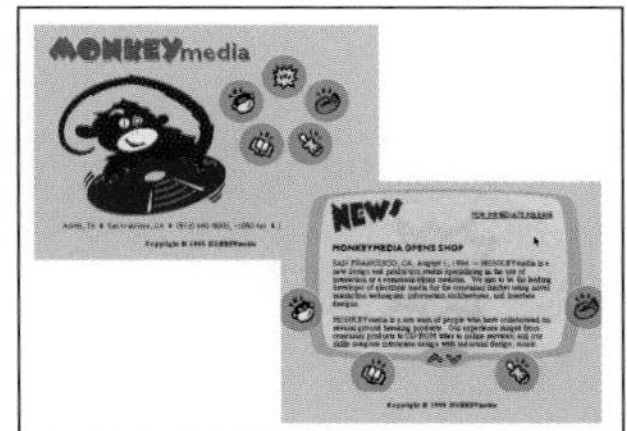

USING SPACE WISELY: THE SHRINK AND STRETCH MODEL

Monkey Media's Web site at *www.monkey.com* features a unique and innovative use of space made possible by Shockwave. Literally, the entire Web site exists on just one page that is only 600 x 350 pixels wide!

The way it works is an elegant shrink and stretch (or fish-eye) model. All content is first presented as small icons. When the cursor rolls over one of the icons, the icon expands to reveal the content within. In the case of *monkey.com*, after the icon expands, the content is interactive! The user can access sub-choices and call different content. When the mouse moves away from the content and towards a different icon in the background, the new icon unfolds.

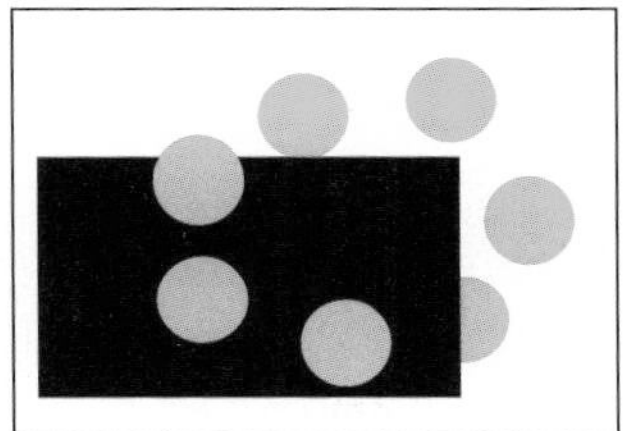

CYCLING CHOICES OVER TIME

Another way to use limited space to convey a lot of content is to space out content over time. There is no rule that says you must place all options on the screen at one time.

In the case of the *Twentieth Century Fox Home Entertainment* Web site, in addition to the normal cross-navigation, the home page needed to showcase 4 to 8 features. With such a range of features, the interface could not look sparse one month and then crowded the next month. The solution was to cycle through the features over time, showing only 3 to 4 on the screen at any one time. In addition, this proved to be a modular structure allowing for frequent updates and the ability to quickly swap one feature for another.

PANORAMIC HORIZONTAL AND VERTICAL SPACE

All Web sites can scroll both vertically and horizontally indefinitely. It is another thing, however, to strategically utilize this attribute of Web pages and plan a user interface that takes advantage of this feature.
Rather than simply having a Web page larger than the browser window that requires users to scroll, think about leading your users off screen in a planned way. For instance, knowing that most users have to scroll if a Web page is larger than 600 x 350, you can design an interface with these cut-off boundaries in mind. Both the *Sony Pictures Entertainment* and the *Nintendo* Web sites incorporate a set of standard navigational icons and a title banner that fit within the bounds of most browser windows. The midsection, however, is an independent, rich collage of choices that bleeds off the edge of the screen tempting users to scroll laterally.

Chapter F

Preparing Graphics for the Web

Previous chapters have focused on creating graphics and interface elements for the Web, but now that you have created them, how do you prepare them for the Web? There is a variety of palette and file format issues to consider once you have a series of final graphics extracted from the original Photoshop-layered files. This chapter explores the common file formats required by both normal HTML and Web technologies such as Shockwave and QuickTime VR. Assuming that you have been using the 216 Web-safe colors in the creation of your Web graphics, you now need to know hexadecimal equivalents as you begin to implement your Web pages in HTML. For this purpose, we've have included a handy chart for converting RGB values to hexadecimal values.

CHAPTER SESSIONS

F1 *From RBG to Indexed Color*

F2 *Maximizing the Web-Safe Color Palette*

F3 *From Indexed Color to GIF Export*

F4 *From RBG Color to GIF Export*

F5 *From Photoshop Layers to GIF Export*

F6 *Preparing Files for Virtual Reality*

F7 *Shockwave and Flash Preparation*

F8 *Batch Processing*

F9 *Creating an Online Presentation*

CHAPTER TOOLBOX

Adobe Photoshop 4.0

Adobe Illustrator 7.0

IMAGES

Image Club, Object Gear

Image Club, Photo Gear

Image Club, Studio Gear

Image Club, Urban Colors

WEB GRAPHIC FILE FORMATS 101

In addition to the common GIF and JPEG graphic formats for the Web, there are a variety of other formats—used especially by Web technologies such as VR and Flash—that you should be aware of. Depending on both the nature of the graphic itself and the technology you plan to use, you will need to prepare graphics in different ways.

GIF VERSUS JPEG

The most common forms of graphics on the Web are GIFs and JPEGs. GIF, which stands for Graphics Interchange Format, is a lossless file format designed for only indexed-color graphics, eight bits (256 colors) or less. Lossless means that it compresses graphics without eliminating detail. The JPEG format, or Joint Photographer Experts Group, is a lossy file format designed especially for displaying 24-bit true color images.

WHEN TO USE GIF

The GIF format works best for flat-colored graphics with crisp, well-defined edges such as cartoon characters and images with type elements. If you have an image that is a mix of flat-color graphics and photographic images, such as type on top of a photograph, you probably should use the GIF format. Keep in mind, however, that GIF only supports images that have been indexed down into a limited color palette. This means that the photographic portion will be dithered, (see Session F1).

Aside from the dithering that results from indexing images, the GIF format is most popular (even for photographs) because of its transparent, interlacing, and animation capabilities (see Sessions F3, F4, and F5).

TIP: *For best GIF results, while you are creating graphics, choose colors from the Web-safe palette—especially for flat-color areas such as type and background colors. Don't worry about photographic elements, let them dither in the indexing process. Then, when you go to index your image, choose Adaptive palette, 7 bits. The Web-safe colors you used will factor into the custom adaptive palette, and the remaining colors will render the photographic portions with minimal dithering. Once on the Web, the image will redither to Web-safe colors, but only on 8-bit displays. Even so, the quality can be excellent.*

WHEN TO USE JPEG

The JPEG format was specifically designed to compress 24-bit, true color photography, and it does an excellent job. The JPEG format is not, however, recommended for images containing crisp, well-defined edges and flat colors such as cartoons and type. These types of images are most adversely affected by the lossy nature of the JPEG format.

While JPEG, like GIF, does support progressive rendering, it does not support transparency. However, a JPEG file can describe a much larger and more photo-like image with less data—making for smaller files and faster downloads. For these reasons, the JPEG format is best used to display purely photographic images.

RGB TO HEXADECIMAL COLOR CHART

In order to ensure that your graphics do not dither when viewed on one computer to the next, you need to use the 216 Web-safe colors while you work. This is especially true when it comes to compositing graphics to a background color in a program, such as Photoshop, that needs to match the background color of your Web site. It's one thing to choose a color from the Web-safe Swatches palette, it's another thing to know the color's hexadecimal number.

Here is a simple chart that you can refer to when you are working with the Web-safe colors and need to know their Hexadecimal codes.

RGB Web-Safe Color Values

Percentage	Decimal Value	Hexadecimal Value
100%	255	FF
80%	204	CC
60%	153	99
40%	102	66
20%	51	33
0%	0	00

There are only six possible values for each of the Red, Green, and Blue values. Hence, there are 216 possible combinations (6 x 6 x 6). In the chart above, the six possible R, B, and G values are in the left column, and their hexadecimal equivalents are listed in the right column.

In Photoshop, find the RGB values for one of the Web-safe colors. To do this, set the foreground color to a Web-safe color from the Swatches palette, and then click on the foreground color in the Tool palette to open the Color Picker. From the Color Picker, write down the RGB values for the color (e.g., R=51, G=0, B=255). Then look up the hexadecimal equivalents for these numbers in the above chart. In this case, the hexadecimal numbers are R: 33, G: 00, B: FF, and together are #3300FF.

Session

F1 From RGB to Indexed Color

After you have extracted a graphic from the original, layered Photoshop file, you need to decide which file format to save it in. Different Web technologies require different file formats; and different file formats require different palette processing.

Changing an image from RGB color to indexed color is a destructive process. You are literally throwing away color information, restricting and image's use of color. For these reasons, indexing an image into a palette is always the last thing you do before saving it into a Web file format. In addition, you should never convert an original source file into indexed color.

ADOBE PHOTOSHOP 4.0 Object Gear: Amusements: Turtle Top

STEP 1: STARTING WITH AN RGB IMAGE

Changing an image from RGB to Indexed Color in the Image > Mode menu in Photoshop, reduces an image's color usage from RGB's almost unlimited 16.8 million color possibilities to a finite palette of select colors. There are a number of standard color palettes to choose from: the 216 Web-safe colors, both the 256-color Mac and Windows systems palettes, or custom palettes. Whichever way, the process of re-rendering an image with such a limited number of colors produces a pixelated effect called *dithering.*

Dithering is a method similar to impressionist painting where to create a smooth gradation of color, alternating dots of just a few colors are used. While it makes for a smaller and more practical data file, it can look poor in solid areas where the effect is more obvious. However, dithering can be avoided in areas of flat, solid color by using a color from the reduced palette. This is why you should use colors from the Web-safe palette as often as possible.

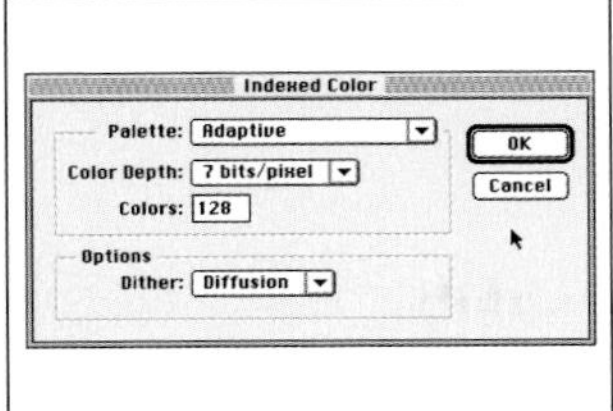

STEP 2: WHEN TO USE THE ADAPTIVE PALETTE

If you need to prepare a GIF image, the two palettes you should consider are the Web-safe color palette or an adaptive palette. Both palettes are accessible from the Photoshop Mode > Indexed Color command from the Image menu.

If the graphic contains photographic imagery and incorporates some flat-color elements that you have already filled with Web-safe colors, you should choose an adaptive palette. An adaptive palette is one that is made up of colors most appropriate for the particular image. The Web-safe colors you use are incorporated into the adaptive palette.

> **TIP:** *If the Web-safe, flat color portion of your image is relatively small compared to the rest of the image (to ensure that the flat color gets included in the adaptive palette), draw a selection around the area before you change the mode to Indexed Color. This gives the area a higher priority during the index process.*

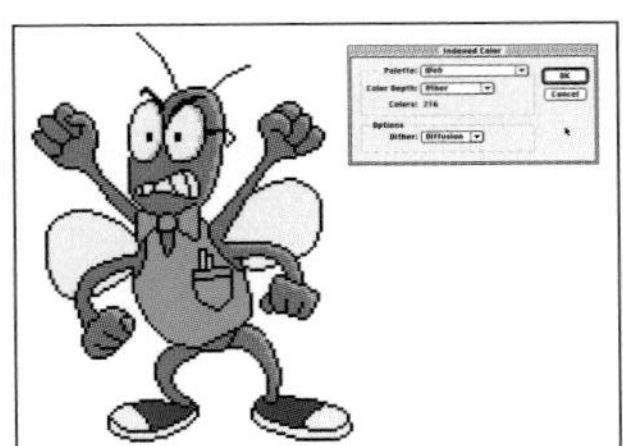

STEP 3: USING THE WEB-SAFE PALETTE

If the graphic consists of mainly flat-color imagery, such as cartoon characters, or text elements, then it makes sense to use the Web palette. Dithering should be kept to a minimum—assuming you have been using the Web-safe colors during the creation process.

Convert the RGB image into the Web palette by choosing Mode > Indexed Color from the Image menu. In the dialog box that appears, choose the Web palette from the pull-down menu. For tips on how to reduce the number of colors further without loosing quality, see Session F2.

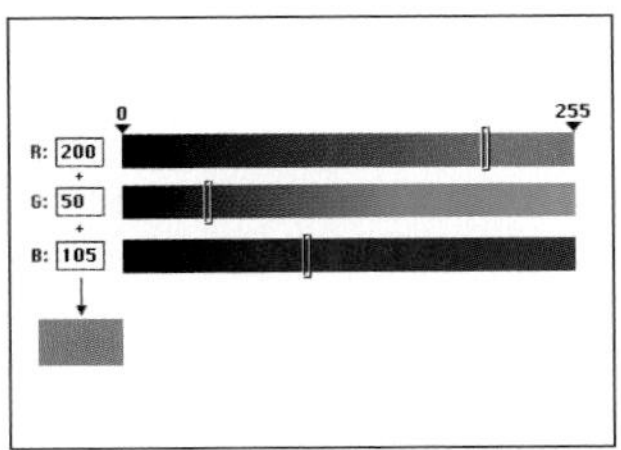

STEP 4: COLOR THEORY

Images are generally referred to by their color bit depth, 24-bit, 16-bit, and so on. But what does that mean in terms of real color and palettes? In the RGB color model, each color (red, blue and green), has a value between zero and 255. Each colored pixel is a mix of the three colors coming together. Therefore, if there are 256 possible values of each red, blue, and green, a pixel can be one of 16,777,216 colors (256 x 256 x 256). The RGB system is capable of displaying any of these millions of colors—rendering images in astounding clarity.

It takes a lot of computer data, however, to display such a large range of colors. In fact, it takes eight bits of computer data to display all 256 possible values for just one of the RGB colors. Therefore, 24 bits are required to display the entire RGB color range (8 bits for red, 8 bits for green, and 8 bits for blue). An 8-bit image, therefore, is one that is only using 256 colors.

Session

F2 Maximizing the Web-Safe Color Palette

Kid's Web Camp, an online Web learning camp for kids at *www.kidswebcamp.com*, features a series of non-dithering characters all optimized into the smallest possible Web-safe palette.

ADOBE PHOTOSHOP 4.0

In cases where it makes sense to index an image into the Web-safe color palette as opposed to an adaptive palette (as in Session F1), chances are you will not need all 216 colors of the palette. By reducing the number of colors you use in a graphic, you can reduce the file size tremendously—which is always a good thing on the Web. In this exercise, you start with a 24-bit, RGB image and reduce it to the smallest number of Web-safe colors possible without comprimising the quality of the image.

STEP 1: STARTING WITH AN RGB IMAGE

Before you index an image into the Web-safe colors, be sure that you have used nothing but Web-safe colors (sampled from the Swatches palette) for all the flat-color areas. If you have not, it is easy to replace the colors of your image (see Session B11).

From the Image menu, select Mode > Indexed Color and choose the Web color palette from the dialog box pop-up menu. If you have accurately replaced all of your colors, you should see no dithering in your image. If you do, select Undo from the Edit menu, replace the dithering color, and index the image again.

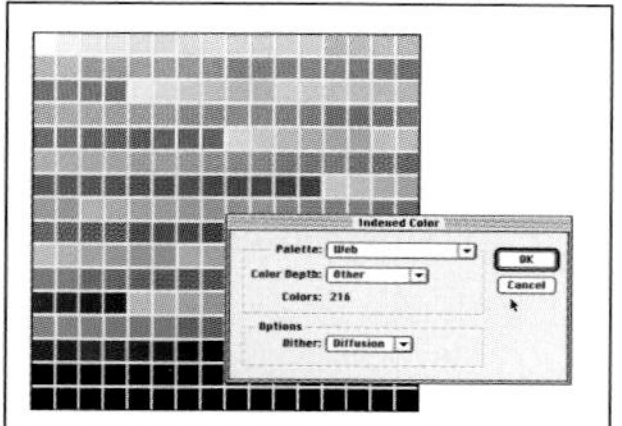

UNNECESSARY COLORS

More often than not, you will not need all of the colors contained within the 216 Web-safe color palette. In this example, the character actually uses only 18 colors. The unused-used 198 colors are unnecessarily adding to the image's file size.

STEP 2: CONVERTING BACK TO RGB MODE

After you have successfully indexed an image into the Web-safe colors without dithering in the flat-color areas, change the image's mode back to RGB.

Changing the image back to RGB mode does not resurrect the lost colors, but allows you to go back again into the Indexed color mode and further index the image.

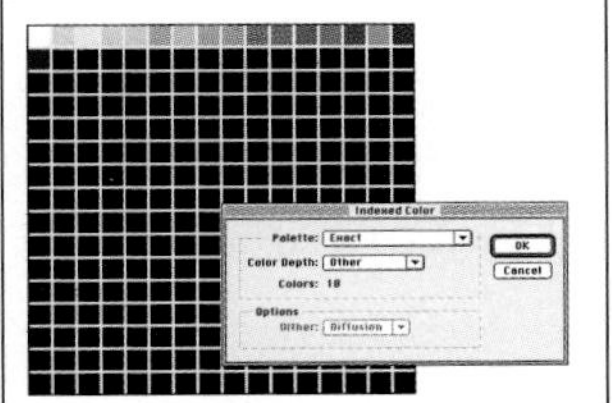

STEP 3: BACK TO INDEXED COLOR MODE AGAIN

Although the image is now in RGB color mode, it still uses only colors from the Web palette. The first time you indexed the image into the Web palette ensured this.

When the image was first indexed into the Web-safe colors, it became an 8-bit image from 24-bit. This means that for each pixel of the image, there are 8 bits of data used to describe it's color from a possible 256 values, far less than 24 bits, but still more than necessary for this example image that uses only 18 colors.

By changing back to RGB, and then choosing Indexed Color again from the Image > Mode menu, you'll notice that the dialog box automatically asks you if you want to use Exact colors this time. Choosing Exact colors causes Photoshop to first reduce the image to only the colors it contains, and then reduce the number of bits per pixel to only the number necessary to describe that number of colors, reducing the file size substantually.

STEP 4: EXPORT AS GIF

After the palette work is complete, you can save the image as a GIF ready for the Web. Choose Export > GIF89a Export from the File menu. For details on using Photoshop's GIF89a Export feature, see Sessions F3, F4, and F5.

Session

F3 From Indexed Color to GIF Export

Photoshop's plug-in GIF89a export feature is a handy way of saving indexed images for the Web. In addition, compared to other GIF creation utilities, Photoshop's does an excellent job of handling transparency and creating small file sizes for faster downloading. This session is designed to step you through the process of using Photoshop's GIF89a Export feature after you have used Photoshop to index an image into a specific color palette.

ADOBE PHOTOSHOP 4.0	Object Gear: Amusements: Turtle top Font: Adobe Chronos

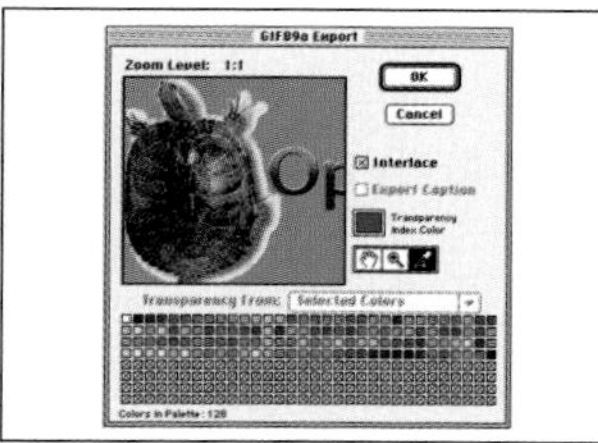

STEP 1: SELECT THE GIF89A EXPORT FEATURE

To take advantage of all the GIF89a Export features, prepare an indexed image that uses a transparent background (see Session D7). Once you have used Photoshop to index the image into a 256, or less, color palette, choose the Export > GIF89a Export command located under the File menu.

When exporting from an indexed image, you also have the option of using a channel to define transparency. This is an especially useful feature if the color you want to be transparent is also being used inside your image.

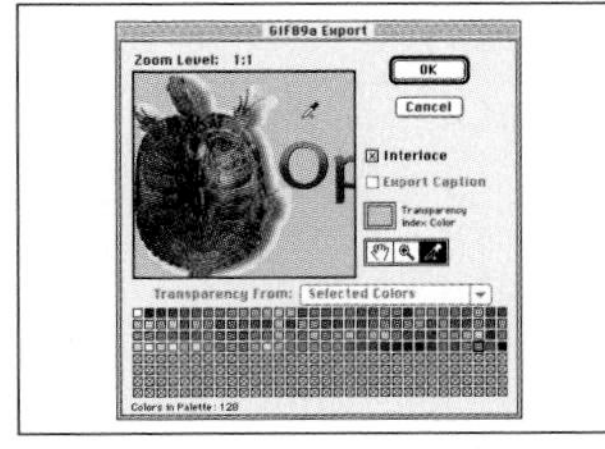

STEP 2: SETTING A TRANSPARENT COLOR

Your image should appear in the middle of the GIF89a interface window. Notice that when the cursor rolls within the image window, it changes to the Eye dropper tool. To set a color as transparent, simply click the color with the Eye dropper tool. If the image is too large and is obscuring the color you want transparent, select and use the Hand tool icon to pan around the image.

Click the color you want transparent. Notice that as you do so, its color swatch in the palette below highlights with a little black border. If you like, you can use an alpha channel to define transparency, simply choose it from the Transparancey From pop-up menu.

> **TIP:** *You can select more than one color in the GIF89a interface window. Make sure the transparency is defined by Selected Colors as opposed to an alpha channel. Then, simply click another color in the image window, or click another color swatch in the palette.*

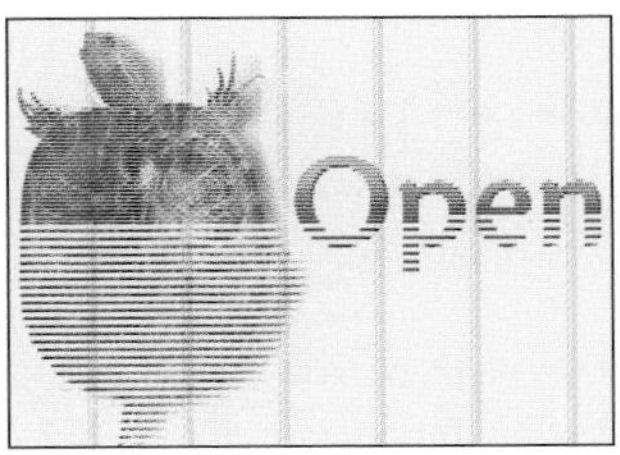

STEP 3: INTERLACING

Before you click OK and exit the GIF89a dialog box, decide whether or not you want the image to be interlaced. Interlaced GIFs are those that draw in gradually on a Web page. The advantage is that a user does not have to wait for the GIF to draw completely; but, rather the user quickly sees a low-resolution version of the graphic while the rest of the image downloads.

Interlacing is recommended for large files that may take the user a while to download. It does add a bit more to the file size, but the effect is negligible. Interlacing is not recommended for GIFs destined to become animated GIFs. Interlacing forces each frame of your animation to fade in before it moves on to the next frame in the series.

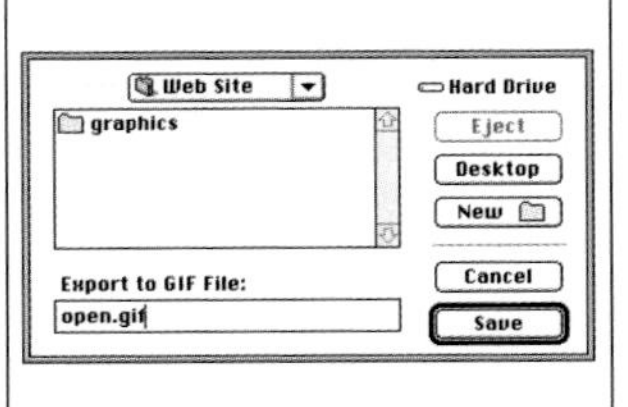

STEP 4: NAMING CONVENTIONS

When you have finished setting your options in the GIF89a dialog, click OK to save the GIF. At this point, the Save dialog box prompts you to name the file with a *.gif* extension. Not only does this naming convention help you identify final art ready for a Web page, it is also generally recognized by software and server platforms.

> **TIP:** *On the Macintosh platform, you can easily see how large your GIF file is by using the Get Info command in the Finder. Locate your GIF in the Finder and click on it once to highlight it. Then choose Get Info from the File menu. The number you should read is the one in parenthesis (e.g., 8,000 bytes used).*

Session

F4 From RGB Color to GIF Export

You can export a GIF from Photoshop without first indexing the image. From the unprocessed, flattened RGB file, you can simply choose Export > GIF89a Export from the File menu. The dialog box looks a bit different, but it is essentially the same process with limited controls.

ADOBE PHOTOSHOP 4.0 Object Gear: Amusements: Turtle Top

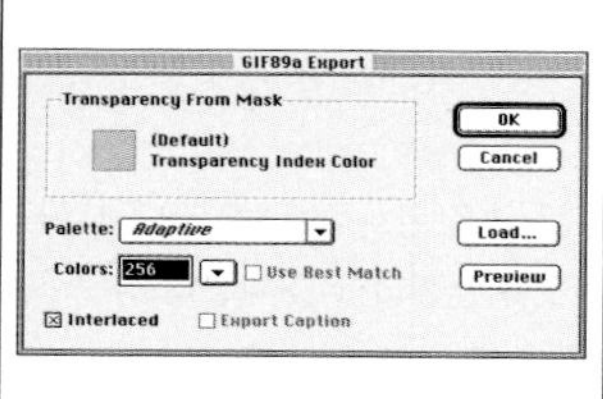

STEP 1: STARTING WITH A FLATTENED RGB FILE

Starting with a 24-bit, RGB, flattened file, choose Export > GIF89a Export from the File menu. Notice that the interface that appears is different for an RGB image than for an indexed image.

TIP: *The GIF format uses Run Length Encoding to compress graphics. The way it works is by reading and compressing one horizontal pixel row at a time. Every time it encounters a differently colored pixel, it makes a note of it—adding to the file size. Therefore, if you are using gradations in your graphics, it is best to use vertical, top-to-bottom gradations, where each horizontal line is one solid color. A horizontal left-to-right gradation can make a GIF file many times larger.*

STEP 2: PALETTE OPTIONS AND TRANSPARENCY

From the GIF89a dialog box, choose an indexed color palette for the image to use. Remember that the GIF format does not accept an image greater than 8 bits.

There are not as many Color palette options from this dialog box as when using the Indexed Color mode options, shown in Session F2. The default choice is to choose an Adaptive palette, but the System and Exact palettes are also available.

The transparency feature is also more limited. The gray Default Transparency Mask swatch refers to Photoshop's transparency. In a flattened, RGB file, there is channel to interpret for transparency. The default transparency mask only works if you are starting from a layered file (see Session F5).

From Photoshop Layers to GIF Export

One of the most convenient functions of Photoshop's GIF89a Export feature is that it allows you to export a series of selected layers. By simply turning on the Eyeball icons of the layers you need, the GIF89a Export function can automatically generate a GIF ready for the Web. In addition, Photoshop's transparency can be automatically translated into GIF transparency.

ADOBE PHOTOSHOP 4.0	PhotoGear: Backgrounds and Textures: Marble 1.tif StudioGear: Business Metaphors: SBM31 Font: Adobe Keplar

STEP 1: PREPARE LAYERS FOR GIF EXPORT

In the same way that you would prepare layers to merge in earlier chapters, turn on the Eyeball icons of only the layers that will become your GIF. Unlike merging layers, however, the GIF89a Export feature does not require that you select one of the visable layers. Choose Export > GIF89a Export from the File menu.

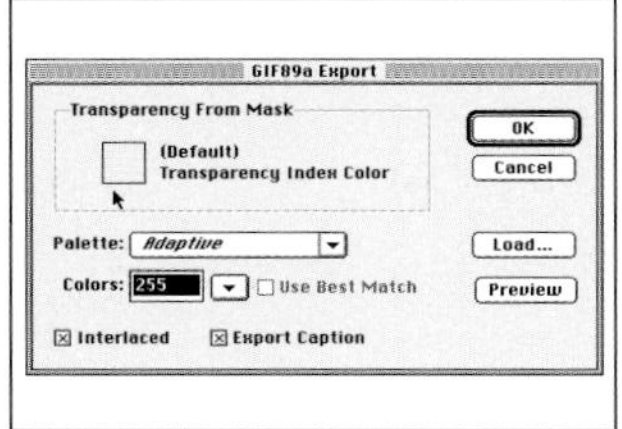

STEP 2: PALETTE AND TRANSPARENCY CONTROL

As when exporting a flattened RGB file, there is limited control over palettes when exporting a series of layers. The best option is to use the Adaptive palette.

There is also less control over assigning transparent colors. If the graphics you are exporting are surrounded by transparency, the GIF89a Export feature automatically keeps that transparency. The problem however, is that the edges of your GIF are anti-aliased to the default gray swatch that appears in the GIF89a window. To anti-alias your edges to a color that matches your background, click on the swatch and enter its RGB values in the Color Picker.

Session

F6 Preparing files for Virtual Reality

The second episode of the *Suspect* series, *Dead Birds Don't Sing*, features 3D Surround Video rooms.

There are two common forms of bitmapped-based virtual reality on the Web: Surround Video (an ActiveX control), and QuickTime VR. The illusion that both create is that of panning in a 360° perspective-corrected environment. QuickTime VR also can rotate in all directions around a 3D object. In addition, both technologies enable you to embed links within the environments—creating a highly exploratory user experience. The second episode of *Suspect*, the online murder mystery series, features a series of Surround Video rooms sprinkled with clues that the user can discover. Both VR formats require similar file preparation; however; generating the imagery in the first place requires some specialized tools or handy illustration.

ADOBE PHOTOSHOP 4.0

STEP 1: DESIGNING A SEAMLESS PANORAMA

The first step in creating a Surround Video or QuickTime VR file is to create a panoramic image by photographing it or by generating it in a 3D application such as Strata 3D. (Strata 3D can output a warped perspective, VR-ready image.) You can illustrate the room or environment from scratch in Photoshop only if you follow the warped perspective required (see Step 2).

If you plan to photograph the scene, you must use a wide-angle 15mm lens mounted on a special tripod that has X, Y, and Z pivot control. In addition, the pivot should be marked off to show 360°, and you must mount the camera so that its focal point is positioned in exaclty the same place as the mount's pivot point. Take twelve shots turning the camera 30° after each shot.

STEP 2: WARPING THE ENVIRONMENT

If you opted to photograph the environment, you must run the series of photographs through a *stitcher* program, which is included with the QuickTime VR development toolkit. The stitcher warps the photographs into a distorted perspective necessary for both Surround Video and QuickTime VR.

If you design the room in a 3D program such as Strata 3D, make sure that the program supports output for VR. Strata outputs a properly warped-perspective panoramic strip ready to be diced into a QuickTime VR or Surround Video file.

STEP 3: SURROUND VIDEO FILE PREPARATION

Surround Video is fully supported in Internet Explorer on a Windows machine, and may soon be supported on Macintosh. Though not yet cross-platform, the image quality of Surround Video surpasses that of QuickTime VR.

A panorama destined for Surround Video must be saved as a 24-bit, flattened BMP file. Also, the pixel dimensions for height and width must be divisible by exactly 16.

TIP: *Once a graphic has been warped using a 3D program or a stitcher program, you can bring it into Photoshop to embellish. In the case of* Suspect, *once the room was rendered in Strata, lighting, textures, plants, characters, and clues were all draw into the scene.*

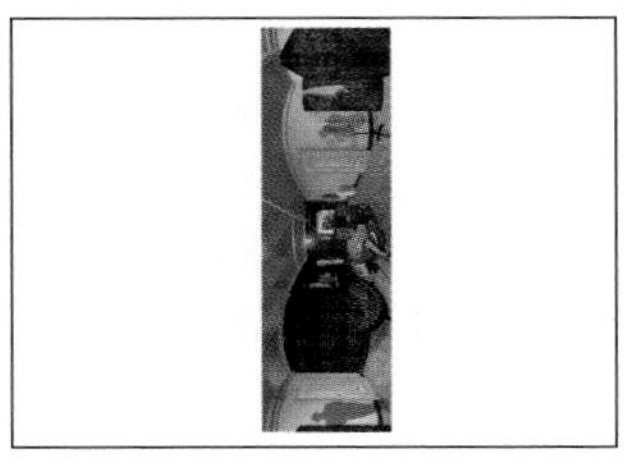

STEP 4: QUICKTIME VR FILE PREPARATION

Preparing panoramas for a QuickTime VR follows the same process as preparing Surround Video files but with one twist. In addition to remaining a 24-bit file with pixel dimensions divisible by 16, a panorama destined for QuickTime VR must be rotated 90° counterclockwise. Once rotated, save the file as a flattened PICT file.

Session

F7 Shockwave and Flash Preparation

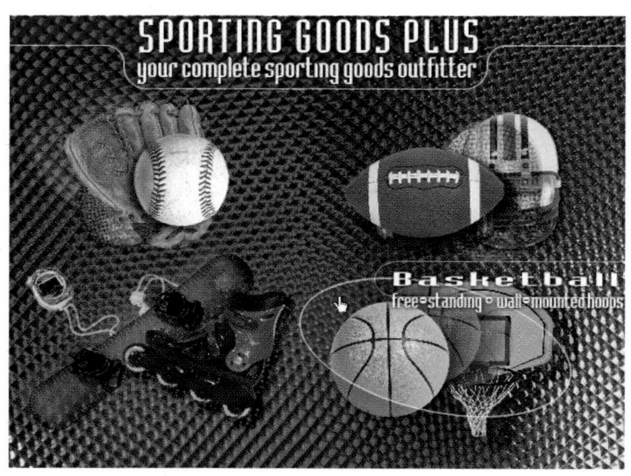

Shockwave and Flash are technologies that you can embed into a Web page to add animation and interactivity not possible using normal HTML. Both technologies, however, require that the end user have the correct plug-in installed before they can view the content. For that reason alone, many people shy away from their use. Even so, these technologies can add great flexibility to your interface design. If you plan to use Shockwave or Flash, you need to prepare graphic files in specific ways.

ADOBE PHOTOSHOP 4.0	Object Gear: Sports Elements (various) Object Gear: Business Elements: Stopwatch PhotoGear: Industrial Backgrounds: Font: Image Club Badlock Compressed and Regular

PREPARING GRAPHICS FOR SHOCKWAVE

Shockwave files are generated from Macromedia Director movies. Director, unfortunately, does not accept vector-based graphics, only PICT (Mac) or BMP (Windows) format. Bitmap files produce larger file sizes than vectors. To reduce the size, it is best to graphics down to their smallest possible size. Wherever possible, use Director to create in-between animation and always use Director to generate your background color. For example, if you want your logo to fade up from black, you only need one file—your logo composited to a black background and then trimmed to its smallest size. With the Blend Ink effect, Director can fade in the logo against a black background.

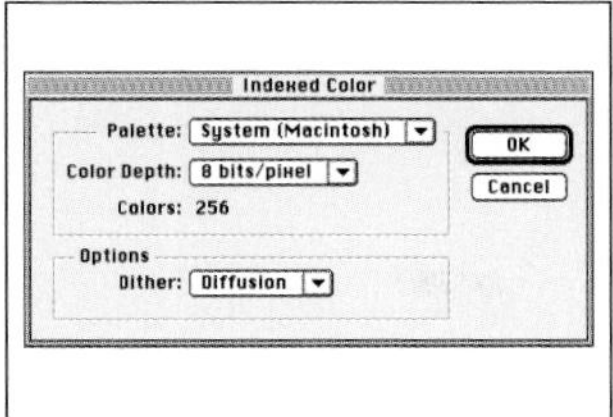

PALETTES AND BIT-DEPTH FOR SHOCKWAVE

Bitmaps for a Director movie can be 8-, 16-, or 24-bit color-depth. For Shockwave purposes, however, it is best to prepare 8-bit graphics; otherwise, the Shockwave file size can quickly become impractical for the Web.

Though it seems logical to use less than 8-bit graphics to trim down file size, Director does not accept less than an 8-bit palette. In fact, before you import graphics into Director, set the monitor to 8-bit color. Director imports graphics according to the monitor's bit depth—no matter what the bit-depth of the graphics.

SHOCKWAVE PALETTE CONSIDERATIONS

Be aware that unlike Web browsers, Director is very particular about palette usage. On a Web page, you can have five images with different palettes on the screen at once. If the monitor is set to 8-bit color, the browser will dither the page to the browser palette. Director, on the other hand, favors one palette on the screen at a time and remaps all other graphics into that palette (notice the loss of color in the rollover label state). For these reasons, it is best to use one palette for all graphics in the project. For simplicity, use the Macintosh or Windows System palettes

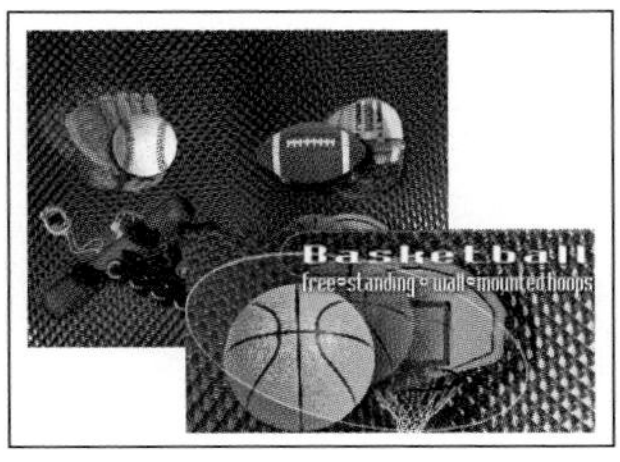

PREPARING FILES FOR FLASH

Flash accepts a wide range of file formats and integrates them seamlessly. You can mix both vector-based graphics saved as normal Illustrator files, and bitmap-based graphics in the form of PICTs, GIFs, and JPEGs. In addition, one nice feature about Flash is that it will automatically anti-alias jagged-looking vector graphics from Illustrator.

As in preparing Shockwave bitmaps, it's always best to rely on the program's internal in-between transitions and background colors. Also, try to keep bitmapped graphics to 8 bits or less, and cropped to their smallest dimensions to keep the file size down.

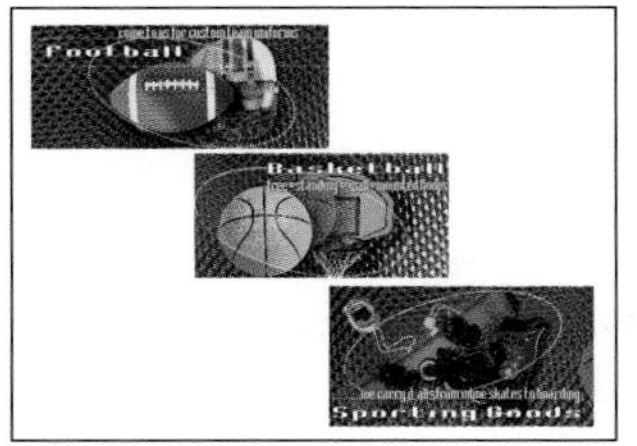

FINAL PROCESSING FOR SHOCKWAVE FILES

For Shockwave, save all graphics as 8-bit and make sure they all use the same palette. When you save them, save them to the same folder and name them alphabetically in the order you would like to import. Director has the ability to import the entire contents of a folder, which saves production time.

TIP: *You can set up a batch save action in the Photoshop Action palette that processes all of your graphics into 8-bit, system palette PICT or BMP files ready for import (see Session F8).*

Session

F8 Batch Processing

Typically, a Web site can consist of hundreds of tiny, individual graphics. Processing all of these into the right palette and saving them in the correct file format can take hours of mind-numbing production. To alleviate is work, you can create a Photoshop action to handle all of the above production steps at the touch of a button. In addition, the Batch processing feature allows you to apply a Photoshop action to an entire folder of graphics, rather than applying an action to one graphic at a time. I find that applying an action to an individual graphic as soon as it is extracted from the layered file is the most efficient use of time. The Batch processing feature applies to images already saved and organized into a folder. In this session, you set up an action to prepare graphics for a Shockwave movie.

ADOBE PHOTOSHOP 4.0

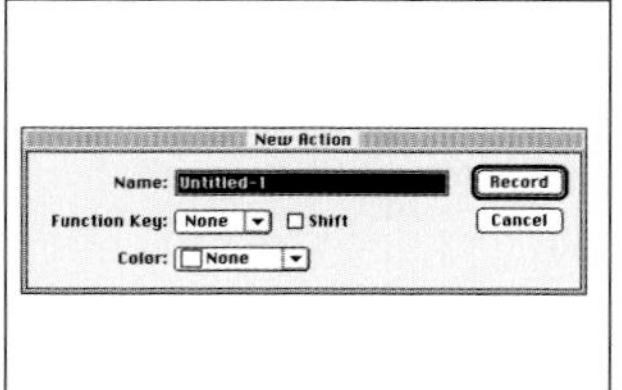

STEP 1: SETTING UP A PHOTOSHOP ACTION

Before you can batch process a selected folder of images, you need to set up a Photoshop action. The action should first index an image into the System palette, and then save the image as a PICT (Mac) or BMP (Windows) file before closing it.

With a sample image ready to process open in Photoshop, open the Actions palette and select New Action from the Action palette's pop-up menu.

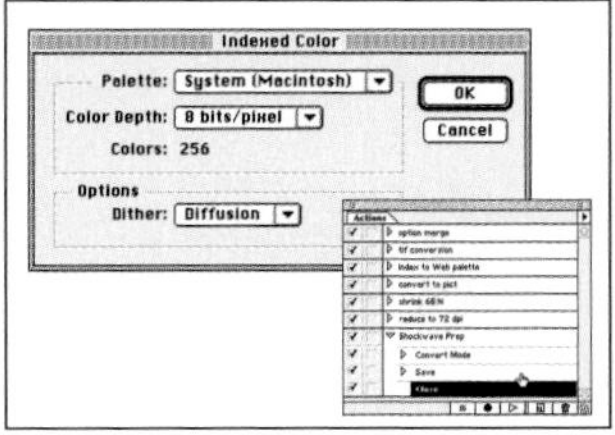

STEP 2: RECORDING THE ACTION SEQUENCE

Assign a name to the new action, such as "Shockwave Prep," assign a function key to it, and click the Record button.

When recording, change the image's mode to Indexed Color. From the Image > Mode > Index Color menu, set the palette to the System palette, 8-bit, and Diffusion dither. Next, save the image as either a PICT or BMP file—depending on your platform—and close the image. Stop recording the action.

STEP 3: TESTING AND SETTING UP A BATCH PROCESS

Prepare a new file and test the new action by pressing the assigned function key. If the action works, then it is ready to use in a batch process.

You can use any action in a batch process; however, as stated before, you must first prepare a folder of saved images, in this case saved as 24-bit, flattened Photoshop files. The batch process is extremely useful for many types of situations.

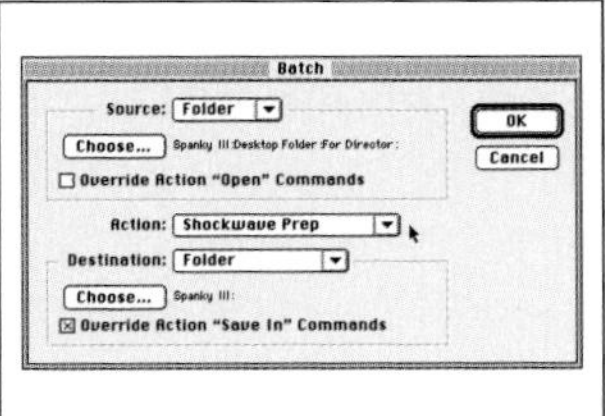

STEP 4: BATCH SAVING

With the perpared folder of graphics, choose Batch from the Action palette's pop-up menu. In the Batch dialog box that appears, first choose the prepared folder of graphics, and then select your action from the Action pop-up menu. Finally, select a destination folder for the final, processed graphics.

Once you click OK, the batch process begins—automatically opening, processing, and closing all graphics within the selected folder.

Session

F9 Creating an Online Presentation

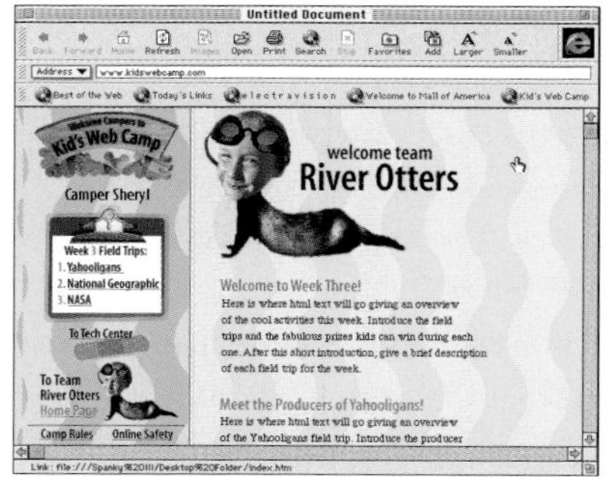

Using PageMill, it is easy to create a simple slide show presentation to show clients user interface or visual design ideas. The advantage to creating a presentation as a Web page is that you can show a proposal for a Web design online in the context of a Web browser. You also can post your presentation on a server at a hidden URL that only your client can access.

The initial design directions for *www.kidswebcamp.com*, an online Web learning camp for kids, were mocked-up in PageMill.

ADOBE PAGEMILL 2.0

STEP 1: PREPARE GRAPHICS

Because the presentation is just a mock-up, you do not have to go through the trouble of chopping up your graphics to their smallest size. Doing so would mean that you would need to reassemble them in PageMill. For purposes of demonstration, you should design the entire Web page as one GIF that you can simply place and center in PageMill (see Session E1). Save the entire Web page as an adaptive palette GIF ready to import into PageMill. In addition, if you plan to use a background tile, which is easy to implement in PageMill, go ahead and prepare a GIF tile, as shown in Session D5.

Assemble all graphics into one presentation folder. This folder will ultimately house the entire click-through presentation.

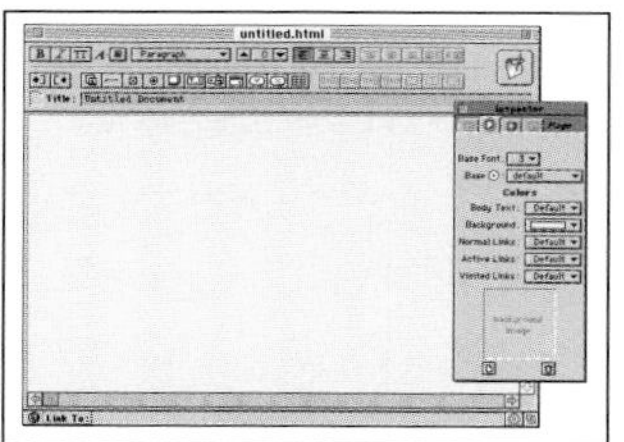

STEP 2: STARTING A WEB PAGE IN PAGEMILL

Open PageMill and from the File menu start a new Web page that will become your home page. A gray, blank page should appear with an editing button bar at the top of the page. PageMill has two modes: an editing mode and a preview mode (which mimics a browser's functionality). By default, you should be in editing mode, indicated by the document-looking icon on the large button at the upper right of the window. This button toggles back and forth between these modes.

Open the Inspector palette, located under the Windows menu, and click on the Page tab icon to reveal the Page panel. Here you can set the color of your text, links, and background color. To set your background color, click on the pop-up menu and choose Custom.

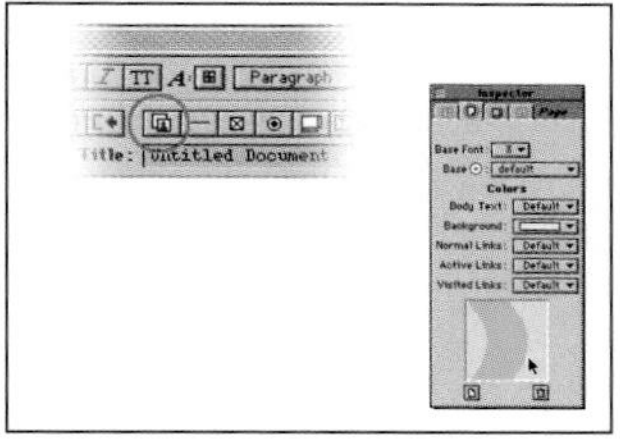

STEP 3: ADDING GRAPHICS AND BACKGROUND TILES

To add the GIF mock-up to your PageMill Web page, you can either drag and drop it from its folder directly into the PageMill window, or you can use the insert graphic button located at the top of the PageMill window. Simply click the Insert Graphic button, as shown, and locate your GIF using the Open File dialog box.

To add a background tile to your Web page, drag and drop the tile GIF into the background tile box in the Page panel of the Inspector palette. You can also click the Backround File button with the Document Icon, and then locate the GIF.

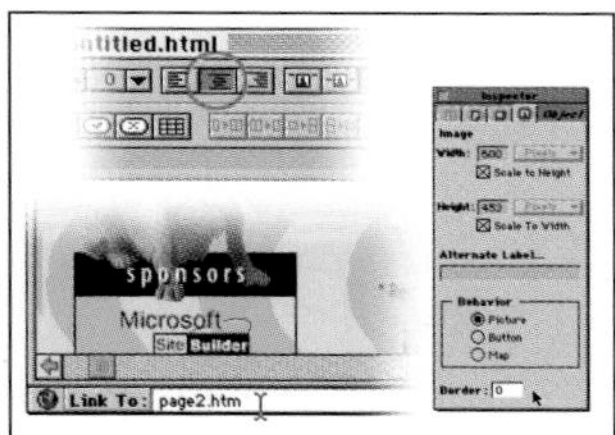

STEP 4: CENTERING GRAPHICS AND ADDING LINKS

Center the GIF mock-up on the Web page by first selecting it (by clicking it), and then clicking the Centering icon located in the top row of icons.

Next, add a link to the graphic so that when a user clicks on it, it simply advances to the next Web page in the presentation. To do this, first select the graphic, and then type the name of the Web page to which it should link (e.g., page2.htm) in the Link To text field at the bottom of the window. After typing in the link, press the Enter or Return key. You can remove the bright blue border around the linked graphic by entering a border of zero in the Inspector palette.

Adding links to text is the same process. First type some text into the Web page, select it, and then enter the link in the Link To text field.

STEP 5: LINKING MULTIPLE PAGES TOGETHER

Once you have created the home page, save it into the presentation folder, naming it either "home.htm" or "index.htm." Create a new Web page for each slide in your click-through presentation. When you have finished assembling its graphics, tiles, etc., remember to name each file exactly as you referred to it in the link from the previous page. If you like, you can link the last page back to the index.htm or home.htm page.

TIP: *Save time and extra work by starting a new page, saving it, and then modifying it to become your next page. Then use the Save As command to create a new file with your changes.*

Chapter G

USING A WYSIWYG HTML EDITOR

Rather than creating Web sites from scratch, you should consider using a WYSIWYG HTML editor such as Adobe PageMill. WYSIWYG (what-you-see-is-what-you-get) is a term used to describe visually based software tools. Using PageMill, you can literally build a Web page before your very eyes. Not only is a WYSIWYG HTML editor great for people who are not comfortable with HTML syntax, it is also good for people of all levels to quickly try different Web page layouts.

CHAPTER SESSIONS

G1 *Creating a Frame Structure with PageMill*

G2 *Creating a Table Structure*

G3 *Building an Order Form*

G4 *Working with Images in PageMill*

G5 *Adding External Objects*

G6 *Fine-Tuning Your HTML*

G7 *Managing a Site with SiteMill*

CHAPTER TOOLBOX

Adobe PageMill 2.0

Adobe SiteMill 2.0

ADOBE PAGEMILL 101

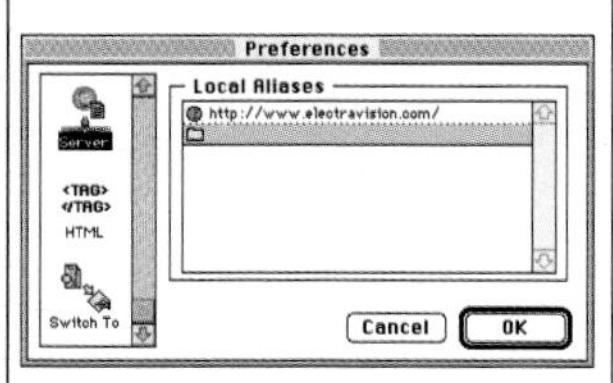

BEFORE YOU BEGIN

Before you begin working with PageMill, you should create a folder on your hard drive that will contain your Web site. The name of the folder does not matter, but you will need to point to it in PageMill. (This folder will become the alias for your server.)

In PageMill, open the Preferences window located under the Edit menu. Scroll down the left column to the Server icon and click it. Next to the small World icon, enter the name of your server and subdirectory (if necessary). Then, click on the Folder icon on the next line. In the subsequent Open File dialog box, locate the folder you created as the alias of your server, open the folder, and click the In Here button.

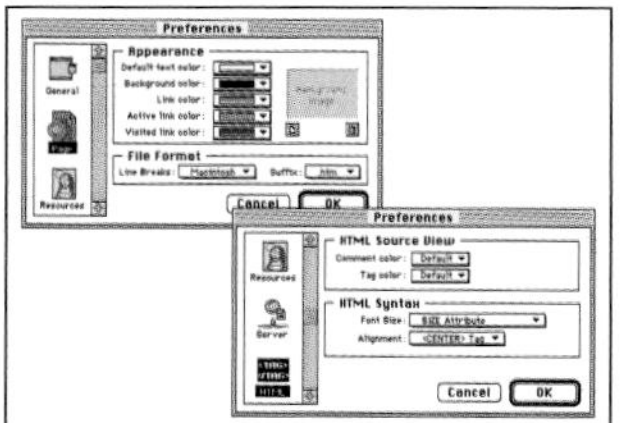

ADDITIONAL PAGEMILL PREFERENCES

There are a number of other preferences that you can set in PageMill. For instance, in Page preferences, you can set the default background, text, and link colors for each page you create, and you can determine which naming extension, *.html* or *.htm*, you want to use for each page. (See Session L2 to decide which extension you should use.)

In addition, certain HTML syntax, such as the *<p>* centering attribute, does not work on older browsers. In order to make a Web site as compatible as possible, you may want to change the HTML preference, selecting the *<center>* tag instead of the *<p>* tag.

TIP: *The Switch To preference, found under the HTML preference, enables you to choose a different application, such as your favorite browser, to view your current Web page. This is a great way to quickly test your PageMill layout in the browser of your choice.*

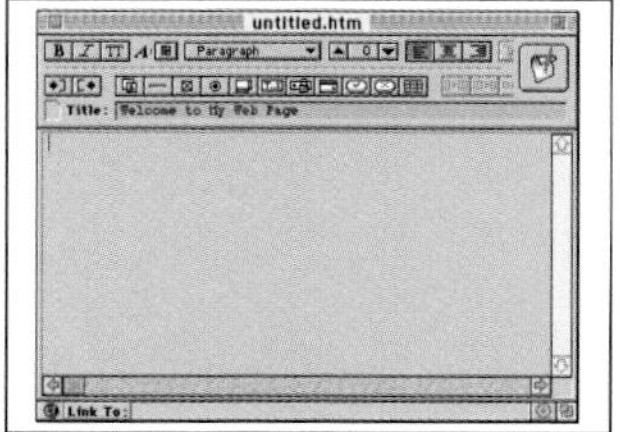

STARTING A NEW PAGE

To start building a Web page layout, select New from the File menu. A gray, blank page appears that has a row of buttons at the top. Just underneath the top row of buttons, enter a name for the Web page. Keep in mind that this is the name that appears only at the top of the browser window, not the name of the actual HTML file.

Adding text and images to your Web page in PageMill is just like working with a word processor. You can simply begin typing directly into the Page window. Use the Return key to start new paragraphs, and then select and edit your text.

To get an image into PageMill, choose Place from the File menu, and click the button with a small Photo icon at the top of the editing window; or simply drag and drop an image directly into the Page window. Like text, images can be selected and centered by clicking on the image, and then clicking on the Center Alignment button.

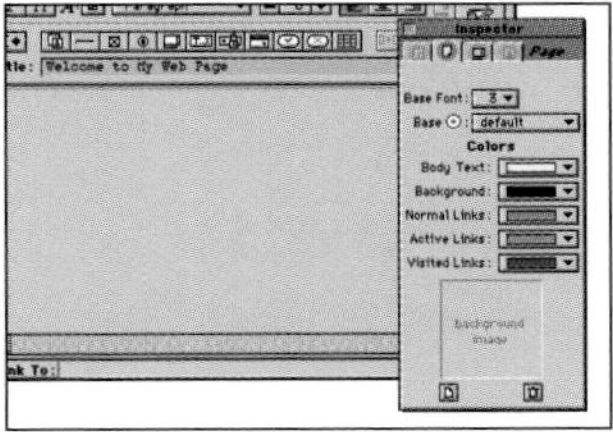

INSPECTOR PALETTE

One of the most important interface windows in PageMill is the Inspector palette found in the Window menu. In it you'll find specific attribute options for every type of object from frames and tables to images and text. You can also specify page attributes such as adding a background tile, setting the background color, and choosing text and link colors.

The four tabs in the Inspector palette display different catagories of attributes. One is for frames. Another tab, pictured here, applies to normal pages. Here you can drag background tiles into the lower box, and assign colors to links and normal text. The third and four tabs display a variety of object attributes.

LINKING

There are two ways to add links to both text and images. One way is to select the image by clicking it like you would in a word processor, and then entering the link in the Link To field at the bottom of the page. When you finish entering the link, it is important to press the Enter or Return key. To remove a link, select the image or text, and then choose Remove Link from the Edit menu.

The other way to add a link is to first select the text or image, and then drag and drop an HTML page from the Finder onto it. If you drop the HTML file onto the PageMill window and miss the selected text or image, PageMill adds a text link to your page automatically at that position.

SAVING YOUR PAGE

Finally, remember to save each of your Web pages from PageMill with the naming convention you have already set up in your links. For example, imagine adding a link such as *product1.htm* to an image on your home page. If you have not yet created the *product1.htm* page, it is easy to forget and give it another name when you create it. If you do make such a mistake, SiteMill can quickly fix such linking problems (see Session 17).

Session

G1 Creating a Frame Structure with PageMill

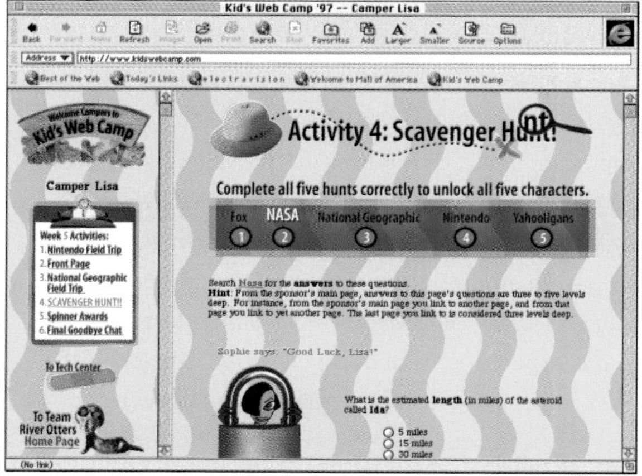

The *Kid's Web Camp* site, at *www.kidswebcamp.com*, uses a frame structure to separate the interface from the content.

The use of frames in a Web page layout is popular because of the added flexibility they afford—especially for user interface design purposes. For example, you can use one frame for interface choices and another frame to display the content of those choices. Not only does this strategy allow you to cache graphics in the interface frame, the interface frame does not need to re-draw every time a user clicks a button. Frames are normally complex to implement, but by using PageMill the process is made very simple.

ADOBE PAGEMILL 2.0

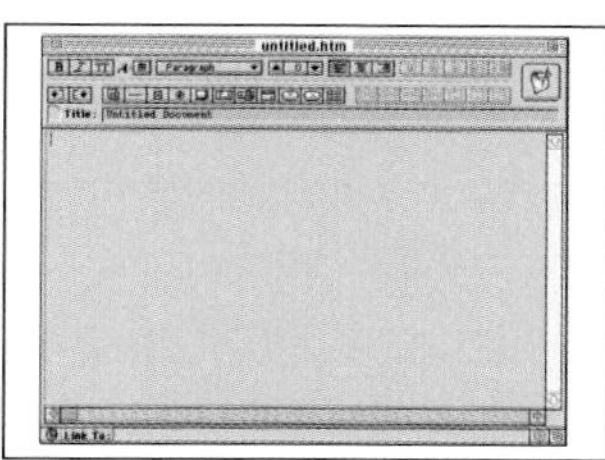

STEP 1: START A NEW DOCUMENT

A Web page layout that uses frames is actually a master page, or frameset, that calls together a collection of different HTML pages. Each frame is actually a different Web page.

To create a frameset in PageMill, start with a blank file by choosing New from the File menu. A new, gray page should appear with a variety of buttons across the top of the window.

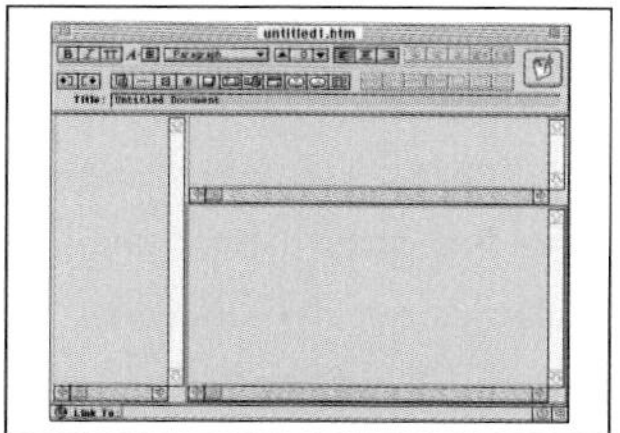

STEP 2: SETTING UP A FRAME STRUCTURE

Before you begin to create frames, think of how you want to divide the screen. For this example, we will create a three-frame structure: an interface (or menu) frame, an advertisement frame, and a content frame.

To create the first frame, hold down the Option key (Mac), or Alt key (Windows) and position the cursor over the left-most border of the Web page. When you see the cursor turn into an arrow, click and drag to the width of the first frame, dividing the page into two parts. The left frame will become the interface frame. Next, drag out a border from the top edge, within the right frame. to define the Ad frame as a portion of that space. Notice that the Content frame—the bottom right section—is the remaining space.

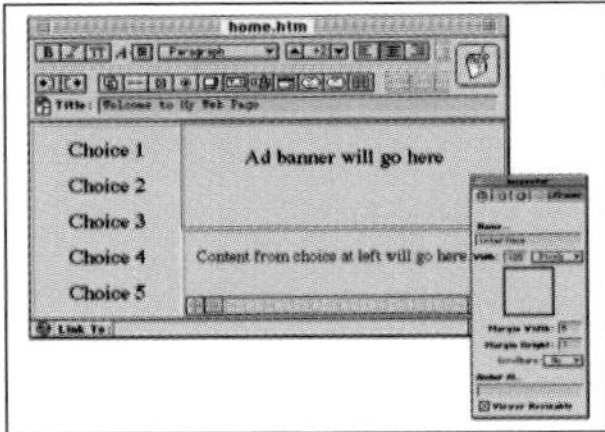

STEP 3: EDITING EACH FRAME

Select one of the frames by clicking within it; a highlighted border should appear around the frame. To edit the attributes of the frame, open the Inspector palette located in the Window menu. First, enter a name for the frame, and set the remaining attributes. In this example, the scroll bars are turned off and the width set to a fixed pixel width. Select the remaining frames by clicking them, and setting their attributes.

Each frame must be saved as an individual HTML page. If there is nothing in the frame, however, you will not be able to save it—simply type some text into the frame as shown. To save a frame, select it, and then choose Save Frame from the File menu.

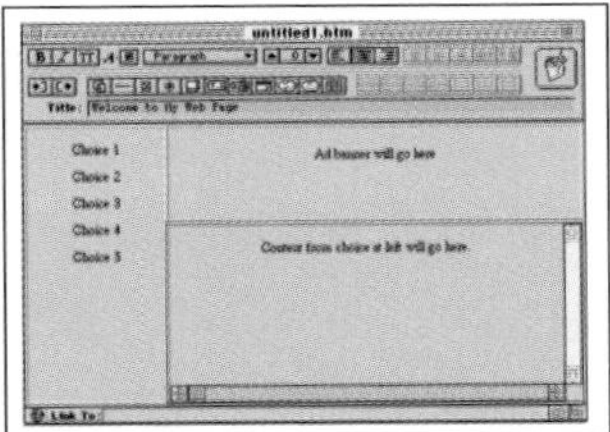

STEP 4: SAVING THE FRAMESET

Now that you have the basic frame structure set and have saved each frame, save the *frameset*. The frameset is the master HTML file that brings all the individual HTML pages together. To save the frameset, choose Save Frameset from the File menu. If this is to be your home page, name the frameset either *home.htm* or *index.htm*.

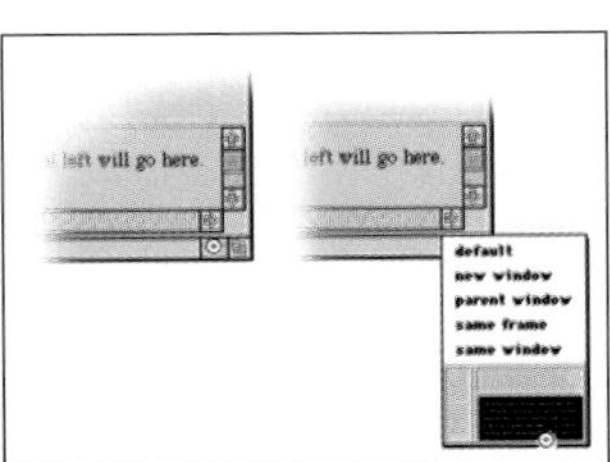

TARGETING A LINK

Normally when you click on a link, the window changes to reflect the new content. The key advantage to using frames is that when you click on a link, say in the menu frame, it changes the content in another frame. How do you set up such a relationship among frames? The key is to *target* links.

To target a link in PageMill, first create a normal link, such as Choice 1 in our example. Select Choice 1 in the menu frame, and type in a link in the Link To field, and then press the Enter or Return key. Once the link is set, it should still be selected. Before you can target a link, you must select the entire link. You can triple click on a link to select it.

Notice that the Target icon in the lower right corner of the window is now red. Click and hold the Target button to reveal a miniature of your frameset. Drag on this menu to highlight the frame you wanted target by this link, where the HTML page should appear.

Session

G2 Creating a Table Structure

One of the most unique uses of tables to organize interface, content, and animation elements is found in the *Cats* feature at *www.nationalgeographic.com.*

Tables are useful in Web page layouts for displaying straightforward tabular information and designing your layout. The *National Geographic Online* feature *Cats* uses tables to organize everything on the page from interface elements to content and animation elements. In this example, you create a table in PageMill, and then learn how to add both text and graphical elements to the table's cells.

ADOBE PAGEMILL 2.0

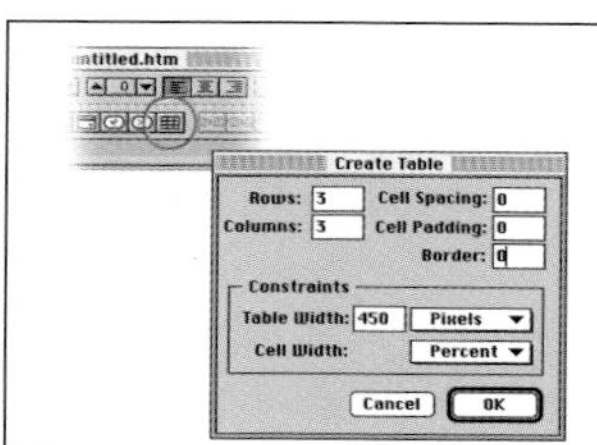

STEP 1: START A NEW DOCUMENT

If you plan to use a table structure to organize graphical elements, it is best to plan your layout beforehand in Photoshop (see Session F1). This is especially important if you are cropping graphical elements to a specific size so they match in the table layout.

In PageMill, begin by choosing New Page from the File menu, and create an initial table structure. There are two ways to create a new table. One way is to click once on the Table button in the window button bar. This opens a dialog box where you can enter the number of table cells with which you wish to start, as shown. Another way is to click and hold the Table button, and drag out the shape of your table. Either way, create an initial table that is 3 rows by 3 columns.

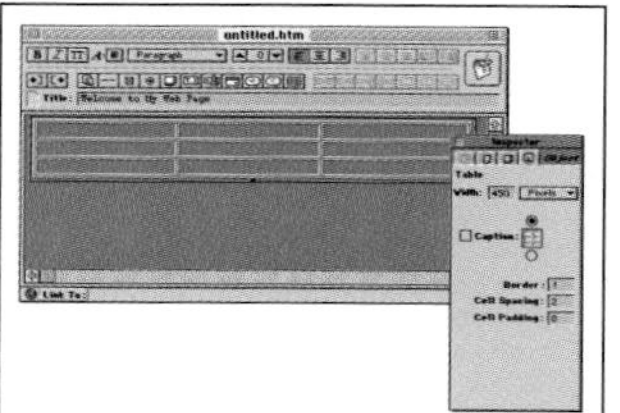

STEP 2: MODIFYING THE TABLE STRUCTURE

Once you have an initial table structure, click on its outer border to select it, and then open the Inspector palette. For the purpose of this example, set both the overall borders and the cell spacing to 0.

Next, resize the table. Notice that when you select the entire table, there are three small handles on the outer right and bottom edges. Simply click and drag these to resize the table. To change the size relationship of the table cells, click and drag the internal cell borders until you get the proportions you want.

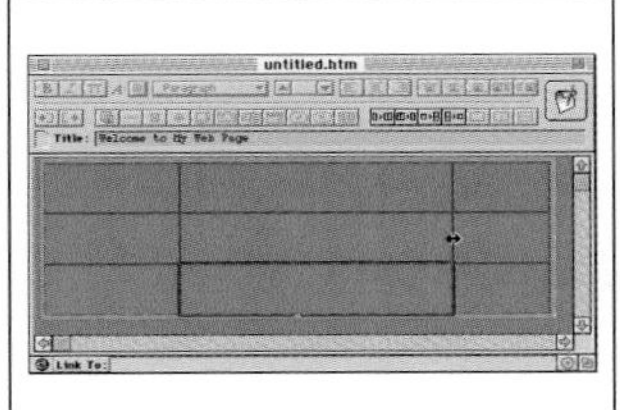

STEP 3: MODIFYING AN INDIVIDUAL CELL

To edit an individual table cell, you must select the cell. This is a little tricky to do; the best way is to first click on one of the cell's borders, and then click on the cell's interior. You may need to experiment with this a few times until you get used to it. When selected, the cell has a black border around it and the Inspector palette changes to display the cell's attributes. In addition to controlling the alignment of text and graphics, you can change the background color of the cell at the bottom of the Inspector palette.

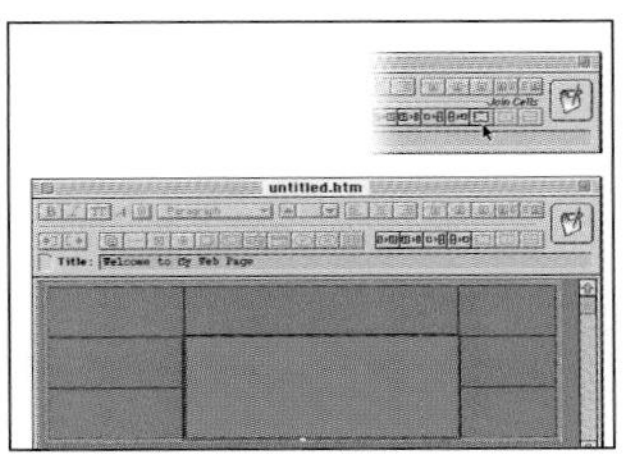

STEP 4: COMBINING CELLS

You are not limited to a perfect, three by three table structure. You can add, subtract, and combine cells so that you do not have a linear grid structure. To combine cells, you must first select them by holding down the Shift key. Once you have selected a few cells, click the Join Cells button at the top of the window.

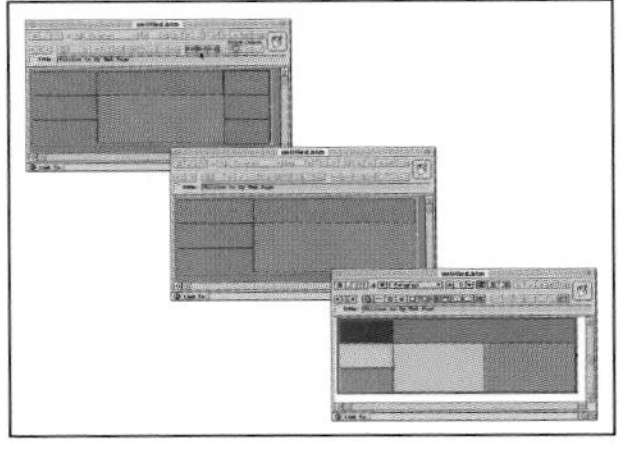

STEP 5: INSERTING AND DELETING ROWS AND COLUMNS

To add or subtract new rows and columns, use the series of buttons at the top of the page. By simply positioning the cursor over each button, a text label appears to remind you of each button's function. Select all the cells in the last column by holding down the Shift key, and clicking the Delete Column button in the top icon bar. By deleting, adding, and combining cells, you can quickly create a complex table structure.

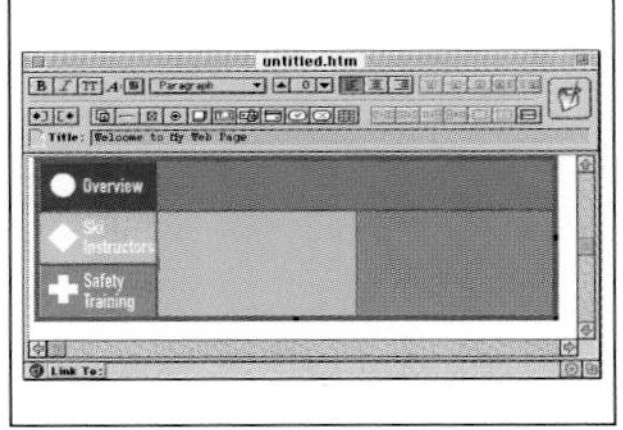

STEP 6: ADDING GRAPHICS AND TEXT

Adding text to each table cell is simple, just click inside a cell until you see a flashing cursor and begin typing. To insert an image or animated GIF, click in a cell, and rather than typing, use the Place Object button at the top of the page or choose Place from the File menu. In addition, you can drag and drop graphics and text directly into a table cell.

TIP: *You can also add new rows and columns to your table structure by Option (Mac), or Alt (Windows), clicking on the interior table cell borders.*

Session

G3 Building an Order Form

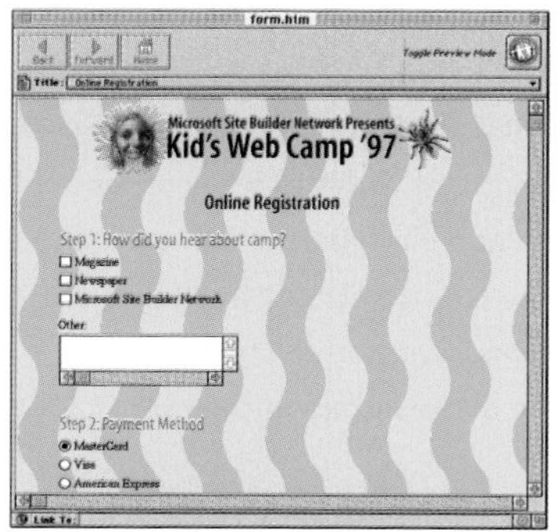

PageMill has an extensive array of form objects from text fields to radio buttons and checkboxes. By using a combination of these together, you can create your own custom order form for online credit card sales, or whatever you like. Of course, creating the forms is one thing, hooking them up with CGI scripts is another—especially when dealing with secure, online transactions. (See Session L5 for more information on CGI scripts.) In this session, we create a simple sign-up form for *Kid's Web Camp*, the online kids summer camp.

ADOBE PAGEMILL 2.0

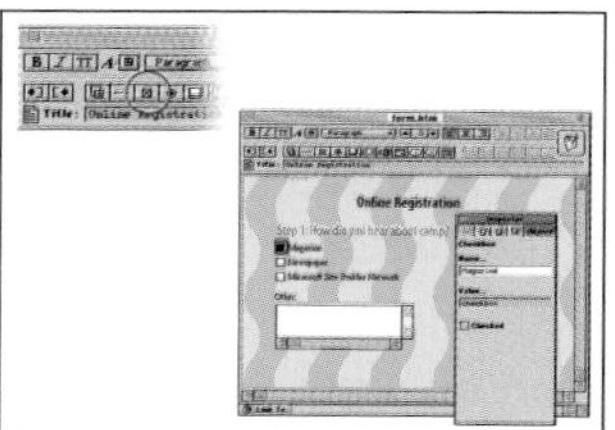

STEP 1: MAKING CHECK BOXES

Checkboxes allow your users to select multiple items from a list. To create a checkbox in PageMill, first position the cursor to the spot where you want the box inserted, and then click on the Checkbox button at the top of the window. A checkbox appears along with a blinking cursor. Type in the text next to the checkbox.

In the Inspector palette, you can change the attributes for each checkbox. Simply click on the checkbox to select it, enter a name in the Inspector palette, and then decide whether it should be checked or unchecked by default.

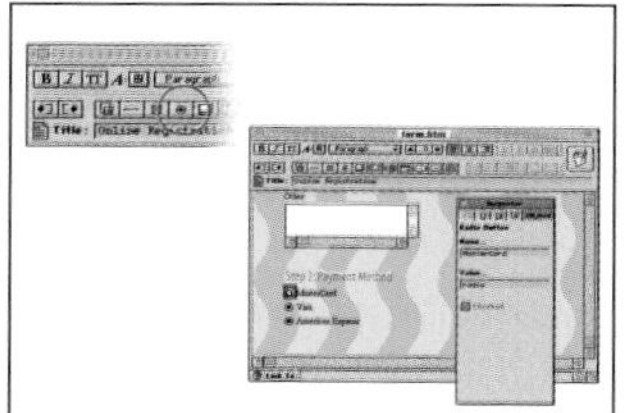

STEP 2: CREATING A SET OF RADIO BUTTONS

Radio buttons are different from checkboxes in that they never work by themselves. Rather, they present muliple options and only one can be selected at a time. But, because it is possible to have multiple groups of radio buttons, you must differentiate each group.

Position the cursor where you want to insert the first set of radio buttons, and then click the Radio Button button at the top of the window. When you go to make the next radio button on a new line (to ensure that it will be linked to the first one), hold the Option (Mac), or Alt (Windows), key and click and drag to duplicate it. If you are successful, you will see the first radio button turn off and the new copy become the selected button in the group.

To modify each radio button, first select it in the page, and then change its attributes in the Inspector palette. Remember that only one of the buttons in the group can be the default button.

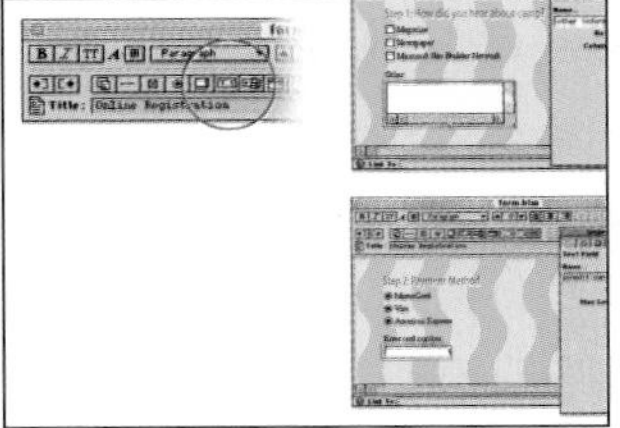

STEP 3: ADDING TEXT AREAS AND FIELDS

Just underneath the set of checkboxes you created in Step 1, add a text area so users can type in additional information. To do this, first position the cursor after the last checkbox, use the Return key to start a new line, and then click once on the Text Window icon. Like the other form objects, you can modify text fields in the Inspector palette as shown.

Next, add a text field under the radio buttons that will allow users to enter their sixteen-digit credit card numbers. Insert the text field as you did for the other form objects, and then use the Inspector palette to limit the number of characters to sixteen. Password text fields are just like regular text fields; however, when a user enters information, it is hidden by a series of bullets as opposed to normal characters.

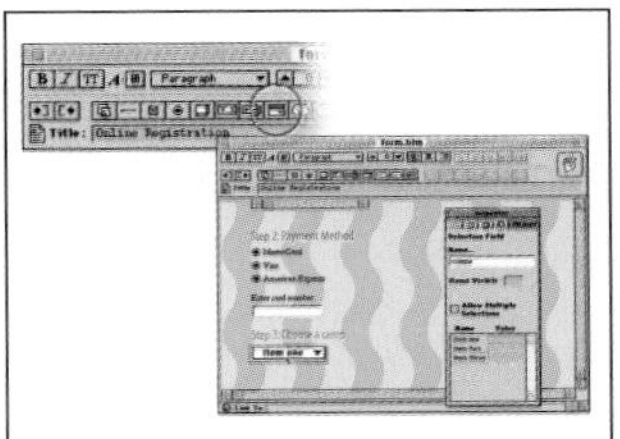

STEP 4: INCLUDING POP-UP MENUS

Pop-up menus are a great way to handle a number of choices in a condensed space. You can insert a pop-up menu by clicking once on the Pop-up Menu button. By default, the menu contains "item one." To change the name of an item, double-click the pop-up menu object, select the text with the cursor, and then type in the new name. To add more items, simply press the Return key and type in the new items.

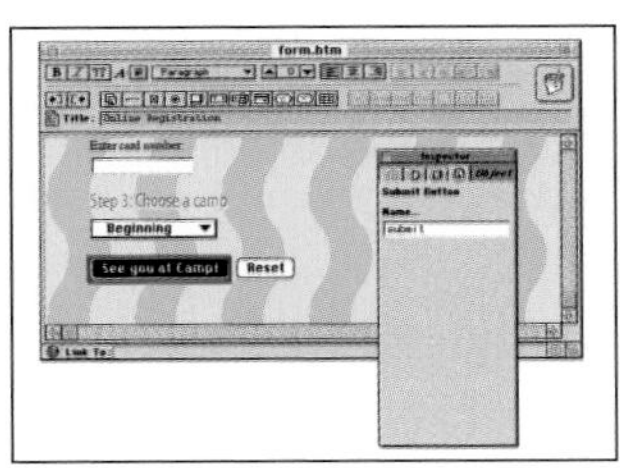

STEP 5: ADDING SUBMIT AND RESET BUTTONS

Lastly, you need to insert both a Submit button and a Reset button. Otherwise, the information that users type in your form has no way of getting to you. Keep in mind, however, that the Submit button must interact with a CGI script in order to assemble all of the information and send it where it needs to go (see Session L5).

Insert the cursor where the Submit button will go, and click the Submit button at the top of the window. Next to the Submit button, insert a Reset button. The Reset button clears all of the form entries so the user can start again. To change the names of either button, select the name in the page and type in the new name. Note that its action remains the same.

Session

G4 Working with Images in PageMill

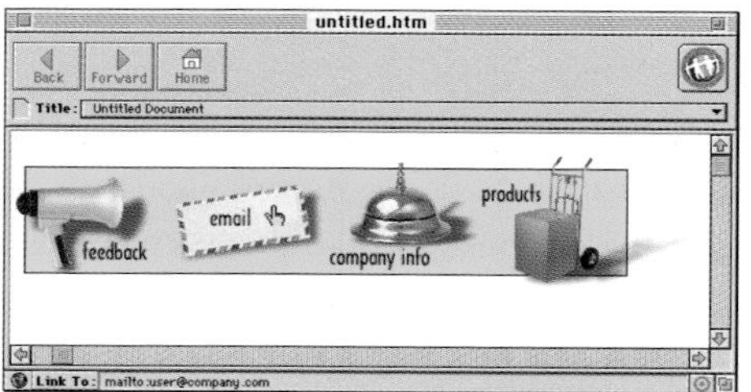

Rather than finalizing images in a graphics program such as Photoshop, you can add your finishing touches directly in PageMill. PageMill can import not only GIFs and JPEGs, but PICTs, BMPs, and Photoshop layers as well. Once in PageMill, you can control transparency, interlacing, and create image maps.

ADOBE PAGEMILL 2.0

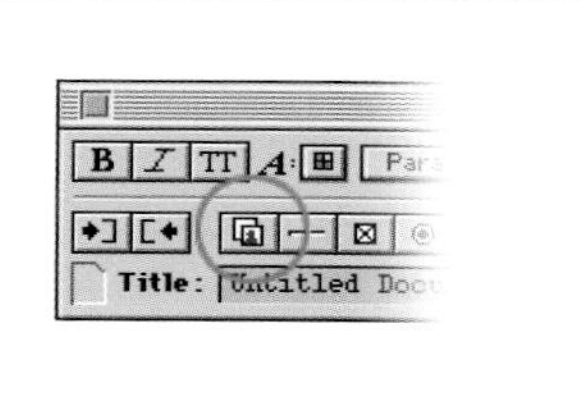

STEP 1: PLACING GRAPHICS INTO PAGEMILL

There are three ways to import graphics into PageMill. One way is to simply use the Place command from the File menu. You also can use the Place Object button, located in the button bar at the top of the window. Lastly, if you have both Photoshop and PageMill open at the same time, you can drag and drop a Photoshop layer directly into PageMill.

TIP: *When you place RBG graphics that you have not indexed into a color palette, PageMill automatically assigns them an 8-bit palette.*

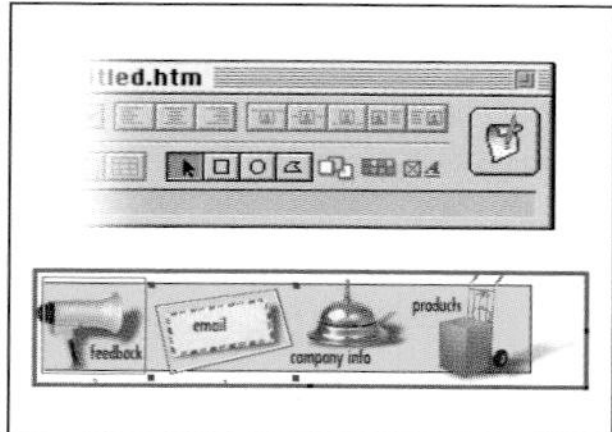

STEP 2: CREATING AN IMAGE MAP

Instead of linking to an entire graphic, often a single graphic (such as an icon banner) needs to have multiple links. In such a case, you need to create an image map.

In PageMill, it's easy to create image maps. To begin, double-click on the graphic; this displays a new set of tools in the top icon bar, a selection arrow followed by three *hotspot* shapes, and a series of image map editing buttons.

Choose one of the hotspot shape tools, and draw a hotspot around a portion of your graphic.

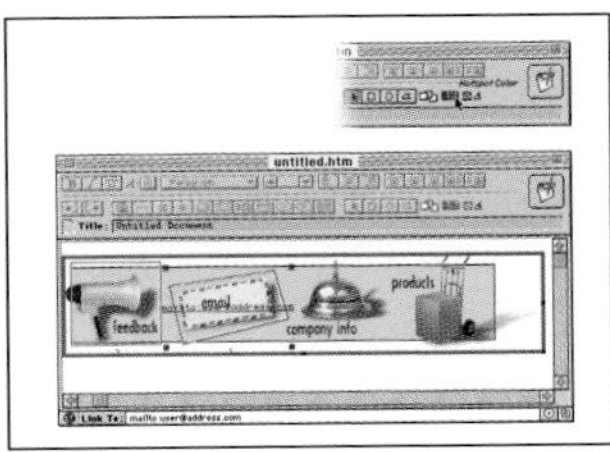

STEP 3: EDITING IMAGE MAPS

Once you have created a series of hotspots, assign a link to each one. Select a hotspot with the Pointer tool, and then enter a URL in the Link To field at the bottom of the window. After entering the link, press either the Return key or the Enter key. You can hide and show the link text that appears inside the hotspot by clicking on the Hotspot Label button at the top of the window.

By default the hotspots are outlined in bright blue. If it is difficult to see your hotspots due to the color of the underlying image, you can change the color with the mini Color pop-up menu in the button bar.

The order in which you create hotspots determines which button is on top of the other. This is very important if the buttons overlap because the top-most button will be dominant. To reorder buttons, select the one to be moved and use the Shuffle Hotspot pop-up menu in the button bar.

Now, you can resize the hotspots by simply dragging their handles. Notice, however, that you cannot edit the points of a polygon shape.

NOTE: *The Inspector palette indicates whether or not an image has an image map associated with it. When you select an image, the behavior section of the Inspector palette reads Map as opposed to Picture or Button.*

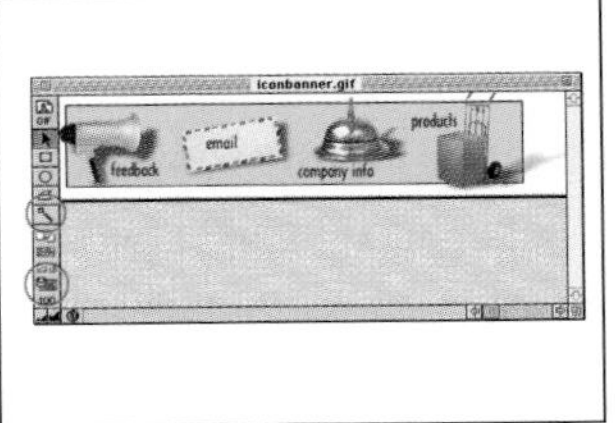

STEP 4: SETTING TRANSPARENCY AND INTERLACING

If you have not already done so in a graphics program, you can set an image's transparency and interlacing attributes directly in PageMill. First click off of the image, and then hold the Command key (Mac), or Control key (Windows), and double-click on the image. A new, smaller window appears with your image and a set of tools.

To make an image interlaced, click once on the lower picture-like icon so that it appears to be covered by venetian blinds. To de-interlace an image, click again so that the picture icon is solid.

To make a color transparent, choose the magic-wand-looking tool and click once on the color to be transparent.

Notice that this window also enables you to create an image map. If you create an image map in this window, however, PageMill will generate an external map file separate from the HTML file. This is the old style of creating image maps required by older browsers, where the server interprets the map.

Adding External Objects

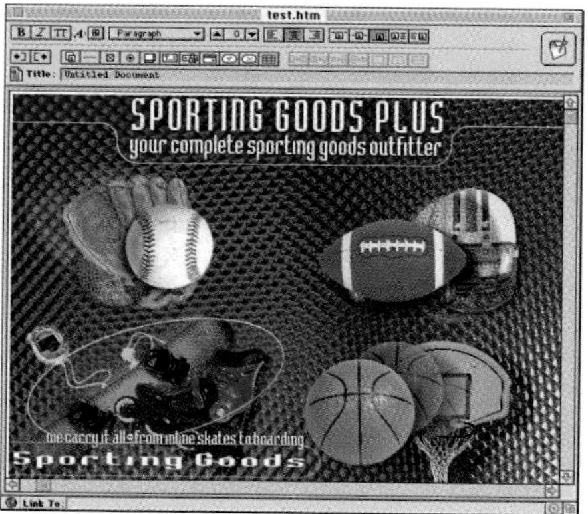

In PageMill, you are not limited to importing only static images such as PICTs, GIFs, and JPEGs. PageMill enables you to create dynamic Web sites by allowing you to import external media objects such as Shockwave, QuickTime, and Flash movies, as well as ActiveX objects, Java applets, and PDF files. Even if PageMill does not recognize the file you are importing, it will create a space for it so that your page can be viewed properly in a Web browser.

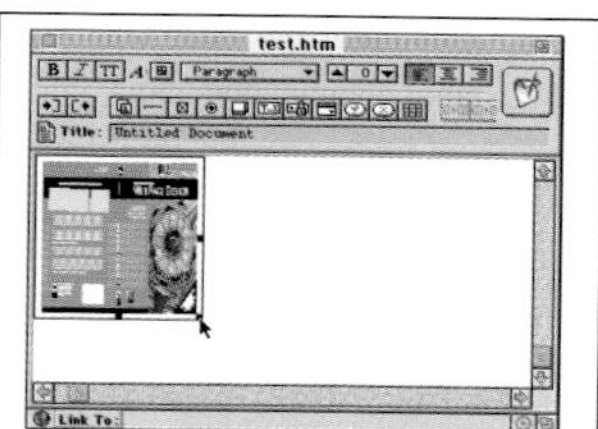

STEP 1: INSERTING A, ACROBAT PDF FILE

Placing Acrobat PDF files into your Web page layout is as easy as placing normal, static graphics. You can use the Place command from the File menu, the Place Object button in the window's button bar, or simply drag a PDF file directly into your PageMill window.

Upon placing a PDF file into your Web page, Acrobat Reader automatically launches in the background to render the PDF image. The PDF file displays in your layout as a tiny thumbnail that you can resize by dragging the handles around the thumbnail.

NOTE: *You cannot add a link to a media object (such as a PDF file) like you can to a static graphic. Also, if you are inserting a PDF file, in order to view it in a browser, you must have the PDF plug-in installed.*

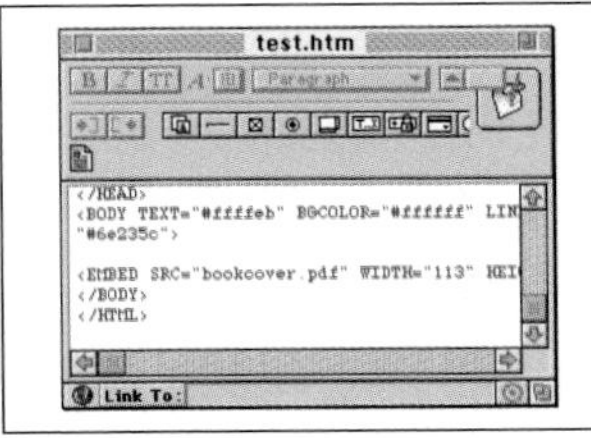

STEP 2: ADDING OTHER MEDIA TYPES

Adding other types of media objects to your Web page layout is just as simple as adding a PDF file. Simply place the object into the layout, using one of the methods described in Step 1. PageMill accepts Java applets, Flash, QuickTime, and Shockwave files as well as ActiveX files. PageMill automatically uses the *<embed src="name">* tag. If you need to adjust any parameters, you can always access the HTML Source from the Edit menu, or make changes in the Inspector window.

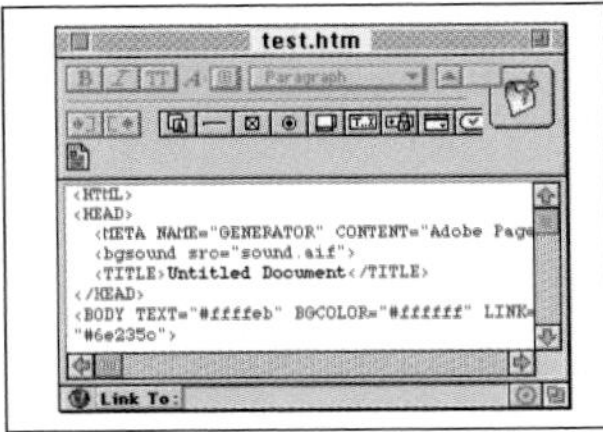

STEP 3: ADDING SOUND

PageMill does not have direct support for importing sounds to your Web page. You can, however, add a background sound by editing the HTML source of your Web page (see Session 18).

You can also create a link directly to a sound file. Simply select the graphic, hotspot, or text and type in the name of the sound file in the Link To field at the bottom of the window.

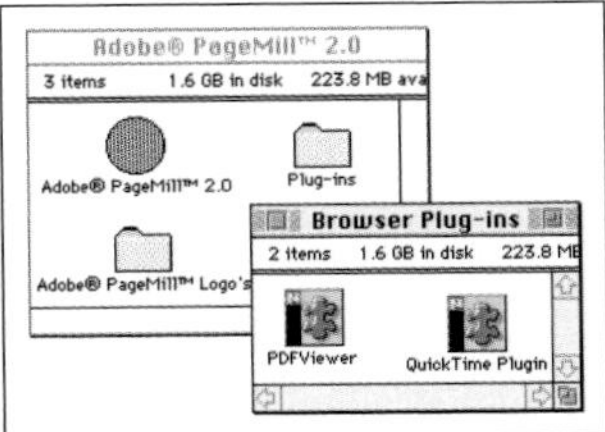

PLUG-INS FOR PAGEMILL

Just as you must add the correct plug-ins to your browser to display content properly, you also must add plug-ins to PageMill. If PageMill does not recognize a media object, chances are you do not have the correct plug-in installed in PageMill's Browser Plug-Ins folder. To install plug-ins, quit PageMill, and place copies of your plug-ins into the PageMill Browser Plug-ins folder. Restart PageMill.

NOTE: *If you do not have the correct plug-ins for a media object, PageMill will not recognize it. This does not, however, prevent PageMill from properly inserting a place for the object in HTML. Just keep in mind that you may need to manually enter the height and width of the object in the Inspector palette—especially in the case of Flash and Shockwave files.*

Session

G6 Fine-Tuning your HTML

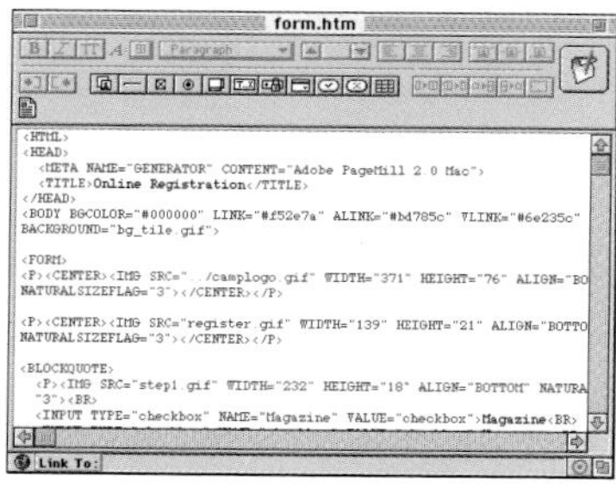

Just as there are two sides to a coin, there are two sides to every Web page, the graphical side, which you have been working in, and the flip side which is the HTML code describing the page. Once you assemble your basic Web page layout in PageMill, there are a number of ways that you can fine-tune your HTML, including typing directly into the HTML source file itself. You can also add invisible items such as anchor links, margin breaks, and comments that appear only while in PageMill.

ADOBE PAGEMILL 2.0

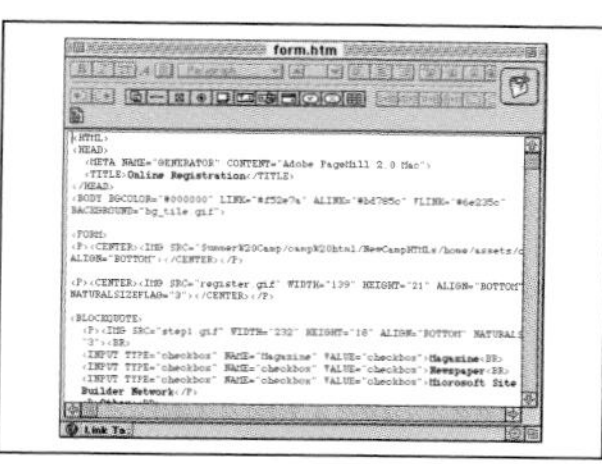

STEP 1: EDITING AND VIEWING HTML CODE

You can quickly toggle back and forth to view both sides of your Web page by choosing the HTML Source option from the Edit menu. To make changes to your code (such as adding JavaScript or CGI scripts) simply type directly into the HTML. Note that PageMill connot interpret correctly some scripts once you flip back to the graphical Preview mode. To prevent PageMill from trying to interpret such scripts, you must use a Placeholder marker at the beginning and end of the scripts, see Step 3.

STEP 2: INCLUDING JAVASCRIPT

You cannot run JavaScript from within PageMill, but you can view and edit a script while in the HMTL Source view. To add JavaScript to your Web page, switch to HTML Source view by choosing it from the Edit menu, and begin your JavaScript after the opening *<BODY>* tag. The syntax to insert JavaScript is as follows: *<SCRIPT language="javascript">*. Follow this opening tag with your JavaScript on the next line, and then close the script using the *</SCRIPT>* tag.

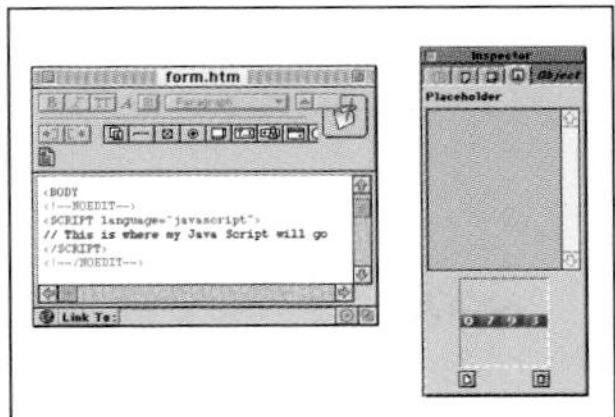

STEP 3: USING PAGEMILL PLACEHOLDERS

If you switch back to the graphical mode, PageMill will try to interpret the JavaScript, and in doing so will display it as text on the page. To avoid this, while you are still in the HTML Source view, position the cursor just before the JavaScript opening tag and choose the Placeholder option from the Edit menu. This inserts an opening and closing *<NOEDIT>* tag. Select the ending *</NOEDIT>* portion of the tag and move it to follow the closing *</SCRIPT>* tag as shown.

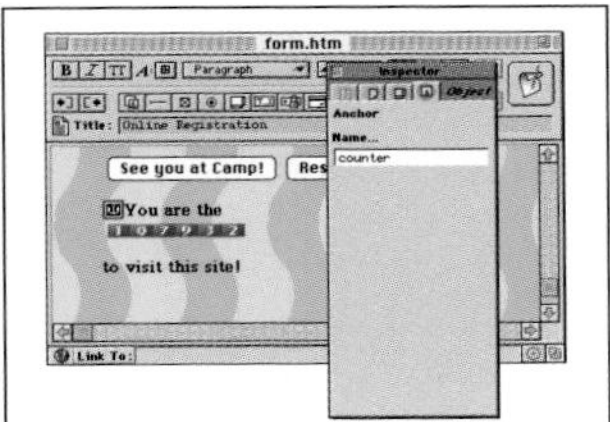

STEP 4: HOW TO MAKE AN ANCHOR-LINK

Anchor-links are links to different parts of the same page. An anchor-link is actually two pieces: the anchor, or point where you will go to, and the link that is clicked to initiate the jump to the anchor. To add an anchor, select the text or object to link to, and then choose Insert Invisibles > Anchor from the Edit menu. After you insert the anchor, click it to select it, and give it a name in the Inspector palette.

Next, select the text or object that, when clicked, takes you to the anchor. In the Link To field at the bottom of the window, enter the name of the anchor proceeded by a pound-sign: *#anchorname.*

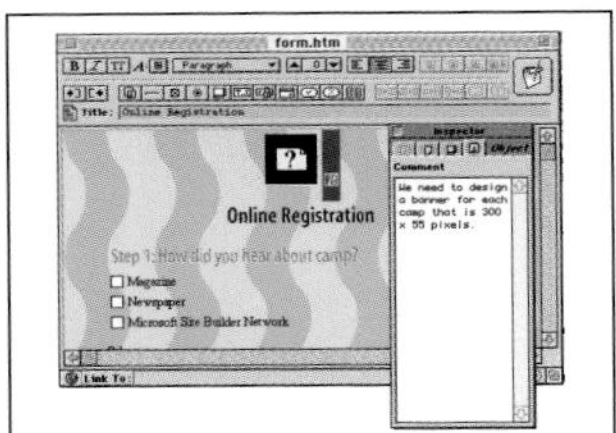

STEP 5: INSERTING AN INVISIBLE COMMENT

To annotate your Web page, without displaying your remarks in the actual layout itself, add an invisible comment to the page. Position your cursor where the comment is to go, and then choose Insert Invisibles > Comment from the Edit menu.

Click on the Comment icon once, and then type your comment into the Inspector window. When you view your HTML source, the comment is in red.

Spinner, the character shown at left, is from the book *Kid's Web Kit.*

STEP 6: ADDING AN INVISIBLE MARGIN BREAK

One of the most practical uses of a Margin Break is to control text alignment to a graphic. For instance, if you are aligning a short paragraph of text to the right of a graphic, and want the next segment of text to resume underneath the graphic, insert an invisible Margin Break just after the short paragraph. Without the Margin Break the text that follows continues to align next to the graphic—even if you don't want it there. This can be especially useful when users enlarge their browser window, potentially confusing the design by flowing text next to the image.

Session

G7

Managing a Site with SiteMill

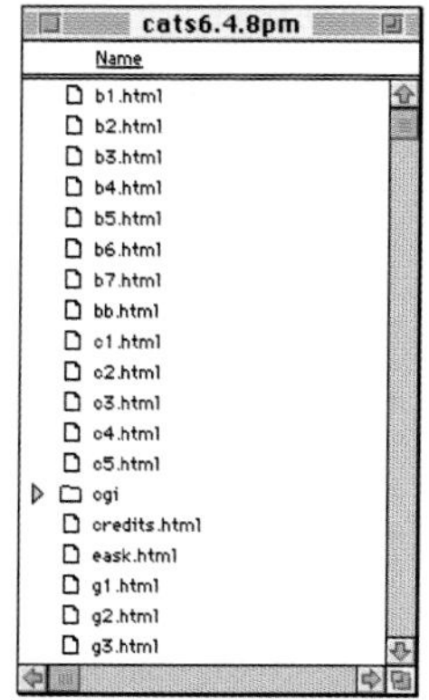

SiteMill, Adobe's companion application to PageMill, is designed to help organize all the pages of your site, automatically checking for missing elements, inappropriate links, and enabling you to change relationships among files. SiteMill has the capability to replace pages on a site as well as add additional directories, automatically updating all necessary links and object references. When you have completed changes to a site, SiteMill has the capability to directly upload it to a server. SiteMill is extremely valuable when working on complex sites that involve many pages; you can concentrate on creative changes without being burdened by editing every file that may be affected by them.

ADOBE SITEMILL 2.0
ADOBE PAGEMILL 2.0

NOTE: *SiteMill 2.0 has been bundled with PageMill 2.0 since July, 1997. SiteMill 2.0 allows you to open Web pages PageMill. Whereas SiteMill 1.0 had PageMill 1.0 features built-in.*

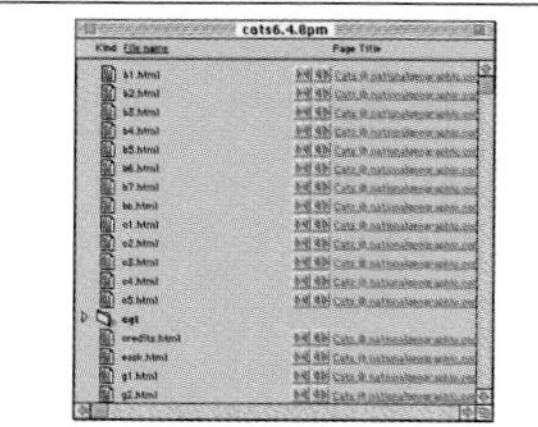

STEP 1: LOADING A SITE

When you first launch SiteMill, it asks you to locate a folder on your hard drive that contains the files of your site. After you select the appropriate folder, SiteMill reads in all the files and folders, analyzes the HTML pages for external and internal links, and displays a status window.

To the right of the list of files, SiteMill displays two columns of pop-up menu buttons. In the left column, you will see either an Arrow button or a red X. An Arrow pop-up button indicates that there is incoming links connecting to that Web page; whereas a red X indicates that there is no incoming links. If you select an item from either of the Arrow button pop-up menus, it opens in PageMill.

NOTE: *SiteMill can only work with one Web site at a time. To load another site, first close the current site, then use the Load command in the Site menu. Alternatively you can reload the same site without closing it.*

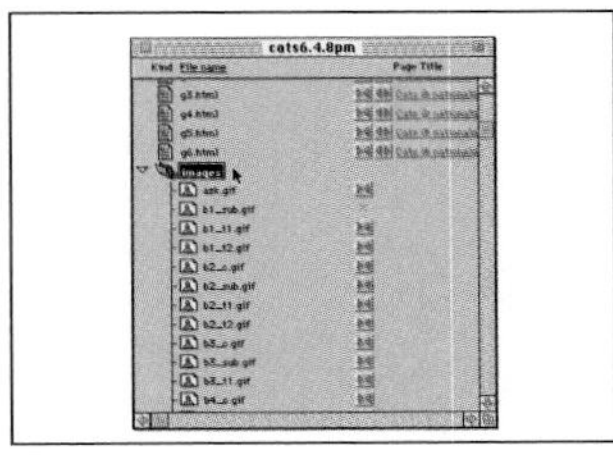

STEP 2: MAKING CHANGES TO A SITE

The advantage of using SiteMill to manage Web pages is its ability to automatically, and universally, redirect links and fix directory changes.

For example, let's say that you need to change the name of a sub-directory that contains all of the graphic files. Normally, you would have to update each link on each page. In a large site, with dozens of pages, a task like this can be daunting. Using SiteMill, you can simply change the name of the folder in the status window. SiteMill quickly updates all the links.

You can also rename HTML or graphic files, add or remove folders (or directory levels), update external URLs, and even delete or redirect links.

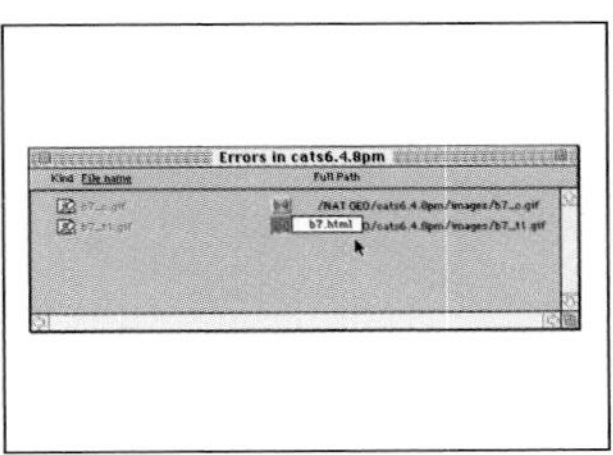

STEP 3: CHECKING AND FIXING ERRORS

When you load a site that has links to objects or HTML pages that can't be found, SiteMill displays them in the Errors window. Again, this can be extremely useful for large sites, saving you from having to test every link on every page.

To fix an error you have two options. The first is to double-click on the file name, displayed in red, and use the subsequent dialog box to locate the missing file (or find another file altogether). The second option is to update the page that contains the bad link.

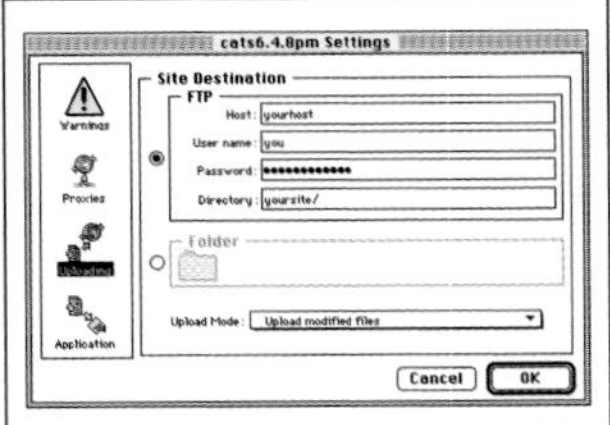

STEP 4: UPLOADING A SITE

After a site is completed, or updated, you can use SiteMill to upload it to your Web server. In addition, SiteMill can recognize which files have been changed, giving you the option to upload only those files.

To upload your site, you must first specify the FTP settings in the Preferences dialog box, found in the Edit menu. Open the Preferences, select the Uploading option, and enter your server information. Then, with an open Internet connection, choose Upload from the Site menu.

TIP: *If you are serving the Web site from your desktop computer or a computer on a local network, you cxan use the Uploading Preferences to tell SiteMill to copy the site into a folder or directory, rather than uploading it via FTP to a remote server.*

Chapter H

HTML: So Much More Than Just Text

HTML is the current language of the World Wide Web. HTML is what communicates from the server to the browser to display what the user requests. When you want to access a Web site and type in a URL (for example *http://www.adobe.com*), you're really asking the server that hosts that site to give you the HTML page designated as the home page for that site. In this chapter, you will work with the basics of HTML, incorporate graphics, frames, and tables, downloadables, and the basics of the hexadecimal numbering system for HTML colors. HTML can be created in two different types of software applications, text editors and visual site editors that allow you to edit a WYSIWYG graphical representation of your pages. To become familiar with the inner workings of HTML, the chapter focuses on the creation of Web pages using a text editor.

CHAPTER SESSIONS

H1 *Incorporating Graphics and Downloadables*

H2 *Create an HTML Table*

H3 *Creating a Frame Structure in HTML*

H4 *Bandwidth and Speed Tips*

H5 *Email Feedback from Users*

H6 *Introduction to Hexadecimal Colors*

H7 *How to Create an Imagemap*

CHAPTER TOOLBOX

Simple Text or Notepad

Adobe PageMill 2.0

Adobe Photoshop 4.0

Pantone® ColorWeb

WebMap

Transparency

HTML 101

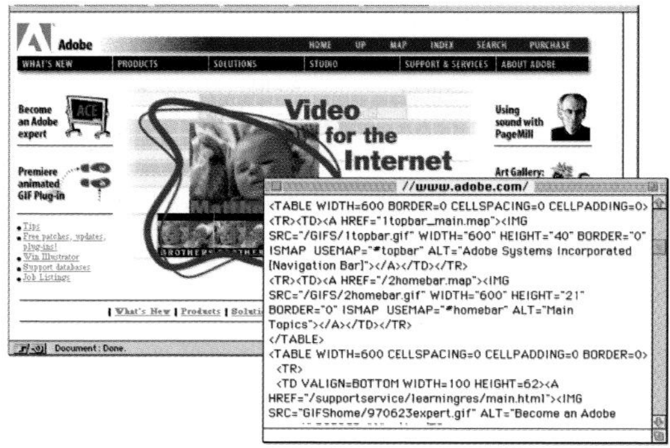

The HTML file of a page itself is generally very small—it contains only text. Graphics are not contained in the page directly; instead, the HTML page contains a tag that references another file on the server. If you're familiar with PageMaker or Quark, or even Macromedia Director, you're familiar with the idea of linked external files—you tell the application where the graphic resides, and when you open your document, the image is located and displayed.

There can be slight differences between how each brand of browser interprets and displays an HTML tag. And some tags are even unique to a specific browser and ignored by others. The creation of standards are constantly in negotiation and many tags are becoming more universally handled by browsers.

PARTS OF AN HTML PAGE

HTML pages consist of two parts: the head and the body. The head portion of the HTML page contains page-specific overview lines, including copyright information, image maps, and meta tags. The body portion of the HTML page contains all other information for the page, including background and text colors, text, graphics, tables, and other media elements used throughout the page.

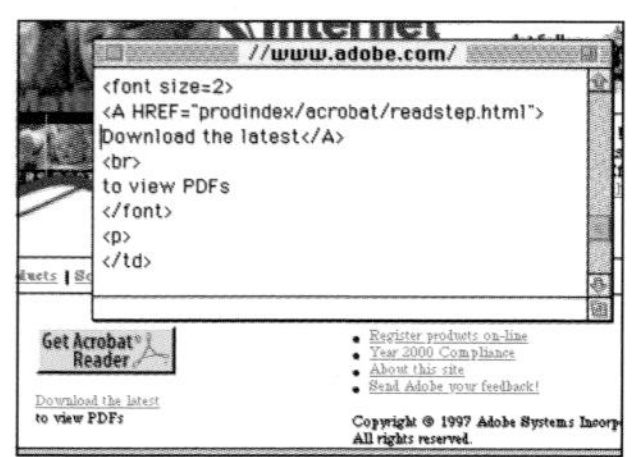

BASIC HTML TAGS USED TO DISPLAY TEXT

HTML tags tell the browser how to perform actions such as displaying text, hyperlinking, and where to place images on the page. Some common text formatting tags that you'll see on almost every page you look at, are:

<P> signifies a paragraph break
*
* new line, but not a paragraph break
<br clear=all> new line, and clears all margins

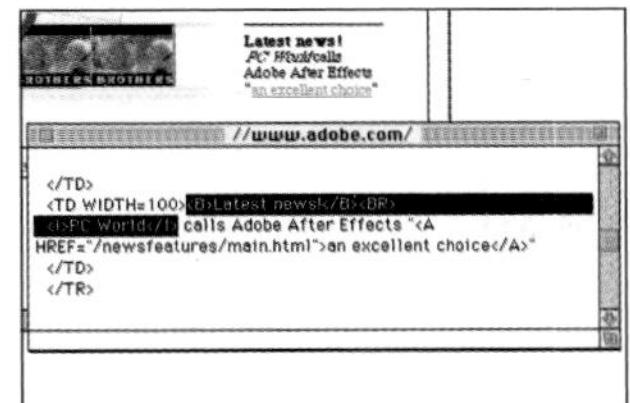

CHANGING THE APPEARANCE OF TEXT

Most tags that format text are used in pairs, enclosing the text they effect. For example:

<*b*>**this pair of tags will make the text bold**</*b*>

<*i*>*or italic*</*i*>

<*font size=+2*>will make this text big</*font*>

<*font face="arial"*>changes the typeface for the text</*font*>

<*center*>centers the text on the page</*center*>

Notice that the tag which follows the effected text is the same as the initial tag with the addition of a slash character. The Font tags in these example use the size and face parameter; parameters are not placed in the closing tag.

```
<ul>
<li>bulleted item number one
<li>bulleted item number two
<li>bulleted item number three
</ul>
```

CREATING A SIMPLE LIST

HTML understands the creation of a bulleted list of items, using the <*ul*> and <*li*> tags. The <*ul*> and </*ul*> tags surround all content to generate a list, and the <*li*> tag specifies an individual item in the list.

TOP 10 CROSS-PLATFORM AND CROSS-BROWSER TIPS

Considering that different platforms and browsers offer different capabilities, you should determine your average user's configuration and design to that standard. However, remember that others will view your site and the design should never degrade to the point of being unusable. Keep the following tips in mind for cross-platform and cross-browser Web design:

1. Test your design and production on as many configurations as possible, including PC and Mac, as well as Internet Explorer and Netscape.
2. Text on a PC is generally larger than text on a Macintosh.
3. Colors generally appear darker on a PC than on a Macintosh.
4. Use Web-safe, non-dithering colors in graphics and HTML for best results.
5. Browsers display tables and frame structures with slight differences.
6. Make sure that a site designed for a 17-inch monitor also works with a 13-inch monitor, at 640 x 480 pixels.
7. Consider the typical user's monitor capabilities; some users have only 8-bit color capabilities.
8. The interrelated use of a background tile and graphics may not be a good idea; the design may not display consistently on different configurations.
9. Scripting languages, like JavaScript and VBScript, are interpreted differently in different browsers.
10. Try to avoid creating multiple versions of your site for different configurations. Unfortunately, this is not always possible.

Session

H1 Incorporating Graphics and Downloadables

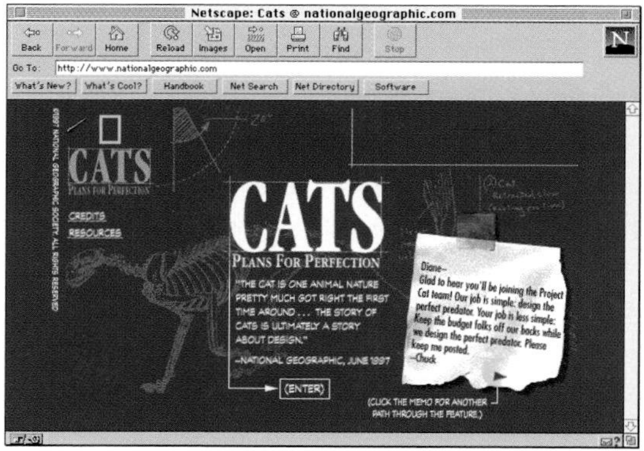

With the introduction of graphics-capable browsers like Netscape Navigator and Internet Explorer, HTML has become much more than just pages of text. This session looks at incorporating images and hyperlinks into the HTML of your Web pages, and takes a look at how to offer downloadable graphics, movies and animations, PDFs, and almost anything else from your site. Keep in mind that you're designing for the Internet and no matter how beautiful your graphics are, if they take too long to download, not many users will wait to see them.

SIMPLE TEXT
NOTEPAD

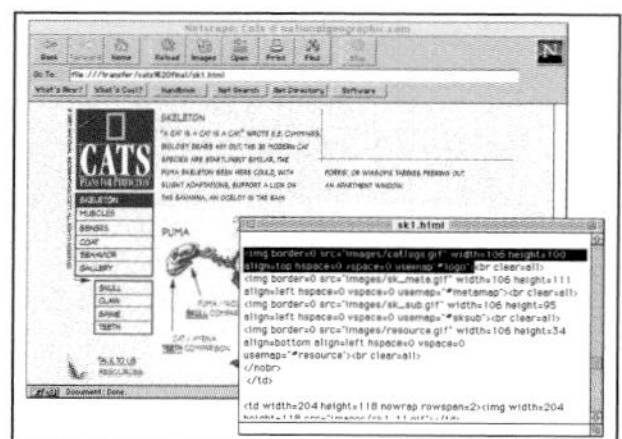
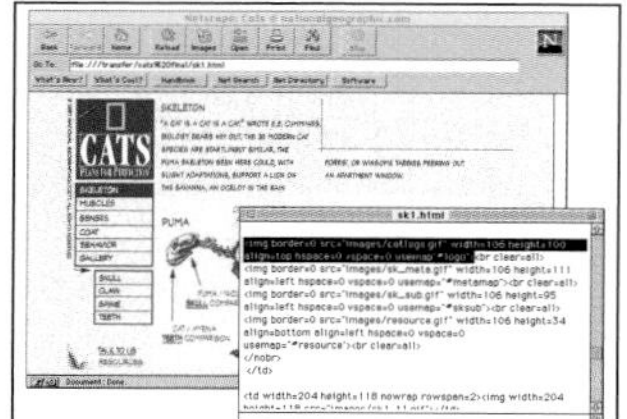

STEP 1: ADDING IMAGES

Graphics are included in HTML by using the *<img>* tag, as in the following:

```
<img border=0 height=120 width=160 src="companylogo.gif">
```

This example places the "companylogo.gif" within the page without a hyperlink border, and it tells the browser the graphic's dimensions ahead of time. Always include height and width tags so the browser can format the appropriate amount of space for the graphic while it displays the text, as text always downloads before graphics.

By the way, line formatting tags like *<center></center>* work on graphics as well as on text.

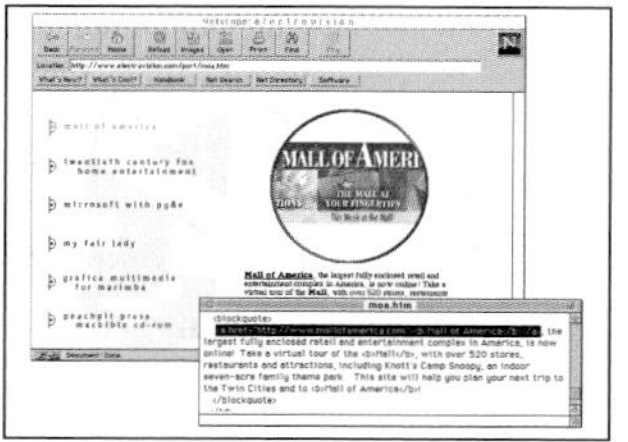

STEP 2: HYPERLINKS

In order to make a piece of text an active link, you use the *<a>* tag, which defines an action for a link:

```
<a href="page2.html">Click here to continue.</a>
```

This line of HTML presumably gives the user the next page within a series when clicked, linking to the file "page2.html." Make sure the text appropriately conveys what will happen when clicked to avoid confusing your user.

STEP 3: HYPERLINKED GRAPHICS

This same tag can also surround graphics to make them clickable:

```
<a href="page2.html"><img src="continue.gif"></a>
```

When the user clicks on the graphic "continue.gif," which presumably implies continue, the next page within a series displays. Just as with text, make sure graphics are intuitively labeled, especially if you're using the *<border=0>* attribute. If the graphic or consequence is unclear, the user won't perform the desired action.

STEP 4: DOWNLOADABLES

A good way to handle avoiding high resolution downloads is to use a thumbnail graphic as a representative graphic the user can click to download a larger image:

```
<a href="picture.jpg"><img src="picture.gif"></a>
```

When the user clicks on the thumbnail "picture.gif," the larger image, in JPEG format "picture.jpg" displays.

You can also offer your viewers links to other types of files like QuickTime movies, screensavers, games, and PDF files via the *<a>* tag. When the link is activated by the user, the file either opens with the assistance of a helper application, or downloads and is stored on the user's hard drive for later use. The following example might be used to retreive a QuickTime movie:

```
<a href="cool.mov">click here to download a cool QuickTime
   movie</a>
```

TIP: *A good rule of thumb for gauging the amount of time a download will take is about 1k per second. This is an average of modem speeds, as well as Internet traffic and means that a megabyte download may take around 15 minutes.*

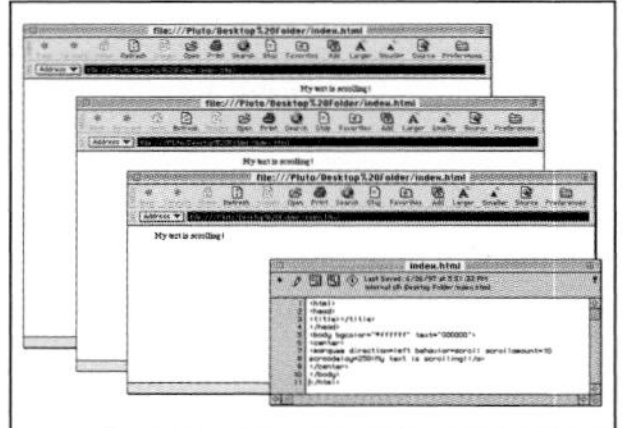

STEP 5: MARQUEE

The *<marquee>* tag is a special animation instruction that scrolls text across the HTML page, kind of like a ticker-tape.

```
<marquee direction=left behavior=scroll scrollamount=10
   scrolldelay=250>My text is scrolling!</marquee>
```

This line causes the words "My text is scrolling!" to animate from the right side of the monitor to the left side at a readable rate. You can also use formatting tags like and *<align>* to change the appearance of your scrolling text.

Session

H2 Create an HTML Table

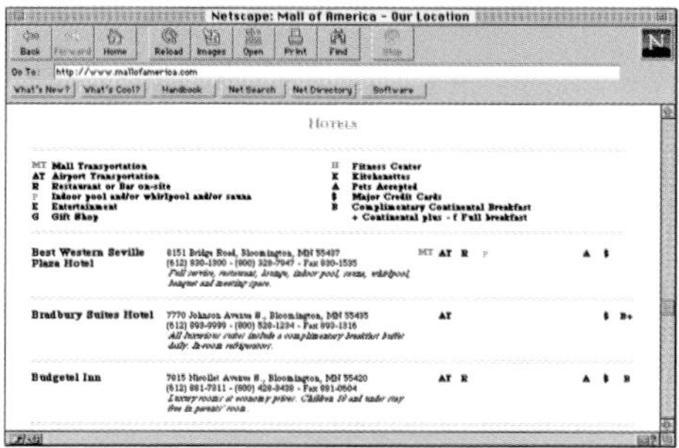

If your site calls for the organization of text and graphics into columns and rows, you need to understand the basics of HTML table creation. Tables can be a little intimidating until you get the hang of the different tags and their attributes. If you find creating a table from scratch difficult, you may want to try using a WYSIWYG HTML editor like PageMill to automate table creation (see Session G2).

A table is created by first defining the table as a whole, then defining the cells starting in the upper-left corner and moving to the right, dividing your text and graphics into columns, and then inserting breaks to begin new rows. While it is easy to get carried away dividing table cells, this session starts with a simple table of 2 columns.

SIMPLE TEXT
NOTEPAD

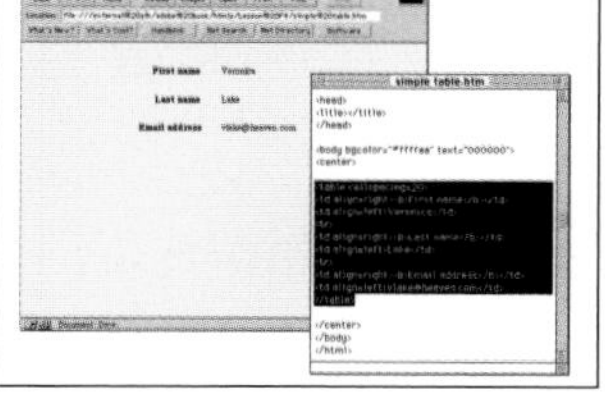

STEP 1: THE VERY BASICS OF A TABLE

Every table starts with a *<table>* tag, and is closed with *</table>*. This lets the browser know that all elements enclosed in these tags are to be tabled.

The following is a simple HTML table for two columns of information:

```
<table cellspacing=20>
<td align=right><b>First name</b></td>
<td align=left>Veronica</td>
<tr>
<td align=right><b>Last name</b></td>
<td align=left>Lake</td>
<tr>
<td align=right><b>Email address</b></td>
<td align=left>vlake@heaven.com</td>
</table>
```

TIP: Do not forget to use the closing *</table>* tag. Different browsers give you unexpected results from this omission.

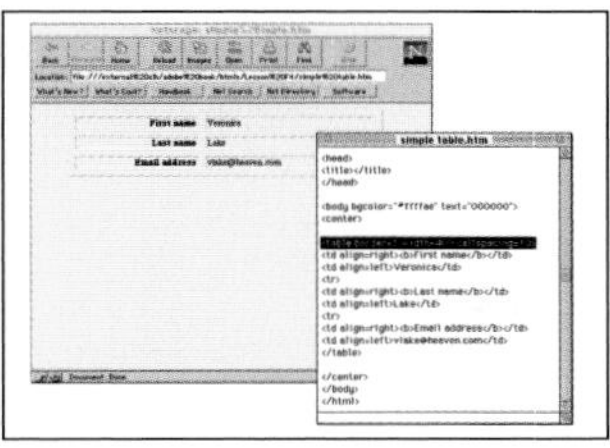

STEP 2: ATTRIBUTES OF THE <*TABLE*> TAG

The <*table*> tag offers a lot of control over appearance by using the attributes available within the <*table*> tag. The *cellspacing=* and *cellpadding=* attributes place more space around the text in the table's cell. The *width=* attribute sets the overall width of the table. You can use the *border=* attribute to set the width of a border surrounding the table. A value of zero hides the border.

When you first view your table, try using the attribute and value of *border=1*, even if you eventually hide the border. It's a lot easier to see where you've got problems when you can see how the table is divided.

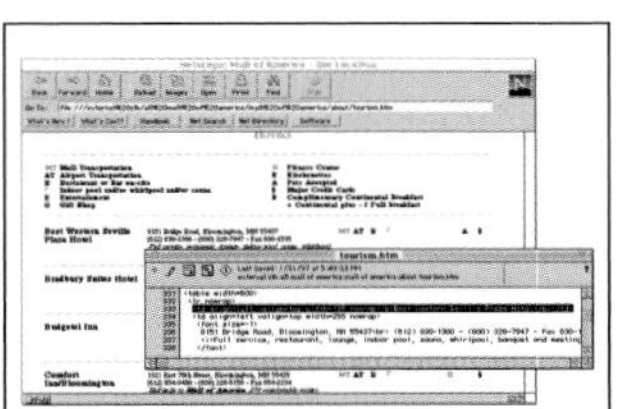

STEP 3: <*TD*> TABLE DATA

To place text or a graphic into a new cell in a table, simply surround it with the tags <*td*> and <*/td*>, which stands for table data and defines each cell in the table and the data within the cell. There's no technical limit to how many cells you can incorporate into a table, just the practical limitations of how much space you have on your page.

NOTE: *If you're creating a large table (e.g. one that scrolls past two pages), consider breaking it into multiple tables. A browser does not display any part of a table until all of its HTML downloads. By creating multiple tables, the first one can display while the others continue to download.*

STEP 4: ATTRIBUTES OF <*TABLE*>

Like the attributes of the <*table*> tag, the <*td*> tag's attributes specify how the cells of information look. The *align=* attribute aligns the graphic or text horizontally, while the *valign=* attribute aligns the graphic or text vertically. The *width=* attribute sets the width of the cell. The *colspan=* and *rowspan=* attributes are tags used to set width or height when you have a column that spans multiple rows, or a row that spans multiple columns.

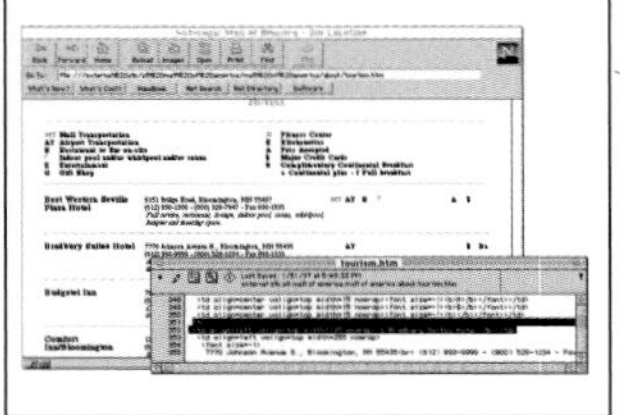

STEP 5: <*TR*> TABLE ROW

After you've finished loading a row of table cells, use the <*tr*> tag to start a new row. Sometimes it is suggested to surround a row of information with <*tr*> and <*/tr*>, rather than only a <*tr*> at the end of each row. However, this leads to consistency problems across different browsers and platforms. The method of <*tr*> at the end of the row works consistently.

Session

H3 Creating a Frame Structure in HTML

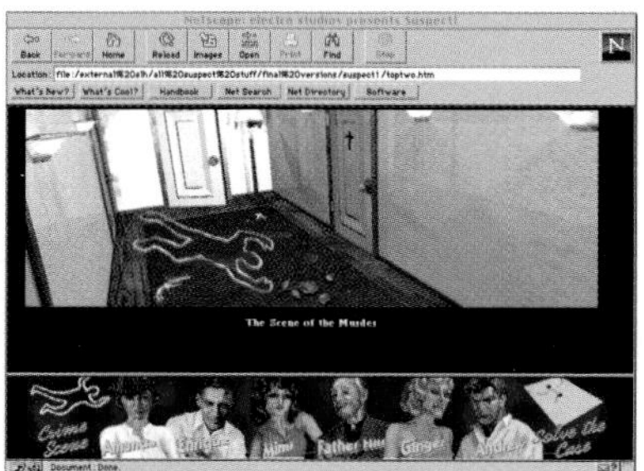

The use of frames can be great in a site when you have navigational choices that are repeated on every page. By placing these repetitive elements into a frame next to the site's content, the user always sees the navigation options in a single place and the graphics do not need to reload and display, slowing everything down. While frames can be great, try not to go crazy designing a site that has 4 or even 5 frames on each page, which can be difficult to program, look cluttered and bulky, and become confusing for the user. An HTML frame structure is created by defining a frameset that references the individual HTML pages to be displayed.

SIMPLE TEXT
NOTEPAD

TIP: *Feel free to use your favorite HTML editor; all of them will support the editing of HTML pages referenced in frames.*

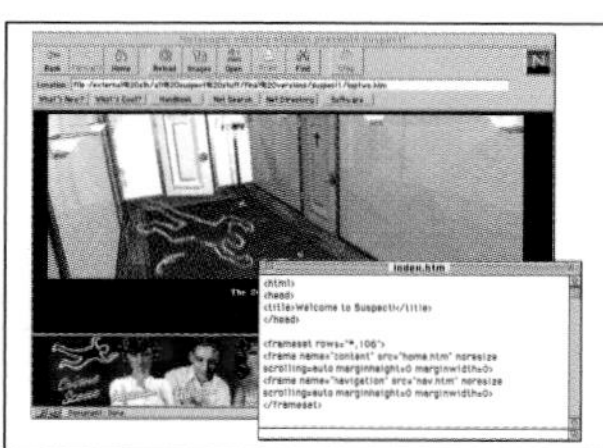

STEP 1: CREATE YOUR FRAMESET

This example page's HTML code (shown below) defines a frameset that divides its window horizontally into two rows, one frame 106 pixels tall referenced second to place it at the bottom of the page, and the other frameset for the rest of the page, represented by an asterix (*), no matter how large the user displays his browser window. The first frame, given the name *content*, is the larger frame where the user sees her choice of pages linked from the *navigation* frame. Attributes to the *<frame>* tag specify options for the appearance of the frames. The *noresize* attribute sets the frame so that the user can't resize this particular window. The *scrolling=auto* attribute and value determine if the frame displays a scrollbar when the the window is smaller than the content it contains. The *marginheight=0* and *marginwidth=0* attributes and values set content within the frame to appear with no extra space at the edges of the window.

The *<noframes>* tag is used in the frame-defining HTML file to tell a browser that doesn't support frames to use the HTML that follows it.

This section of "Index.htm" demonstrates the creation of a frameset:

```
<html>
<head>
<title>Welcome to Suspect!</title>
</head>
<frameset rows="*,106">
<frame name=”content” src=”home.htm” noresize
   scrolling=auto marginheight=0 marginwidth=0>
<frame name=”navigation” src=”nav.htm” noresize
   scrolling=auto marginheight=0 marginwidth=0>
</frameset>
```

STEP 2: CREATE YOUR NAVIGATION FRAME

In our example HTML file that defines the frameset, the page *nav.htm* is specified to display in the frame named *navigation*. Navigation options on this page link to the various content pages that will display in the content frame.

If you want, you can make this navigational menu a list of simply text-based links. However, because the user only has to download the page and its referenced graphics once, you should consider using a graphic, even though it takes longer to download. And because this page appears constantly while viewing the entire site, you'll want to make it look good.

In a frame structure, you need to specify which frame is replaced with the new page. To do this, reference the destination frame using the *target=* attribute, as in the following example:

```
<a href=“overview.htm” target=”content”>Display
   Overview.</a>
```

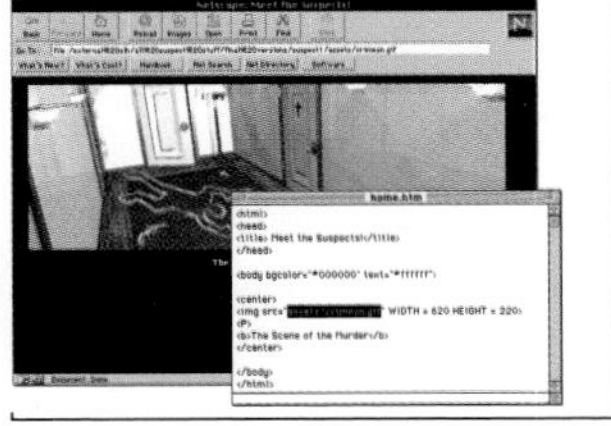

STEP 3: CREATE YOUR FIRST CONTENT FRAME

After defining the page for the *navigation* frame, create the first content page for the *content* frame. This example defines the first page loaded into the *content* frame as *home.html*. Because this is the first page that users will see, just like the navigation page, you'll want to make it visually stunning.

TIP: *Try to use graphics on this page that are referenced in later pages. That way, the user will already have them cached as she moves through the site.*

Session

H4 Bandwidth and Speed Tips

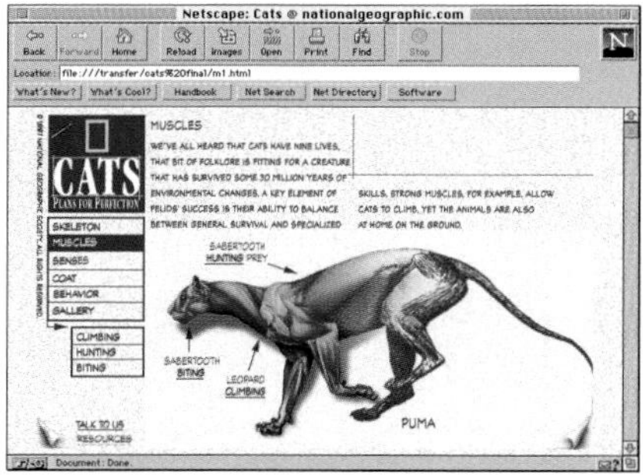

Given the state of the Internet today, one of the main concerns for any designer and producer should be that of bandwidth. If your user is forced to wait too long for your site to download, they won't stay nor return to your site. Statistics say that if a user makes a choice and sees no response for 30 seconds, she gets impatient and leaves. Make sure during the design process that you test frequently on the average anticipated computer configuration.

SIMPLE TEXT OR NOTEPAD
TRANSPARENCY

CACHE AND REUSE GRAPHICS

When a page is requested from your site, the user's browser temporarily stores a copy of the downloaded HTML pages and their associated graphics on the user's hard drive. At this point, these files are cached, and if later in your site you reference a graphic again, the browser can use the stored copy.

Consider caching a graphic that appears frequently, for example, a company logo or product branding. Graphics for navigation choices that appear throughout the site can be cached as well. Avoid referencing resized or altered graphics of essentially the same thing.

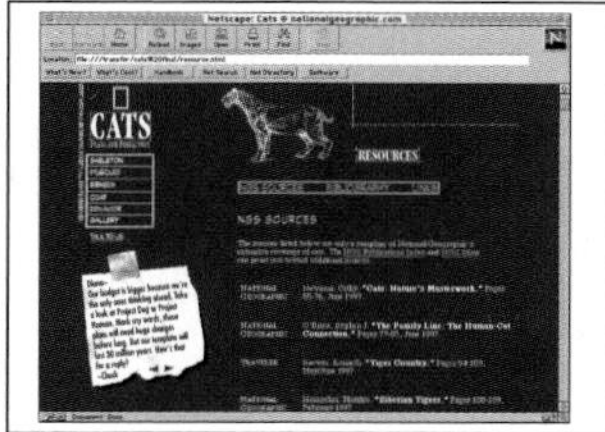

TEXT VERSUS GRAPHICS

Text is always significantly smaller than graphics; therefore, a text download is always faster than a graphic download. This makes a text-based design a good foundation on which to add images that are of secondary importance. Try to make an appealing design with the fewest possible number of graphics, using instead font styling and text formatting HTML tags in place of over-the-top images of typeset headlines or menus.

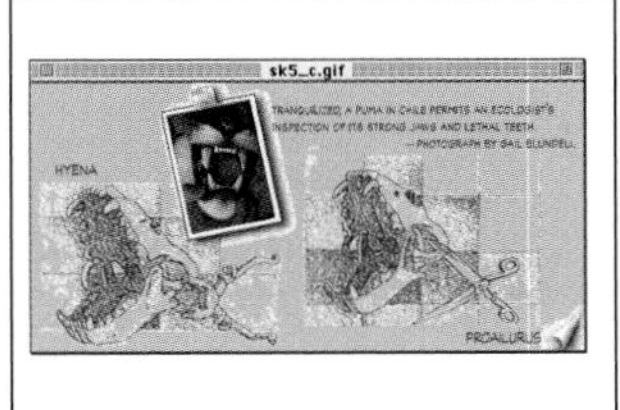

OPTIMIZE SIZE OF GRAPHICS

Due to the nature of how GIF files are compressed, try to use, as often as possible, flat Web-safe colors to minimize dithering. Crop the graphics as small as you can and use the *<hspace>* and *<vspace>* HTML tags to create necessary margins.

If you're using a background tile behind all of your graphics, make the space surrounding the graphic a solid color, and then make it transparent.

TIP: *A Mac shareware application called Transparency allows you to easily choose a 1-bit color to designate transparency.*

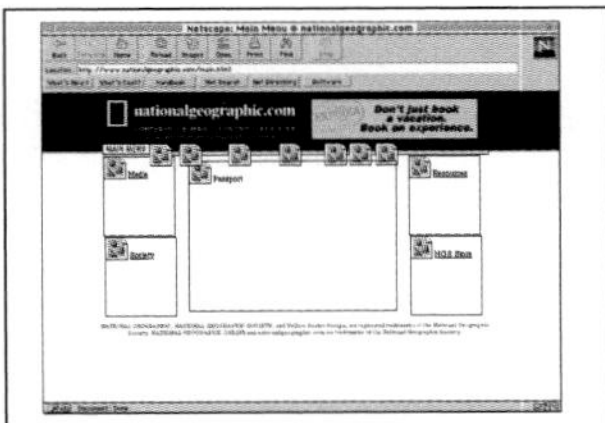

HEIGHT AND WIDTH TAGS

While this method doesn't make your graphics smaller, it gives the appearance of quicker interactivity. By setting the *height* and *width* attributes for an image, the HTML text will display first, giving the user something to read while waiting for the graphics to load into place.

Also, try to remember the *alt* attribute of the *<img>* tag, which allows the user to know what the graphic represents before it download by placing a text label in its position.

TIP: *If you replace an image after using the* height *and* width *tags, make sure you change the values appropriotely. Otherwise, your graphics might appear distorted.*

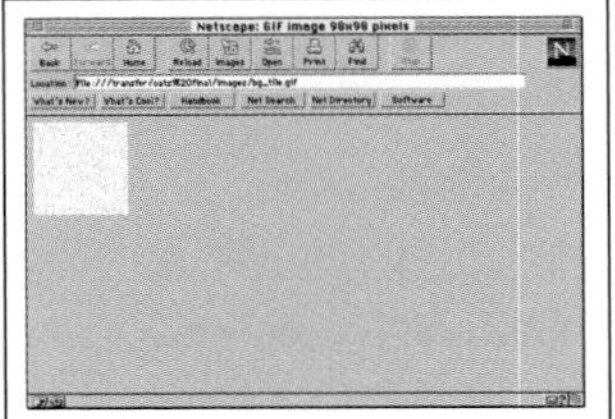

ADDITIONAL DETAILS

Other small details to consider that help minimize download, or at least minimize the appearance of download time:

- using a small background tile or just a solid background color gives the appearance of a richer site, with very little additional download time.
- use an optimized or reduced color table, like the Web-safe palette, specific to the needs of each graphic
- chop large graphics into reusable smaller graphics for caching
- break large tables into multiple smaller tables; a browser will wait until it finds a *</table>* tag before displaying the contents of the table
- investigate methods of actively streaming media, as opposed to offering large downloads

Session

H5 Email Feedback from Users

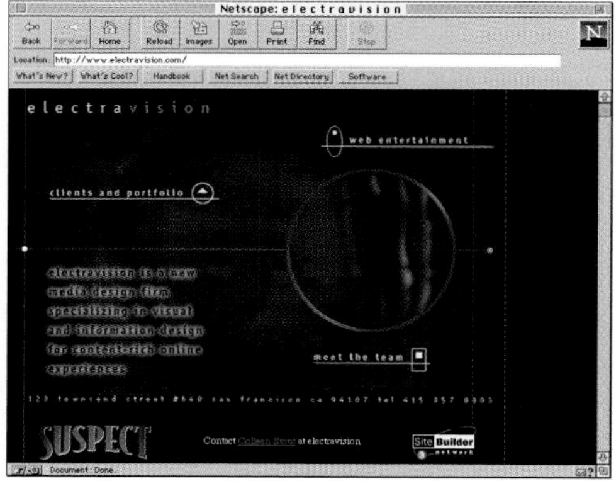

There are a couple ways to giveusers the ability to send you feedback from a Web page. If you want their email addresses, shoe sizes, and the kind of soda they drink, you should make it easy for them by creating an HTML form and a CGI script, as in Session L5. But, if you want to make it easy for yourself, and you only want the user to send you an email message, use the *mailto* value with the *HREF* attribute of the *<a>* tag.

SIMPLE TEXT OR NOTEPAD
ADOBE PAGEMILL 2.0

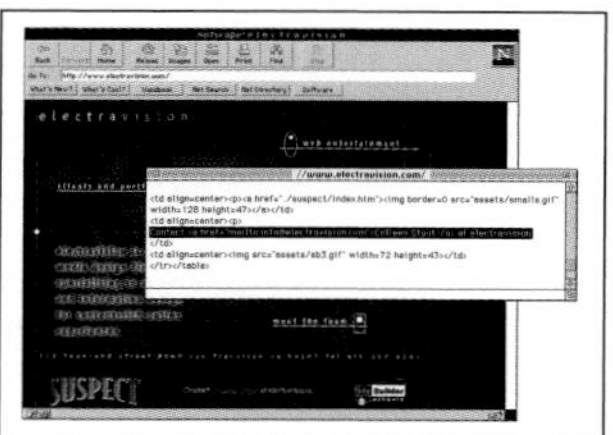

STEP 1: INCORPORATE *MAILTO:* INTO YOUR HTML

Try this line of HTML:

```
<a href="mailto:me@mydns.com">Let me know what you think
   of my site!</a>
```

Fill in your own email address in place of *me@mydns.com*, and when the user clicks on the activated text, the browser automatically opens a window to create and send an email message, already addressed!

> **TIP:** *For this to work properly, the user must have already configured her browser and email options. Most people know to do this, but you may want to include a hint on your page if you're counting on response.*

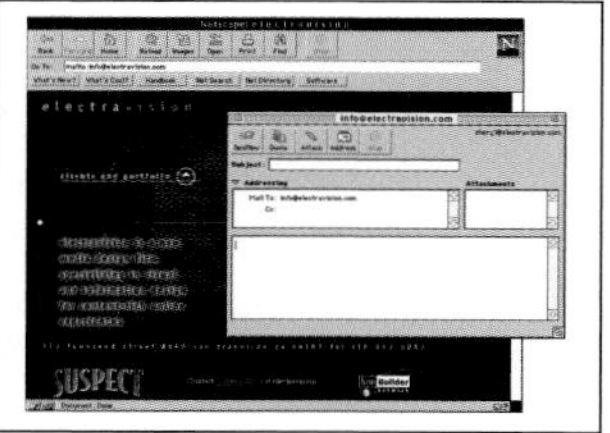

STEP 2: TEST IT!

Always make sure you test your HTML before posting it to the world. A good way to test the *mailto* is to send yourself an email.

There's nothing more frustrating to your user than wanting to go somewhere and cannot because of faulty HTML. One common mistake is to place a space between the colon in *mailto:* and the email address that follows, causing the link to incorrectly address the email.

Introduction to Hexadecimal Colors

Browsers recognize colors referenced in HTML by their numerical component values of the red, green, and blue. And while newer versions of some browsers are beginning to recognize standardized names of colors (such as red, orange, yellow) to really understand the color scheme of the Web, you need to use and understand the basic web hexadecimal color references.

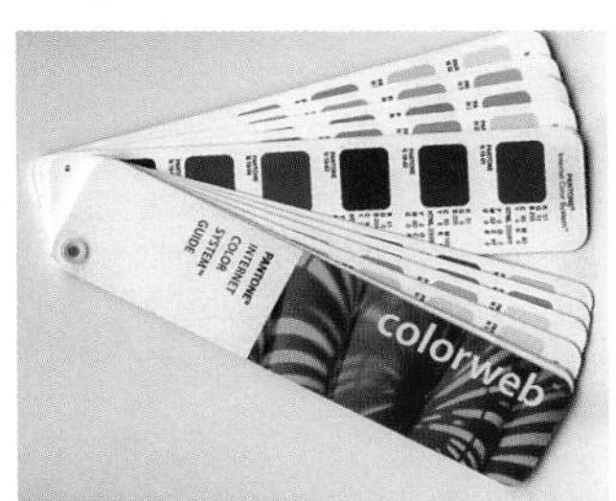

SIMPLE TEXT OR NOTEPAD
COLORWEB

TIP: *Pantone has created a utility called ColorWeb, which is a Photoshop plug-in that comes with a handy book for quick reference.*

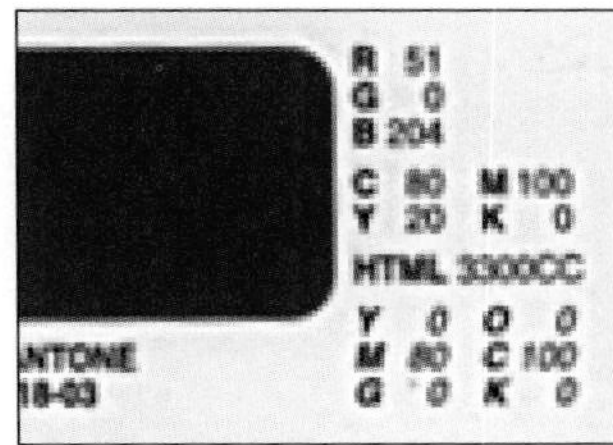

There are 216 standardized Web-safe colors that all HTML browsers recognize. Pantone has created a product called ColorWeb™ to help match these colors to printed inks as well as translate them to other computer color models, making it easy to match colors in Photoshop, Illustrator, and many other publishing software applications.

STEP 1: THE HEXADECIMAL NUMBERING SYSTEM

Hexadecimal is a numbering system based on 16 single digits. These are: 0, 1, 2, 3, 4, 5, 6, 7, 8, 9, A, B, C, D, E, F.

As with the decimal system (based on ten single digits), the value increases the larger the digit. Therefore the value of 0 is zero, and the value of F is the highest.

STEP 2: RRGGBB

HTML color references appear in the following format: RRGGBB. RR refers to the two-digit value of red in the color, GG refers to the two-digit value of green, and BB refers to the two-digit value of blue. Now keeping that in mind, and each digit's value goes from 0 to F, see if the following color values make sense to you:

- 000000 corresponds to black
- FFFFFF corresponds to white
- FF0000 corresponds to red
- 00FF00 corresponds to green
- 0000FF corresponds to blue

The basics are that simple. All the colors available can be generated using the different values of these six numbers. (See "RGB to Hexadecimal Color Chart" on page 117 for further Web color information.)

Session

H7 How to Create an Image Map

In the early days of graphics-based Web browsers, a Web page could only have one hyperlink from each individual image. When image maps were then introduced, the user could click in defined regions of an image, he could navigate to multiple areas from a single graphic. Early image maps were implemented via separate text files that were accessed and processed on the server at the time the user clicked on the image. Now, browsers have incorporated the recognition of image maps locally, making it possible for the image map to be embedded into the HTML page.

In this session, you create an HTML image map by finding the pixel coordinates of areas of an image within Photoshop. There are shareware applications that somewhat approximate the syntax for image maps automatically, but they still require a bit of manual fixing. You might find it just as easy to create your own image map structure in a text editor.

SIMPLE TEXT OR NOTEPAD
ADOBE PHOTOSHOP 4.0

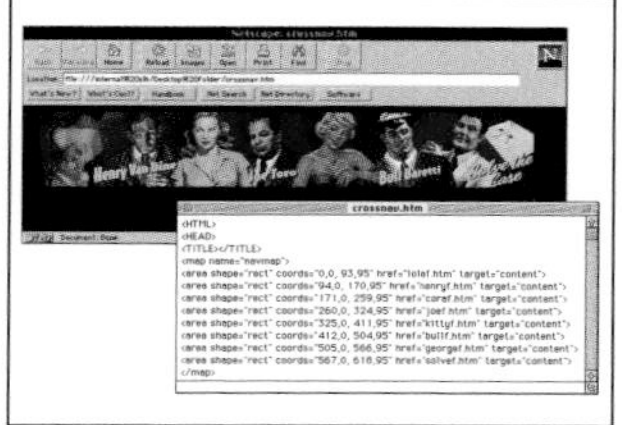

STEP 1: START THE BASIC HTML

Each image map is surrounded by the *<map>* and *</map>* tags, and must have a name attribute that can be referenced later in the HTML. Each region in the image also needs its own tag line that includes the following attributes:

- geometrical *shape* of hot spot (*rect*, *poly*, etc.)
- x and y coordinates for each intersection of the shape
- the *href*, or page to go to when the user clicks
- target, used when you're working in a frame structure

The HTML image map structure:

```
<map name="navmap">
<area shape="rect" coords="10,6, 104,22"
   href="lolaf.htm" target="content">
<area shape="rect" coords="10,23, 104,40"
   href="henryf.htm" target="content">
<area shape="rect" coords="10,41, 104,58"
   href="coraf.htm" target="content">
<area shape="rect" coords="10,59, 104,75"
   href="joef.htm" target="content”>
<area shape="rect" coords="10,76, 104,91"
   href="kittyf.htm" target="content">
<area shape="rect" coords="10,92, 104,110"
   href="bullf.htm" target="content">
<area shape="rect" coords="10,92, 104,110"
   href="georgef.htm" target="content">
<area shape="rect" coords="10,92, 104,110"
   href="solvef.htm" target="content">
</map>
```

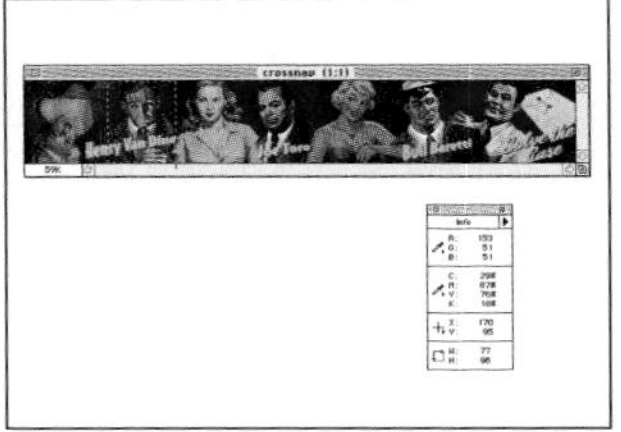

STEP 2: GENERATE COORDINATES IN PHOTOSHOP

Open the image file in Photoshop, and display the Info palette. Hover your mouse above the first coordinate at the upper left of the region you are defining, and make a note of the pixel coordinates shown in the Info palette. Now move the mouse to point at the lower right of the region and note this second set of coordinates. Create pairs of these coordinates for each region in the image.

> **NOTE:** *Make sure the mapped regions don't cross over each other or your user could get unexpected results when clicking between them.*

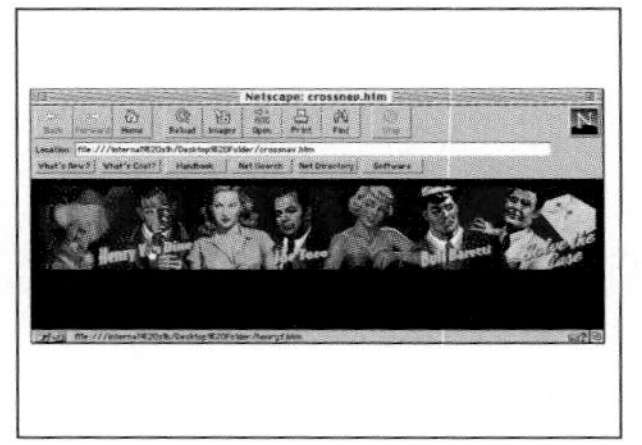

STEP 3: FINISH IMAGE MAP, OTHER TIPS

Now, incorporate the coordinates into the HTML image map and test it. Reference the image map within the <*img*> tag. Such as in the following line:

```
<img src=“choice.gif” border=0 usemap=“#navmap”>
```

Other tips to keep in mind when creating image maps include:

- put all image maps in the <*head*> of the document for easy updating
- if you can, use rectangular shapes, instead of polygon shapes—polygon shapes are harder to adjust, especially if they have a lot of vertices.

Chapter I

Adding Animation to Web Pages

Animation can be a quick and easy way to spice up your Web site, providing you use it sparingly and appropriately. If you choose to incorporate animations on every page, filling them with big, beautiful graphics and CD-quality audio, you may lose users and keep them from coming back because of file size. This chapter looks at various kinds of animation available for Web use. We'll cover simple GIF animations, Shockwave, and Flash2, as well as how to incorporate these animations into your HTML pages. Also included are tips and tricks to help you minimize download time for your users. The chapter closes with a short tutorial on a panorama technology called Surround Video and an introduction to Microsoft's ActiveX.

CHAPTER SESSIONS

- 11 *Creating a GIF Animation*
- 12 *5-Minute Introduction to Macromedia Director*
- 13 *Timing Your Animations*
- 14 *Timing Animations with Audio*
- 15 *Shockwave in HTML, Hints and Tips*
- 16 *5-Minute Introduction to Macromedia Flash*
- 17 *Creating a Panorama in Surround Video*
- 18 *Linking Surround Video in HTML*

CHAPTER TOOLBOX

GifBuilder

Macromedia Director

SoundEdit Pro

Macromedia Flash

SimpleText or Notepad

Surround Video v2.0 Development Kit

WEB-BASED ANIMATION 101

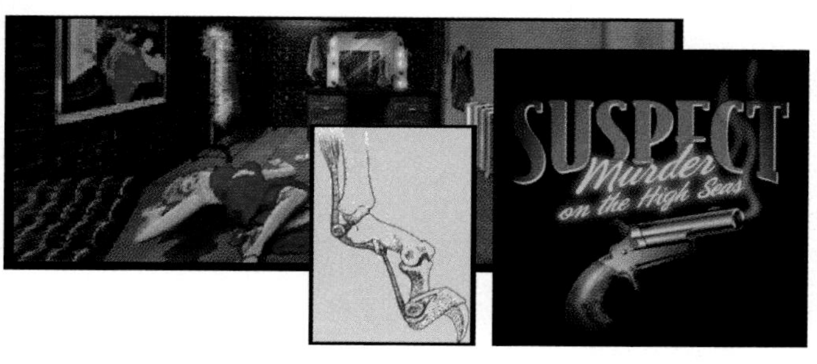

GIF animations, Shockwave, and Flash files have advantages and disadvantages. Choosing the right format for your application depends on your content and needs. GIF animations are a series of bitmap images that play back from the user's hard drive after the animation downloads, kind of like a flipbook. Shockwave files are made from bitmaps as well; however, its capabilities are much more expanded. Shockwave files, made with Macromedia Director, also offer transitions, synchronized audio, and sprite movements (animation of individual elements.) And the latest version of Shockwave supports streaming downloads, which means the animation starts playing while downloads. Flash, which also streams, supports animation of vector-based graphics, making file sizes very small. Both Shockwave and Flash files require the user to have first installed the appropriate browser plug-in to support their files, while GIF animations do not require special plug-ins.

BITMAP VERSUS VECTOR-BASED ANIMATIONS

Bitmaps are graphics that are made of pixels with color values assigned to each individual pixel. Their files are always rectangular in shape; even if the uneven edges that surround a graphic are created using a transparent value selected within the file. Photoshop is a bitmap-based graphics application. Vectors utilize less space than bitmaps because the file contains instructions to create geometrical objects. The information that is stored within a vector-based file is a combination of x and y coordinates, instructions on how to connect those points, and references to particular color fills. Illustrator is a vector-based graphics application. Therefore, Flash files, which are vector-based, can be much smaller than Shockwave's bitmap-based files.

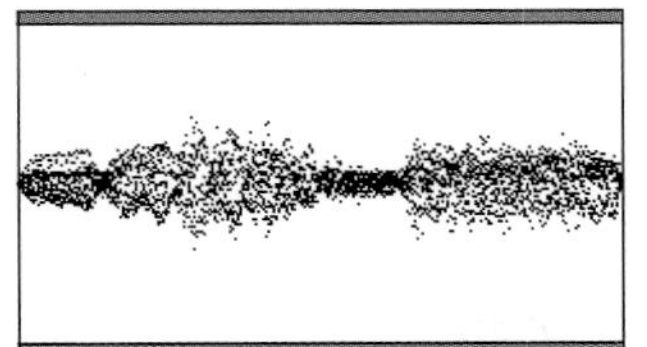

AUDIO

The addition of audio into an animation can add quite a bit in terms of user experience, as well as, unfortunately, file size. Essentially there are three types of audio can be incorporated into animations: voice-over or musical score, looped ambient background music, and individual feedback sounds. Each one of these types has advantages and disadvantages; the main disadvantage usually being that of file size and download time. A voice-over or musical score that continues through the entire animation most will likely be the largest of these three. A clip of music that seamlessly loops is a very effective use of audio in terms of file size; however, this can become a bit too repetitive. Individual small sounds that are activated by user input provide good feedback and can take up very little download time. (See Chapter J, "Adding Audio and Video to Your Site," for more information about audio, including step-by-step audio production sessions.)

MICROSOFT ACTIVEX

Microsoft has released a technology and set of standards for handling interactive media called ActiveX. Prior to the introduction of ActiveX, the only way to reference complex objects that weren't directly supported by the browser was through the referencing of a plug-in. The use of a plug-in is a good solution, except for the time required to download and install the plug-in. Under some circumstances, large plug-ins can take up to 30 minutes or longer to download, and it takes the user away from your site and therefore can dilute your content and your message.

Microsoft has created the ActiveX standard for inclusion of these types of complex objects. Similar to plug-ins, the browser needs to understand a wide variety of file types. Internet Explorer and other browsers that are ActiveX-capable have a built-in understanding of interactive media, and only require a few details in the form of a *.cab* file to comprehend a new file type which lowers the download time for the user. The added bonus of ActiveX is that the browser understands what is needed, and automatically downloads the specific details for that file type, without user input or decisions.

TIP: www.microsoft.com *is the most informative source of information about ActiveX Controls and their capabilities.*

Session

11

Creating a GIF Animation

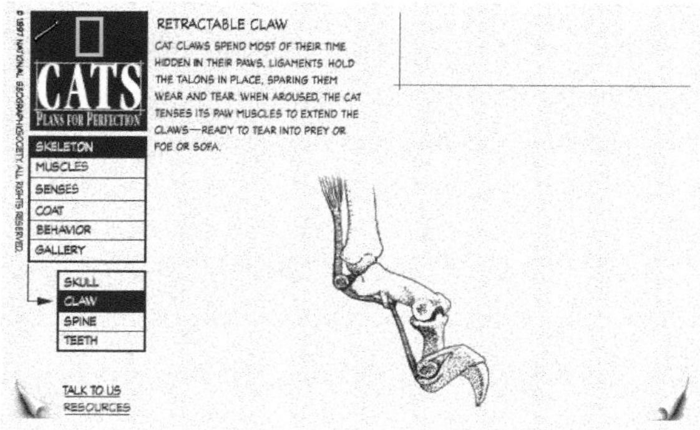

The simplest animation, in terms of both production and output, is the GIF animation. This is a series of GIFs that have been assembled to display in rapid succession to give the illusion of movement. Although GIF animations support no audio, they still can be very effective, given their small size and lack of required plug-ins.

GIFBUILDER 0.3.2

GIFANIMATOR

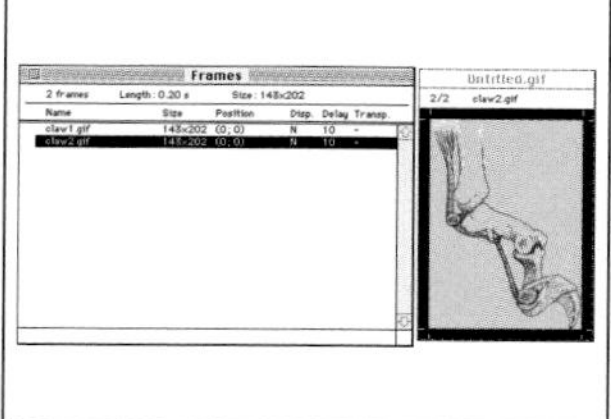

STEP 1: IMPORT AND PLACE ALL GRAPHICS

In GifBuilder, import all your graphics (you can use the keyboard shortcut Command-K) in the order of the animation. Preview the default animation speed and movement by choosing Start. Don't worry about the speed just yet; focus instead on the movement of the graphics. Reposition any graphics within the frame by clicking and dragging, or you can manually change their x and y coordinates using the arrow keys.

TIP: *If you accidentally import the graphics in the wrong order, don't worry. You can drag and drop individual frames into a different order.*

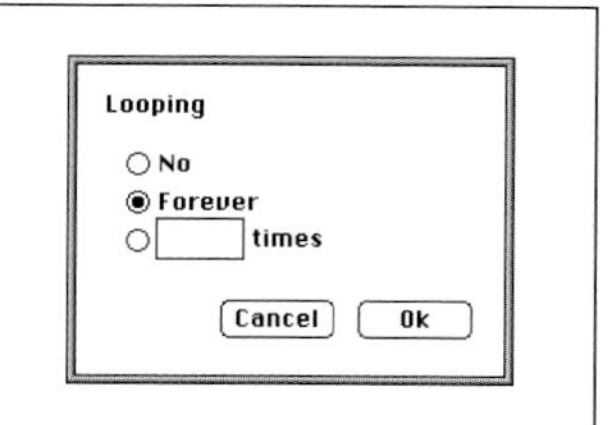

STEP 2: SET THE LOOP VALUE

Your GIF animation can play through once, loop forever, or loop a specified number of times. Open the Loop window and set the number of times for your animation to play.

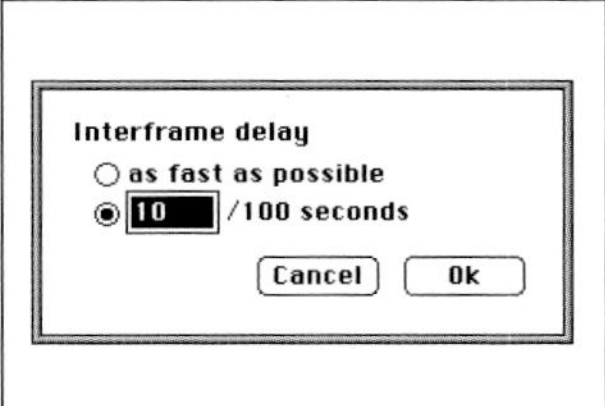

STEP 3: SET THE SPEED OF THE ANIMATION

You can set the speed of the animation universally or individually for each frame. Select one or multiple frames and open the Interframe delay window, which prompts you for a value less than 100. A good speed that implies motion is the value of 10, but the best way to determine your desired speed is to test different values. GifBuilder allows you to immediately see the results of your changes. If your graphics include text, make sure that they display long enough for the user to read them.

TIP: *The speed of the computer affects the speed of the animation, so try to test the animation on a machine that's similar to your typical user's configuration.*

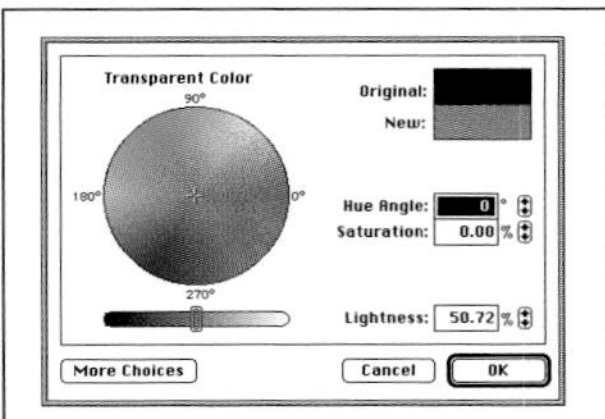

STEP 4: SET THE SPEED OF THE ANIMATION

You can select the transparent color of your graphics before you import them into GifBuilder, or you can set it within the application. If you haven't already set your desired transparency, choose Transparency Color under the Options menu. Here, you have four options: No transparency, White color, First Pixel is transparent, and Other, which gives you a color wheel from which to choose the color.

If you're using a transparent color, make sure that your background is a solid RGB value, or you could get an unclean background filled with random specks.

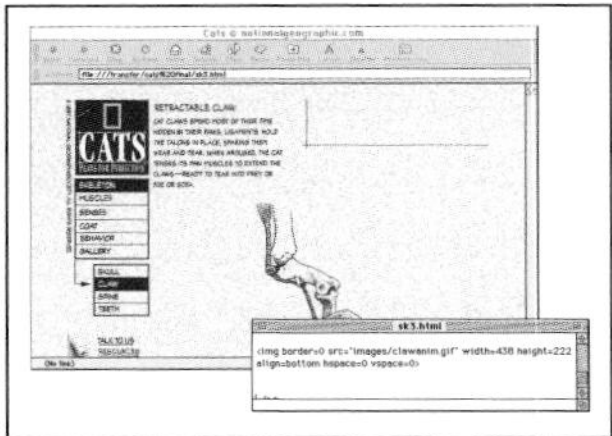

STEP 5: LINK GIF ANIMATION IN HTML

Adding an animated GIF to an HTML page is as simple as adding a normal GIF image. Use the *<img src>* tag, set the width and height, and any hyperlinks you want to use. You can also incorporate an image map into the HTML if your design calls for it.

Session

12

5-Minute Introduction to Macromedia Director

Macromedia Director has been the standard for years in creation of multimedia projects like corporate presentations, CD-ROM front-ends, kiosks, and now animation on the Web. Director is one of those great programs that you can use if you're a beginner, intermediate, or advanced animator. It has a powerful scripting language called Lingo that enables you to do almost anything—from simple looping animations to complex interactivity. This session and session 13, give you enough information to start animating.

MACROMEDIA DIRECTOR

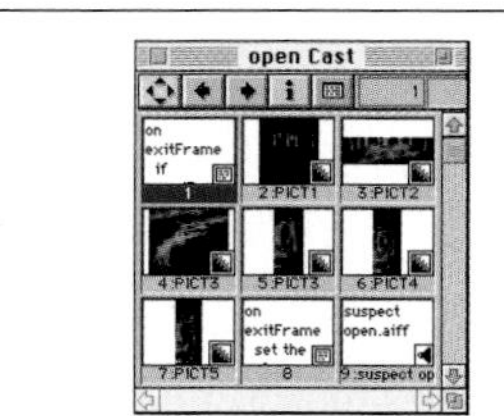

CAST WINDOW

The Cast Window stores all of the cast members of your animation. To start your project, import all of your graphics, audio files, text, and palettes into the Cast Window. Each cast member is indicated by a letter and a number combination. (You'll refer to them later by the numbering system.) To edit a graphic in Director's Paint Window, double-click on the graphic in the Cast Window. To edit text generated within Director, double-click on the text in the Cast Window.

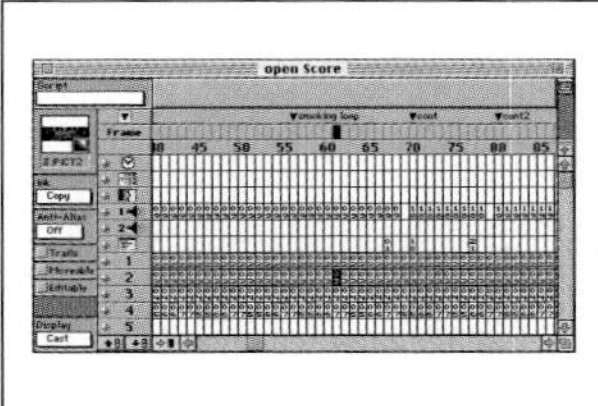

SCORE WINDOW

The Score Window is the most important window in Director. It consists of multiple channels displayed on the left side of the window, each for different types of elements and layering; and it displays frames across the top of the window for length of animation and timing. The basis for the frames analogy is that of time; as you move from left to right, you are moving in time.

Along the lefthand side of the window, you have controls for accessing options for elements:

- tempo channel
- palette channel
- transition channel
- 2 separate audio channels
- scripting channel
- multiple graphics channels for layering and compositing

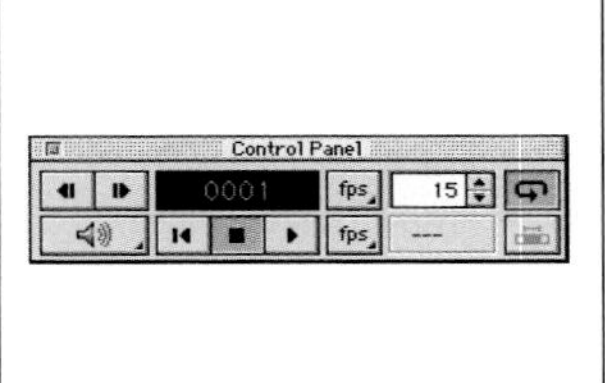

CONTROL PANEL AND STAGE WINDOWS

The Control Panel is used to play, stop, rewind, and fast forward your animation—kind of like a VCR remote control. Using the Control Panel, you can also set the number of frames per second, loop your animation, and turn sound on and off.

The Stage Window is where the action takes place. Upon starting a project, set the height and width of the Stage to create your animation. Here, you'll see the effect of your handiwork in the Score Window.

Session

13 Timing Your Animations

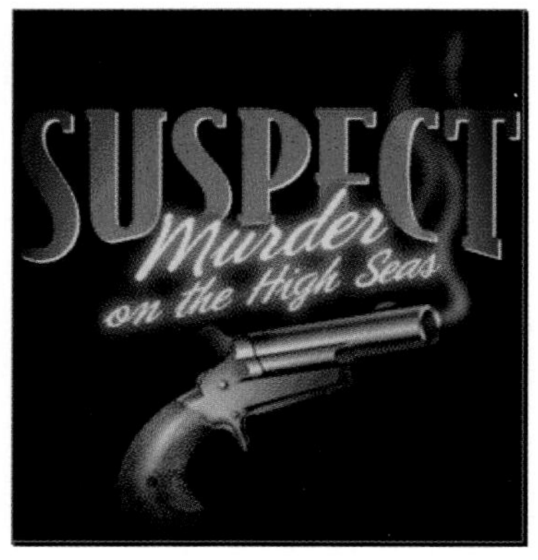

No part of an animation is more important than timing. Make a mistake with the timing of an animation, and it distracts the user from your site's content. This session focuses on the timing of an animation that doesn't include sound. In this example animation from our *Suspect* site, you set the speed of the animation, and interact with the pages of a Web site. See Session 14, if you plan to use sound (in which case you time the animation to the audio).

MACROMEDIA DIRECTOR

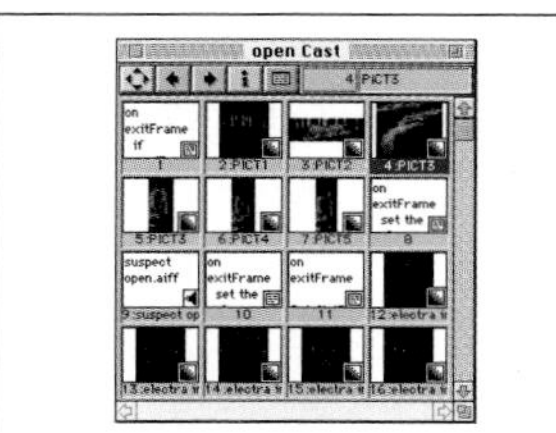

STEP 1: IMPORT ALL CAST MEMBERS AND PLACE THEM ON THE STAGE

Import all cast members into Director by choosing Import. In the Import dialog, you have the choice to import elements individually, or as an entire folder. Also, make sure you have chosen the right type of media to import. On the Macintosh, your choices are PICT, MacPaint, Sound, Scrapbook, PICS, Director movie, and QuickTime movie. Select the file format in the pop-up menu of the Import dialog.

The imported images, sounds, and elements appear in the Cast window.

From the Cast window, drag and drop an individual cast member into the Stage window. Position the cast member with either the mouse or the left and right arrow keys. Keep in mind, every cast member will be in one channel for a certain duration of time. So if you want multiple cast members to appear in the same frame, use a different channel for each.

TIP: *Remember that you're layering graphics here, with Channel 1 consisting of the background image, or the cast member that will appear on the bottom layer. You can later copy and paste, or drag and drop cast members into different channels.*

STEP 2: ANIMATING THE SMOKING GUN

In this example, there are three variations of wafting smoke, so let's alternate between them to create the illusion of movement. Because the individual graphics should be as small as possible, cut the gun out of the smoke graphics. The gun doesn't move at all, so position it once, and then place the alternating smoke graphics in another channel (see Session C2).

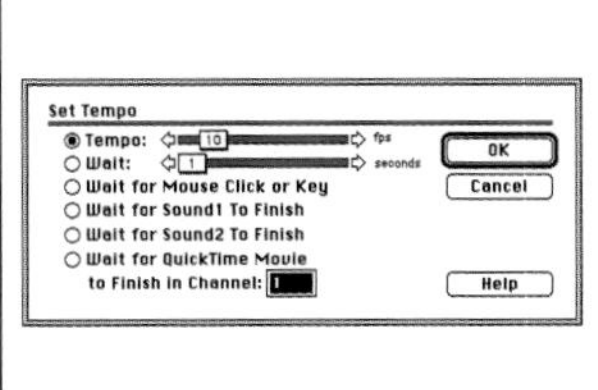

STEP 3: SET THE TIMING

Now that you have placed the smoking gun graphics, test and set the timing for the animation. Play the animation at its default speed by clicking the Play button in the control panel. There are a couple places where you can adjust the speed of your animation. The best place to start is the Tempo channel in the Score window. Double-click on one frame in the Tempo channel to display the Set Tempo window. The default speed is set to 30 fps, which may be too fast for your animation. Set the speed between 1 and 10 to slow down the animation and see the effect.

Another way to lengthen the timing of an animation is to repeat frames of the same cast member. In this example, each smoking gun graphic is placed in the timeline twice, displaying each frame for twice as long.

TIP: *Keep in mind, the speed of the animation is sometimes affected by the speed of the computer viewing it. Make sure you test your Shockwave on your average user's configuration.*

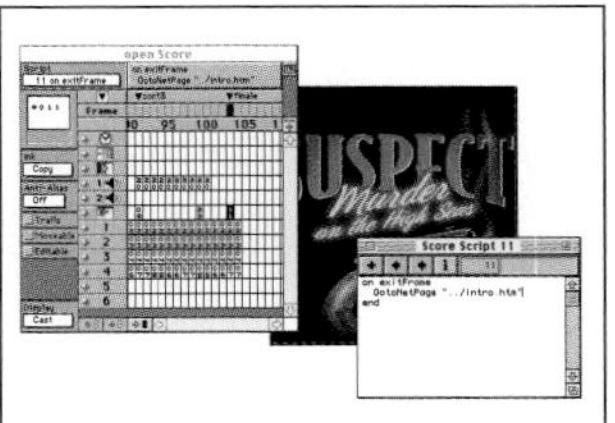

STEP 4: AUTOMATICALLY GO TO ANOTHER PAGE

The Script channel in the Score window is where you place your Lingo commands. (Lingo is Director's scripting language.) In the Script channel, you have additional control over the timing of the animation, user interactivity, and coordination with other parts of your Web site. There are about 10 Lingo commands specific to Shockwave and its inclusion into HTML, the most common being *GoToNetPage*. This command, placed in the Script channel of the last frame in the Score, tells the Shockwave file, upon reaching this frame, to automatically request the specified HTML page. Don't worry if you get an error message from one of the Shockwave-specific Lingo commands within Director. The browser understands the command when the movie is converted to a Shockwave file (see Session I5).

Session

14 Timing Animation with Audio

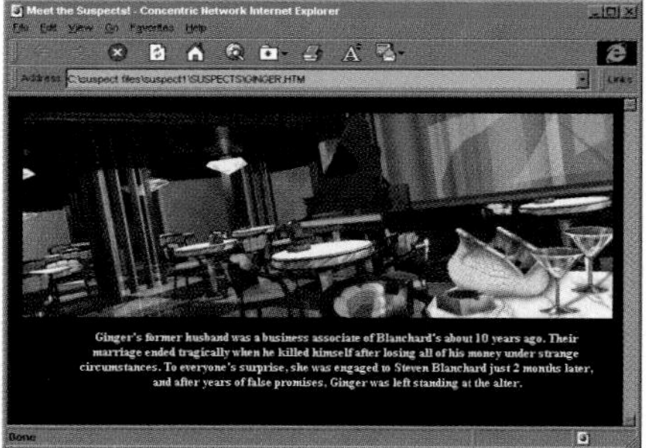

MACROMEDIA DIRECTOR

Adding audio to an animation can add quite a bit in terms of user experience, as well as file size. Therefore, you may want to minimize the amount of audio you incorporate. Still, there are options for integrating audio without adding greatly to the overhead: voice-over or musical score (suggested for Web applications when streaming), looped ambient background music (if small and looped well, these can be very effective), and individual feedback sounds (good feedback for user input).

When incorporating audio, try to place the audio first, and then time the animation to make sure they match. This is, however, an iterative process with plenty of trial and error.

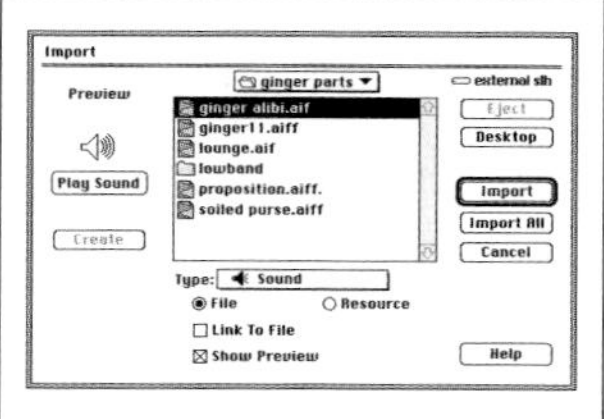

STEP 1: CREATING A PATH IN ILLUSTRATOR

Digitize or create your audio files in SoundEdit Pro or your favorite audio program. (See Chapter J, "Adding Audio and Video to Your Site," for more information on creating audio files.) Incorporate any loops in SoundEdit Pro that you want to use. Director does a fine job of looping a sound in its entirety. If you need to set an internal loop-back, where an introduction plays once and the remainder of the file loops, set that first within SoundEdit Pro. (See Session J2 to set a loopback.)

Import your audio files into Director by choosing the Import command, and set the Type pop-up box to the sound file type to see the complete list of audio files on your hard drive. The files now appear as cast members in the Cast window.

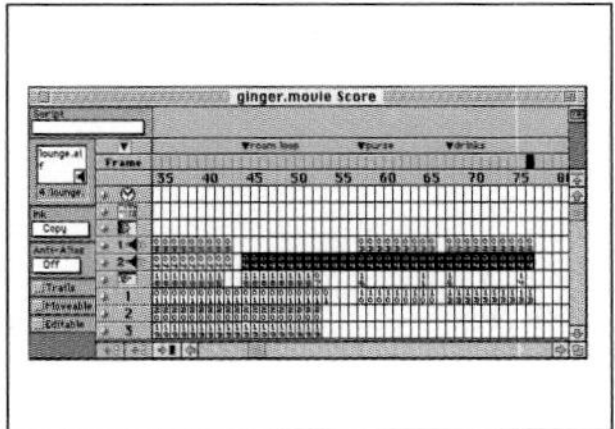

STEP 2: PLACE AUDIO IN AUDIO CHANNEL

Highlight the frames in the Audio channel where you want your audio to play. Choose Set Sound in the Score menu. Select the audio file and double-click. If you have accidentally chosen only the first frame of the Audio channel, don't worry, you can always highlight the additional frames later, and use the In between linear command to lengthen the selection.

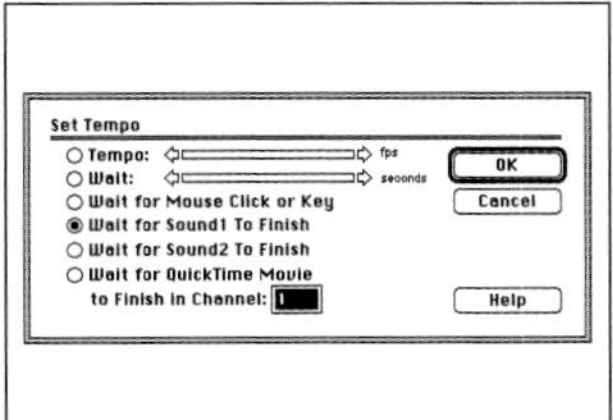

STEP 3: TIME ANIMATION TO AUDIO

When adding audio to a Shockwave file, you may want to pause the animation at some point, until the audio finishs playing. There are a couple ways to do this, the simplest is the Set Tempo window. To access this window, double-click on the frame in the Tempo channel where you want the animation to pause. Then choose the radio button titled Wait for Sound1 to Finish if you placed your audio file in the first Audio channel.

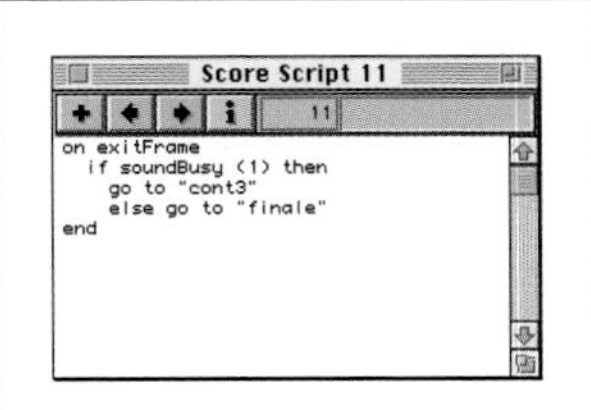

STEP 4: SET AUDIO LOOPS

If, however, you need an animation to keep moving as the audio plays, set the animation to loopback. Our example loops from frame number 99 back to frame number 91, while the audio in that section plays. To set your loopback, double-click on a frame in the Script channel, and in between the lines *on exitFrame* and *end*, enter the following, customized to your animation:

```
on exitFrame
  if soundBusy (1) then
  go to “cont3”
  else go to “finale”
end
```

Now, you need to create two comment markers called *cont3* and *finale* for the script to understand where you want it to go. In the Score window, drag and drop triangles from above and right of the channel numbers, positioning them at the frame that your animation should go to in both of these circumstances, and then type in the descriptive title referenced in the script. You can also use the following code to accomplish the same task by referring to the individual frame numbers. This isn't the best method for loops as any changes to the animation needs to be reflected in the script.

```
on exitFrame
  if soundBusy (1) then
  go to 91
  else go to 99
end
```

Session

15 Shockwave in HTML, Hints and Tips

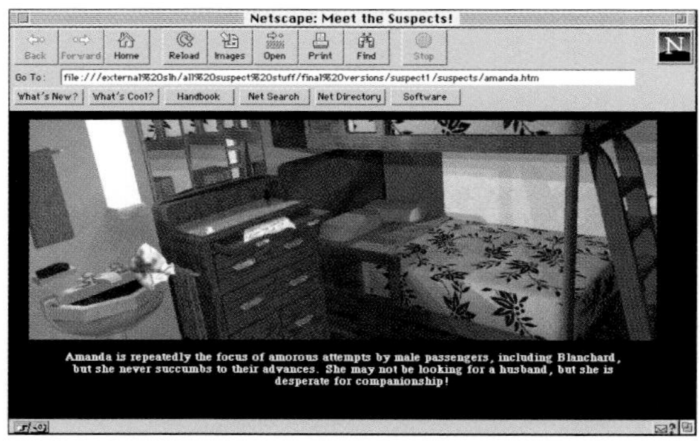

Once your Director movie is complete, you need to output it to a Shockwave file format that browsers can read. After convering to a Shockwave file, the animation should be incorporated in the HTML page where it will reside. In addition to these necessary steps, optimization of the file is a must. This session touches on some of the basics for optimization of a Shockwave file. There is a big difference between just creating a Shockwave animation and creating a good Shockwave animation. The keys to this process are twofold: compelling content with a good reason to be animated, and solid optimization of the Shockwave file for the Web.

MACROMEDIA DIRECTOR
SIMPLETEXT OR NOTEPAD

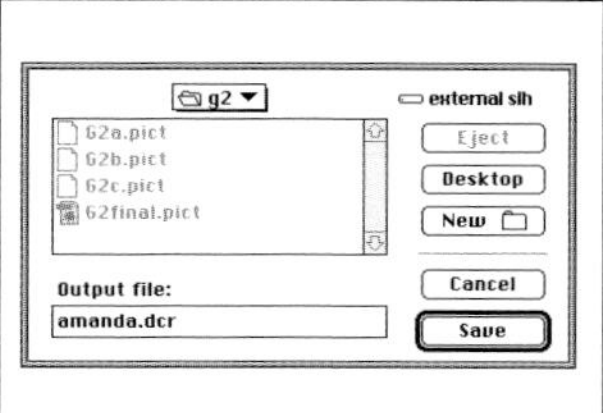

STEP 1: CONVERT MOVIE INTO A SHOCKWAVE FILE

Once your animation is very near completion, start testing performance the Internet on a couple different machines. Play your animation in Director one last time, making sure the animation, interactivity, and audio are working as desired. While your movie is still open and active in Director, choose Afterburner under the Xtras menu. It prompts you to name the Shockwave file, which includes the extension *.dcr*. Save the Shockwave file.

TIP: *As performance of your animation is affected by the speed of the user's machine, make sure you test your file on a common configuration.*

STEP 2: LINKING SHOCKWAVE IN HTML

There are two ways to reference a Shockwave file within HTML, embedding a HTML tag or using Microsoft's ActiveX.

The *<embed>* HTML tag is supported by all browsers that support the Shockwave plug-in. The *<noembed>* tag is a backup tag for browsers that don't have Shockwave capabilities. This means if the browser doesn't support Shockwave, this graphic still will be placed on the page. When using either of these tags, make sure you include values for the height and width of the *.dcr* file.

```
<EMBED SRC="assets/open.dcr" WIDTH=256 HEIGHT=277>
<NOEMBED><IMG SRC="assets/open.gif" ALT="alternate text"
   WIDTH="256" HEIGHT="277" ALIGN=bottom></NOEMBED>
```

The other option for referencing Shockwave files is using the ActiveX control. Microsoft's ActiveX technology offers interactive media without the burden of downloading a plug-in. The user's browser automatically downloads the necessary components to view the interactive file. Rather than requiring the *<embed>* tag, the browser supporting ActiveX recognizes the *<object>* tag. (See Session 18, for a more detailed introduction to ActiveX. For more technical information about ActiveX, take a look at *www.microsoft.com.*)

SHOCKWAVE HINTS AND TIPS

For your Shockwave file to be effective, you must optimize it for the Internet. Optimization for any media-rich file format generally refers to reducing the size of the file as much as possible. A good rule of thumb for relating file size to download time is to expect 1k to take one second to download. Of course, faster connections download faster, and if your user is not on the Internet during peak times, the download time is shorter as well. A second rule of thumb is to try to keep large files, including Shockwave files, to under 200k.

Try to minimize file size by using small clips of reusable audio, and cropping graphics and animation frames to the smallest possible size. You also can try to minimize the overall pixel dimensions of the Shockwave movie. Try interesting designs such as placing the Shockwave movie directly next to a still graphic to make it appear bigger. Don't create 24-bit Shockwave files for the Web. They're far larger and don't look significantly better than color-depth optimzied 8-bit images.

TIP: *A great place to find all kinds of tips and tricks, as well as a gallery of Shocked sites and the latest information on Director and Shockwave is* http://www.macromedia.com.

Session

16 # 5-Minute Introduction to Macromedia Flash

Flash is a great animation tool built specifically for Web-based animations. Originally called FutureSplash, it was bought in early 1997 by Macromedia, and since then has only gotten better. Macromedia has incorporated some of the key features for animation that have been offered in Director for years. This session will give you a basic overview of Flash and its functionality.

MACROMEDIA FLASH2

TIP: *Macromedia currently allows a 30-day evaluation download of the software, which is a great way to try before you buy. The software comes with an excellent set of tutorials to help you get started.*

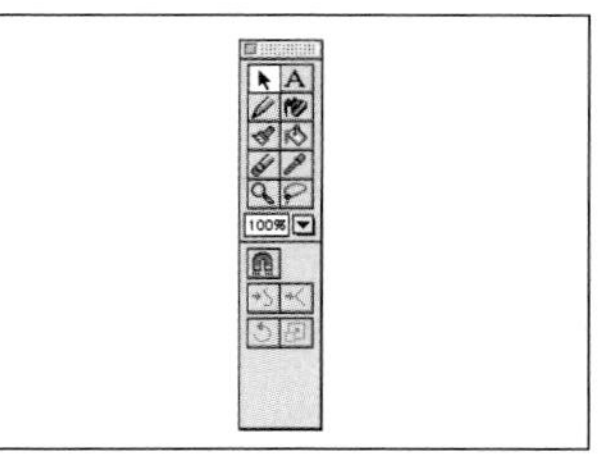

DRAWING TOOLBAR

Flash supports importing of graphics from other applications, and it also offers simple drawing capabilities. Existing files in the following formats can be imported bitmaps (PICT, JPEG, GIF), vector-based (Adobe Illustrator and AutoCAD DXF), and sound.

Limit the number of bitmaps you import into Flash; instead use more vector-based illustrations. Remember the application's unique advantage is that it enables the use of vector-based graphics on the Web, along with a user-friendly interface.

If you choose to create new graphics, use the drawing tools offered by Flash (such as the Pencil, Brush, Eraser, Text tool, Ink Bottle, and Paint Bucket). Flash's unusual Pencil tool offers modification and object effects that make it easy to draw rectangles, ovals, and straight and curved lines.

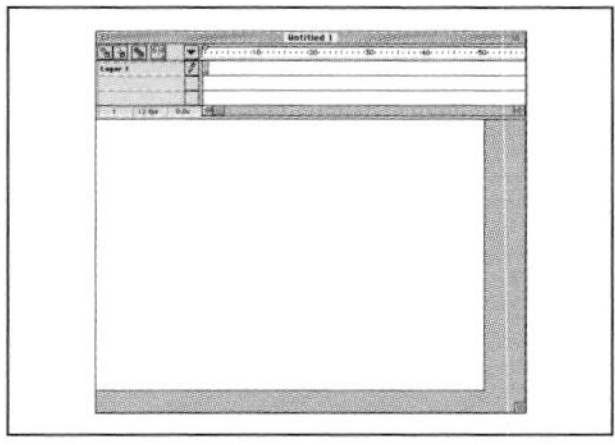

ACTIVE MOVIE WINDOW

The Active Movie window is where most of your action takes place. This window consists of two parts: the current active animation timeline at the top of the window, and the animation area where you see the results of your timeline modifications.

The timeline consists of multiple layers displayed on the left side of the window for different types of elements and layering, and the frames displayed across the top of the window for length of animation and timing. The basis for the frames analogy is that of time; as you move from left to right, you are moving in time.

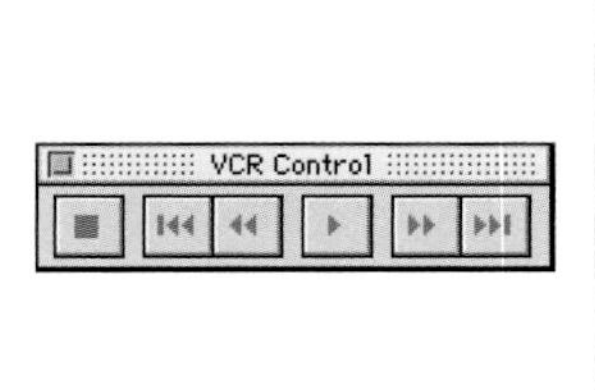

CONTROLLER WINDOW

The Controller window, similar to a VCR controller, allows you to play and stop your movie. It also has rewind, step forward, and step back buttons to maneuver quickly through your animations.

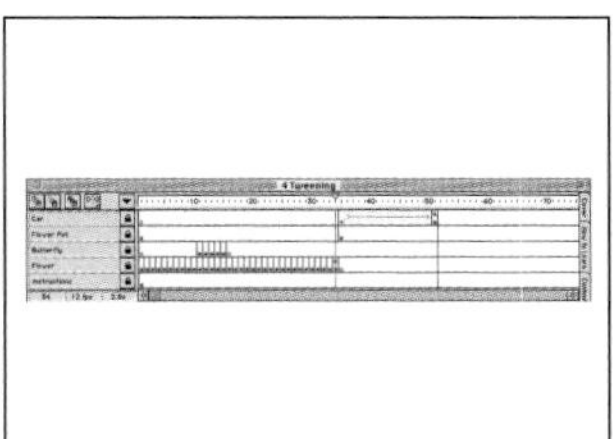

THE BASICS OF FLASH ANIMATION

There are two types of animation in Flash: frame-by-frame and *tweening*. Frame-by-frame animation consists of a number of similar, but not identical graphics, in each frame of an animation. Each frame that contains a new graphic file is called a key frame. Tweening, animation jargon for in-betweening, consists of two, spaced key frames with some kind of movement, scaling, or rotation in-between the frames. These frames between the key frames are generated automatically by the application.

Within each frame of each layer of your animation, you have access to a Frame Pop-up menu that includes options (such as tweening, sound, actions, inserting frames, etc.) for the element in that layer.

Session

17 Creating a Panorama in Surround Video

Surround Video is a panorama technology—supported by ActiveX controls—created by a company called Black Diamond. The application accepts flat images and converts them into moveable, pan-able files that the user can explore. There are a number of applications that create files in similar formats, but Surround Video is by far the easiest to use. There are two ways to create the base image: stitching photographs together to create one large canvas, or using an flat file created in a graphic application that outputs a long format image. In this session, we'll create a Surround Video panorama image from the input source of a flat file created in StrataVision.

BLACK DIAMOND'S SURROUND VIDEO V2.0

CONVERT A FLAT IMAGE TO A PANORAMA AND CROP THE IMAGE

Start with our image in *.bmp* file format, and open it in SVEdit. There are two sides to the main window: the right side displays the origin of the file, or the opening view the user has of the final file; the left side allows you to make any changes to the file. There are two modes to SVEdit: Crop, which allows cropping of the image horizontally and vertically; and Normal, which allows the addition of linking and text additions for hot spots.

Within the Crop mode, you have various options to set. The origin option defines which view is the default when the final file opens. This defaults to the left and right edges of the flat image. The cropping option enables you to crop the image horizontally and vertically in SVEdit. Move your mouse to the top of the main window to drag and drop crop marks to affect cropping on the height of the image. Move the origin of the image to affect cropping on the width of the image. The final option is horizon which defines the horizon line of the panoramic file.

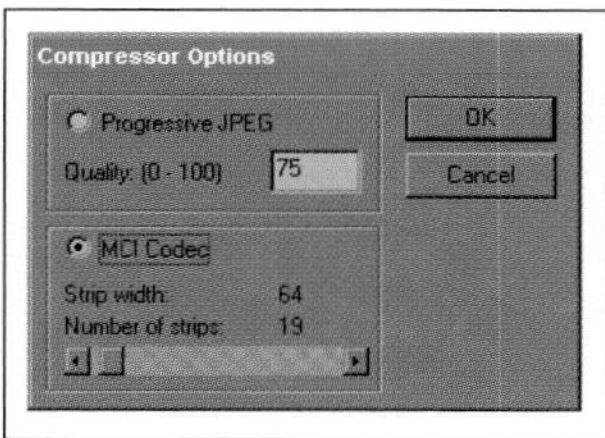

CONVERT FLAT IMAGE TO PANORAMA AND COMPRESS THE IMAGE

Whether or not the image has been altered by cropping or setting a new horizon, and before hot spots can be defined, the image needs to be cut into strips and compressed. Compress your image using the MCI Codec (as opposed to the progressive JPEG option); and for a full 360° panorama, choose 19 strips with a width of 64 pixels to create smooth movement within the panorama. The compressor will be Cinepak Codec by Radius. To maintain the highest quality, set the Compression Quality setting to 100. Save the compressed file, and the image is ready to add hot spots.

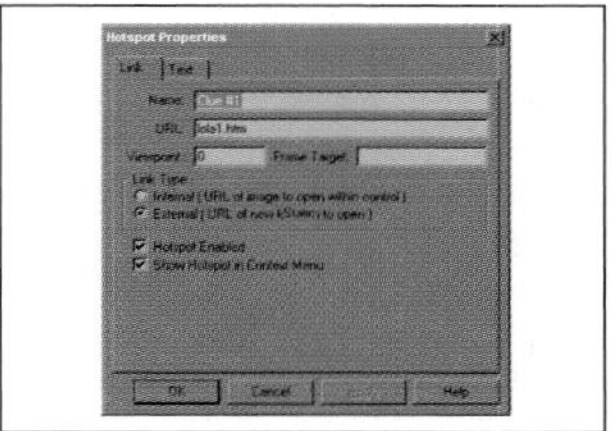

CREATING HOT SPOTS WITHIN PANORAMA

Switch the mode from Crop to Normal to get access to the hot spot options. Using either the compass or the control panel buttons at the bottom of the window, navigate through the image to the spot you want to make into a button. Using the left mouse button, draw either a rectangle or a polygon. Once you have defined the hot spots, the Hotspot Properties window opens with two options: Link and Text.

The options within the Link window include Name (of the hot spot), URL (the file to link to which might be another HTML page or a static graphic), and the frame target. If you're using a frame structure, you can target the new URL to the appropriate frame.

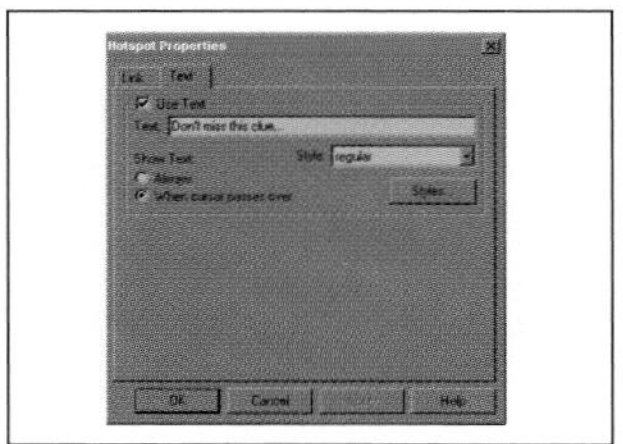

FORMATTING HOT SPOTS WITHIN PANORAMA

The Text window allows you to define the font, size, and color of text associated with a hot spot. You can also choose whether the text should constantly over the hot spot, or if it should just appear only while the user's mouse is over the hot spot. You can incorporate hot spots with links, text, or both.

After you have specified the hot spots, save the file again, using the extension *.svh*. Check out Session 18, to learn how to access your panorama file on the Web.

Session

18 Linking Surround Video in HTML

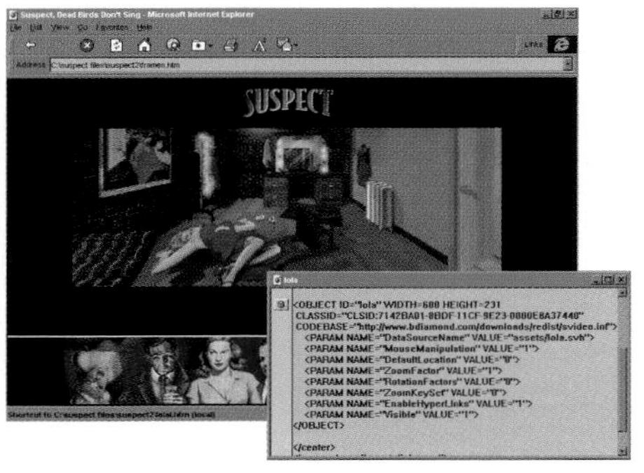

Surround Video interacts with HTML via ActiveX, which enables interactive content like multimedia effects, interactive objects and sophisticated applications—in the Internet Explorer Web browser.

In this session, you incorporate an ActiveX Control into HTML that accesses our Surround Video panorama, using a handy ActiveX development application from Microsoft called Control Pad.

MICROSOFT CONTROL PAD
SIMPLE TEXT OR NOTEPAD

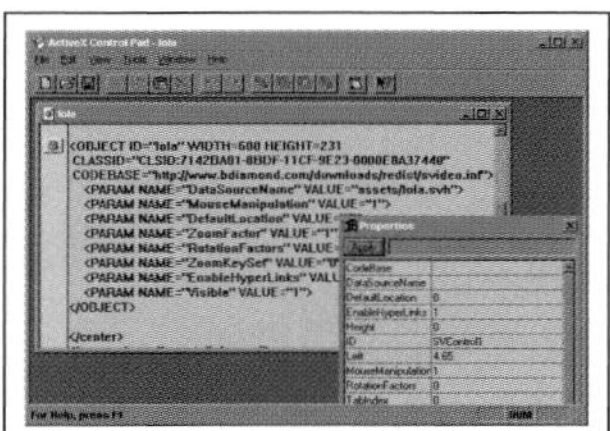

INCLUDING A PANORAMA IN HTML

Starting Control Pad automatically generates a new HTML page for your ActiveX Control. To incorporate your Surround Video panorama, select Insert ActiveX Control under the Edit menu. This opens a window that lists all available ActiveX Controls. Choose the Surround Video Control Object, and Control Pad automatically opens a list of properties for the Control you've chosen. The most important aspect of this Properties window is the text box requesting the CodeBase. The CodeBase specifies the location, as a URL, of the minimal information that needs to download for the browser to understand the Control. Closing the Properties window takes you back to the HTML page that is now updated with a new *<object>* tag specifying your choices.

One good option you have with the Surround Video Control is to have the panorama automatically start rotating upon download of the page.

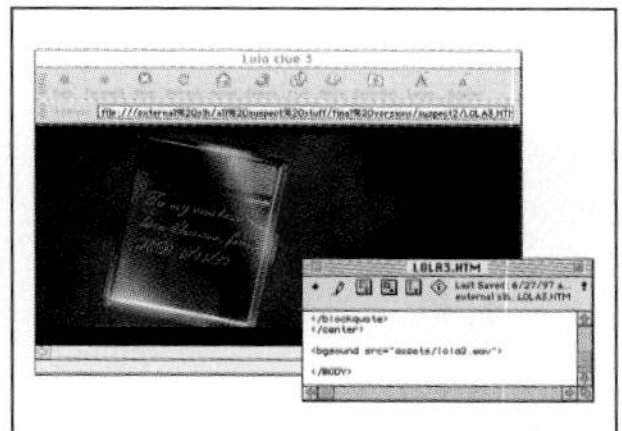

THE <*BGSOUND*> HTML TAG

While future versions of Surround Video will support audio capabilities, there's a simple HTML tag that is now supported by Internet Explorer.

The <*bgsound*> tag enables you to easily integrate audio into your Web pages; browsers that don't support the tag just ignore it. Place the <*bgsound*> tag anywhere on your HTML page, and as soon as the page downloads, the audio file starts downloading. You can set the number of times to play the sound by using the parameter loop, which causes the file to loop as long as the user displays that page.

TIP: *Make sure the audio files you choose are small enough to download without too much disruption of the user's activity.*

Chapter J

ADDING AUDIO AND VIDEO TO YOUR SITE

Audio and video can be a great addition to your site. Many Web sites currently exist with the sole purpose of promoting a non Web-related product, like a movie, TV show, or a music CD. Offering previews of products can be one of the key marketing benefits of a Web site. Offering behind-the-scenes materials and information the user can't find anywhere else also draw users to the site. There are many ways you can offer audio and video elements to your user: streaming files, downloadables, and incorporating sound and video into your animations. Your choice of these options depends on the content and circumstances in each case. This chapter looks at digitizing and editing audio and video, downsampling techniques, compositing graphics on video, output options, and incorporating of these files in HTML. As streaming technologies, in most cases require additional server software and/or configuration, this chapter does not address the specifics of these techniques.

CHAPTER SESSIONS

J1 *Digitizing Audio*

J2 *Mixing and Looping Audio*

J3 *Digitizing Video*

J4 *Editing Video and Adding Transitions*

J5 *Compositing Graphics*

J6 *Synching Video to Audio*

J7 *Output and Compression*

J8 *Animating Layers in After Effects*

J9 *Linking Audio and Video in HTML*

CHAPTER TOOLBOX

Adobe Photoshop 4.0

Adobe Premiere 4.2

SoundEdit Pro 1.0

SoundApp 1.5

Adobe After Effects 3.1

DIGITAL AUDIO & VIDEO 101

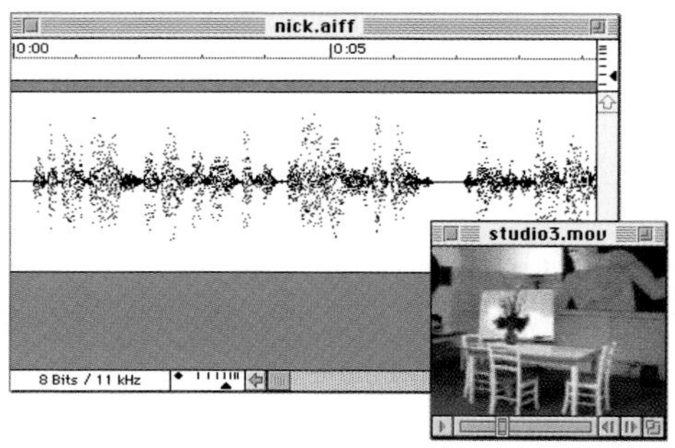

Currently, it's not feasible to expect 16-bit, 44KHz files (or CD-quality sound) over the Internet. Audio files can be very large. Your favorite song, for example, is probably about five minutes long. For the song to have the quality comparable to a CD, it would need at least 10 megabytes of space. Obviously, this is not a reasonable download for the average user. Be selective about the clips you offer on your site, and make them small enough in size to reasonably download. Audio samples of less than 30 seconds, which translates to just under a megabyte, at 8-bit, mono, and 11KHz or 22Kz, are greatly appreciated by your users.

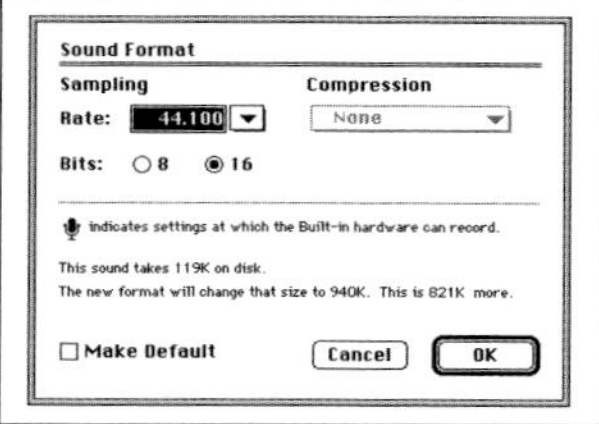

SAMPLING AUDIO

Digital audio is measured using a method called sampling. While digitizing there are three aspects to this measurement and conversion: bit depth, which is the depth at which the audio is sampled. (This is similar to the bit depth of graphics where 24 bits looks better than 8 bits.) KHz, which is the frequency of sampling. (Kilohertz is thousands per second); and channels (mono, one channel or stereo, and two channels).

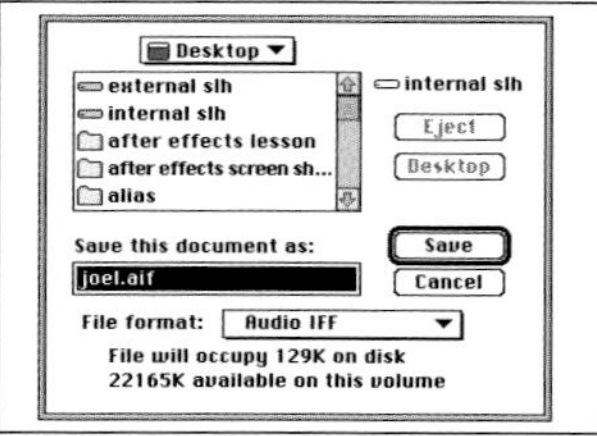

DOWNLOADABLE AUDIO

Offer your users one or more of the three common audio file formats: *.wav* (standard PC format), *.aiff* (standard CD and Macintosh format), and *.au* (standard UNIX format). You can configure most browsers to download and play all of these file formats, with the addition of a helper application. But, make it easy for your users. Offer as many options as you can. You may not want to force your users to download another application to access all of the elements of your site.

Analog video, like that which you see on television or videotape, plays at 30 frames per second, at a size similar to the resolution of a small computer monitor (640 x 480 pixels). With the recent introduction of high-end video components for your personal computer, video can now be digitized, stored, and outputted at that rate and size with little degradation of quality. However, given the bandwidth limitations of the Internet today, this rate and size offered from your Web site would not work.

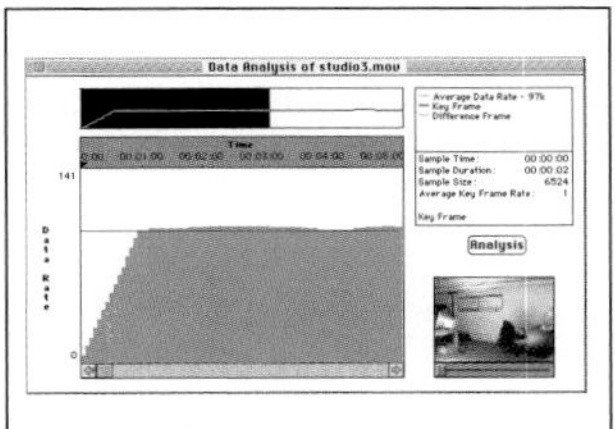

DIGITAL VIDEO OPTIONS

QuickTime is the accepted standard for digital video files. A helper application exists for every computer platform to play QuickTime movies, so you don't have to offer more than one kind of file format to make sure everyone can view your video files. There are three variables to consider when creating downloadable video clips: pixel resolution, frames per second, and transfer rate, which translates into image quality.

The maximum pixel resolution you should offer for downloadable video clips is approximately 160 pixels wide by 120 pixels tall. Ten or 15 frames per second is a good compromise for smooth movement within these video clips, and for minimizing file size. Even at this small size and lower frame rate, your 15-second video could take up as much as a megabyte in size. Testing various image quality settings during output can help reduce file size, but at a certain point, determined by your specific content, the image quality can be less than acceptable.

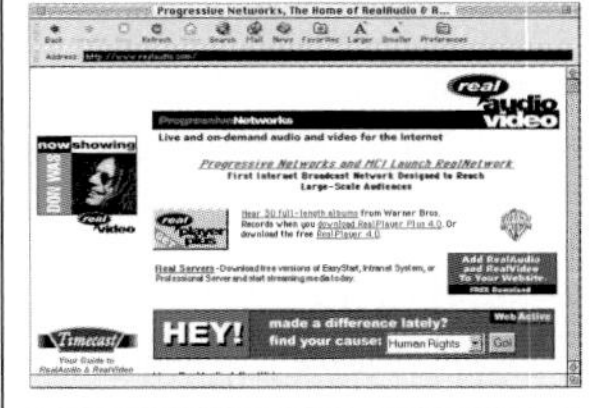

STREAMING AUDIO AND VIDEO

Streaming audio and video are great, new technologies that offer the playing of files while they download. Offering video over the Internet requires the reduction of bandwidth by limiting pixel resolution, as well as reducing detail and color. Streaming audio offered by a Web site also requires a reduction of bandwidth, and translates into lower quality sound.

Streaming technologies include RealAudio, NetShow, and Interactive Music Architecture (IMA). These types of technologies are improving rapidly, but they still have limitations currently, such as a lack of accepted standards means that not everyone is readily equipped to access your files, limited bandwidth means lower quality, and in some cases, limits the number of simultaneous users.

Session

J1 Digitizing Audio

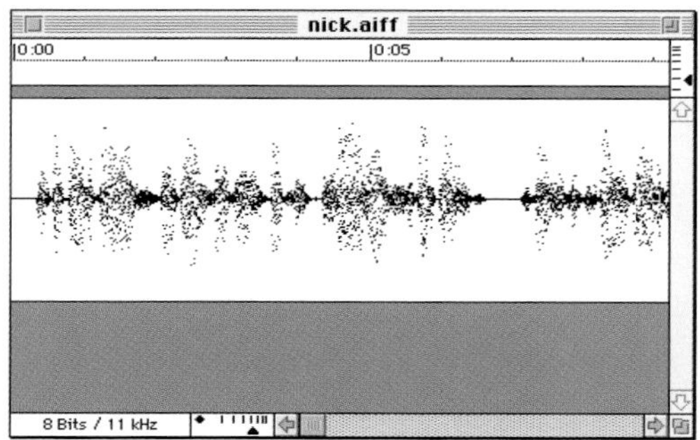

As with any kind of digital signal, the phrase, "Garbage in, garbage out," is especially true when digitizing audio. Always try to use the original source of audio, and therefore the highest quality—whether it comes from a CD, a tape, or just a microphone recording your voice.

SOUNDEDIT PRO 1.0
SOUNDAPP 1.5

STEP 1: CONFIGURE YOUR AUDIO EQUIPMENT

Begin by connecting your audio source to your computer. You can either use a built-in microphone port on your computer, or in some cases you may need an audio digitizing board. Most consumer audio devices offer an audio-out port. A headphones port will work just as well for your connection. Connect the audio source to your computer using a standard audio cable. Depending on the connections on both ends, you may need to find an adapter at your local electronics store.

Test the connection by recording a short sample. With this test, you can make sure your connection is clear; it also gives you a chance to adjust the incoming signal volume. If you're using a Macintosh, you may need to increase the incoming volume within the Sound control panel, as well as on your source audio equipment.

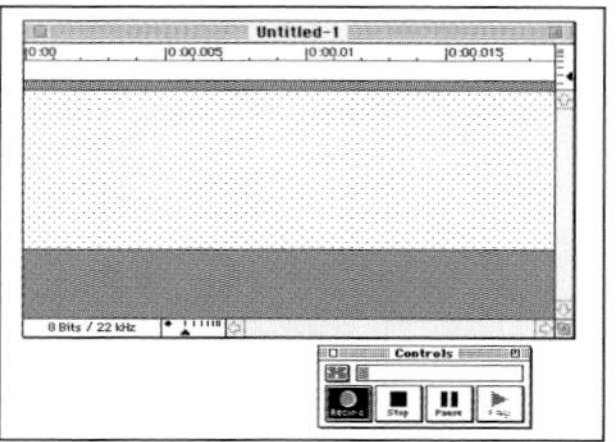

STEP 2: START DIGITIZING

In SoundEdit Pro, choose Record under the Sound menu. While digitizing, make sure the volume is at the correct level. This is indicated by the volume status bar. Most audio software packages have this kind of feature. The bar shows the volume level of the incoming sound and generally reads left to right—the higher the volume, the higher the sound. Some applications color-code these levels; and, similar to a piece of home audio equipment as long as the bar stays green, the level is in the correct range. If, however, it dips into red on the high end, you should turn down the volume of your incoming source.

After you've digitized the sample, look at file using the Waveform view, accessible from the View menu. If the Waveform appears chopped off at the top or bottom, try redigitizing at a lower volume.

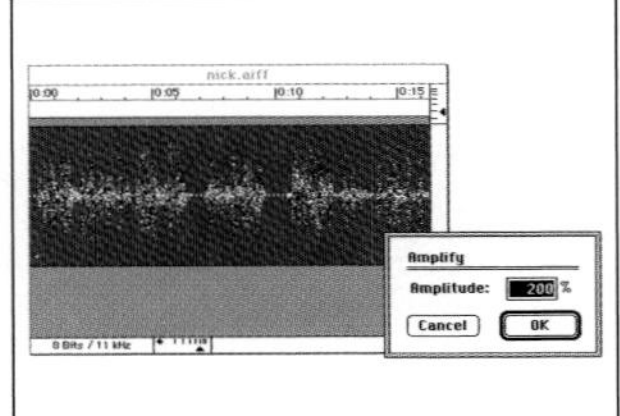

STEP 3: SPECIAL EFFECTS AND DOWNSAMPLE

After you've digitized, you have plenty of options for affecting the sound. If the volume of the clip is too low, try the Amplify command (accessible under the Effects menu). Set the variable to 200% and check your results. Make sure the Waveform doesn't clip at the top or bottom; in which case, you should Undo the command and try a lower percentage. Any clipping in the Waveform translates into a lower quality sound, usually with static.

Under the Effects menu, there are a variety of effects that allow you to alter the sound of your audio files. Try them out to hear which ones generate the sound you want. The Pitch command is helpful if you want your sounds to be either higher or lower in pitch. Be aware, however that this also affects the speed and length of your file. The Echo command is effective in creating a file that has a low, spooky sound to it.

When you've got just the right sound, it's time to downsample and output. If you've digitized anything other than an 8-bit, mono, 11 KHz file, you'll need to reformat it. Keep in mind that, given the current limitations of the Internet, this is your optimum format. In the Sound menu, choose Sound Format, and set your options to the above settings. Click OK and save the file in the *.aiff* format.

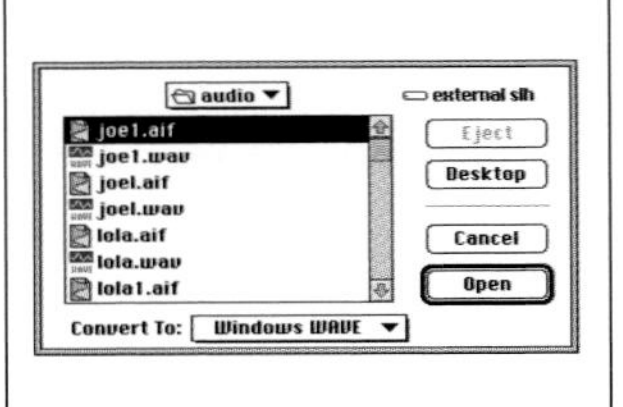

STEP 4: SAVE IN VARIOUS FILE FORMATS

PCs and UNIX machines constitute the majority of the World Wide Web audience. To ensure that all users can access your sound files, offer as many standard formats as possible. The most common format for both of these platforms is *.wav* files, and there are shareware applications for Macintosh that allow the playback of these files.

SoundApp is a Macintosh utility that easily converts *.aiff* files into *.wav* files. Under the File menu, choose Convert, and then select your *.aiff* file from the Convert window. Choose *.wav* from the Output pop-up window, and hit the Open button. Your file is automatically converted.

Session

J2 *Mixing and Looping Audio*

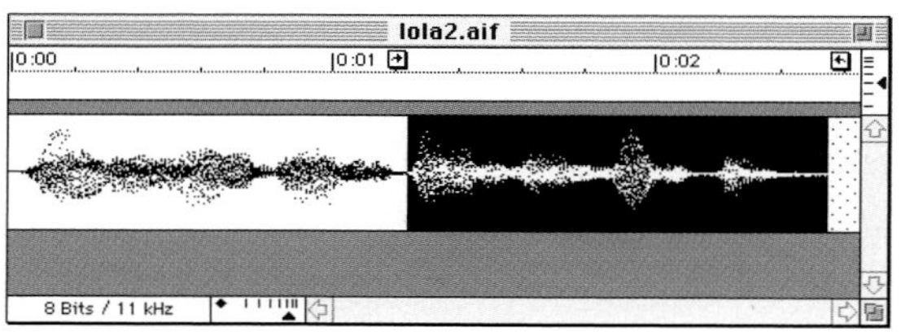

The biggest difference between creating files that will become independent downloadables and files that will be incorporated into animation files is length and size of the clip. Downloadable audio files are best optimized for the Internet in 8-bit format, mono sound, at 11KHz. At these setting, an audio file of about 30 seconds can take up as much as a megabyte in space. Incorporating a file this large into an animation would generate an unwieldy download.

The most effective types of audio to incorporate into animations are small sounds that can be used in association with interactivity. As multiple instances of the same sound does not affect the animation file size, you can reference the sound as many times as you want. While taking up little space, these types of files give the user audio feedback associated with their input.

SOUNDEDIT PRO 1.0

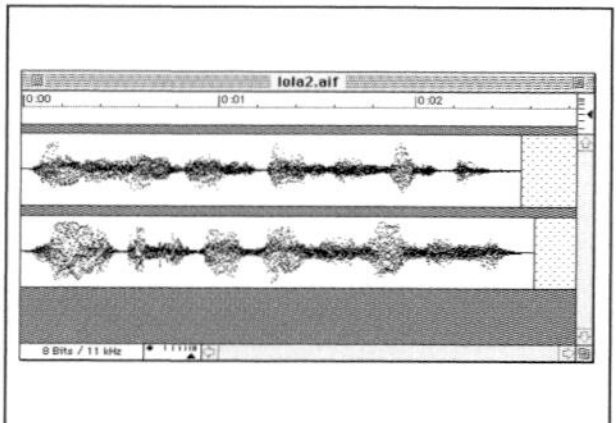

MIXING AUDIO

Multiple audio files can be easily mixed to create a complex background sound. Open one audio file in SoundEdit Pro and choose Add Track under the Sound menu. This creates another channel, into which you can copy and paste the second file. Continue adding tracks to accommodate all the sounds you want to use. Hitting the Play button in the Control window plays the sounds which are mixed automatically. You can then adjust their combined sound by moving the tracks individually to the right or left. After your sounds are in the right place, mix the channels together using the Mix command under the Sound menu. Within the Mix window, you have the option of mixing the sounds into your current file, or creating a new one.

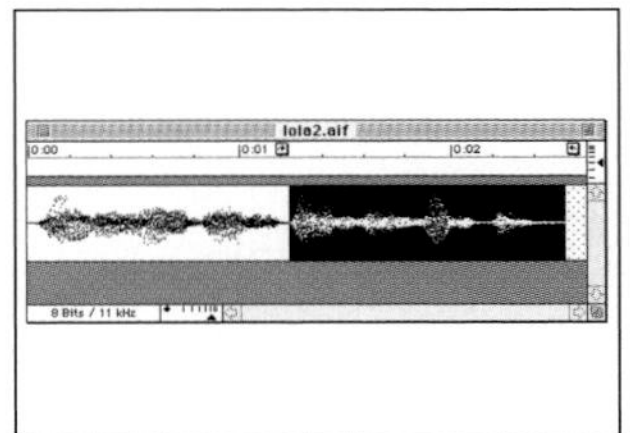

LOOPING AUDIO

Looping an audio file can be an efficient way to add musical interest without using too much bandwidth. Audio files can be looped a couple of ways, depending on how they will be accessed. The HTML tag *<bgsound>* allows incorporation of a loop within the HTML page. (See Session 18, for more information on *<bgsound>*.)

If you incorporate your audio file into a Shockwave animation, you can loop the file in its entirety using Macromedia Director's scripting language, called Lingo. (See Session 14, for Lingo implementation.)

Director, however, can also accept a file that plays with an introduction, and then loops the remainder of the file. To create this type of file, open your file in SoundEdit Pro, and highlight the section of the audio to be looped using your cursor. Choose the command Set Loopback under the Sound menu to set the portion to loop. To hear the results, hold down the Option key while clicking the Play button in the Control window. This plays your file, including the loopback, and allows you to adjust the beginning or end of the loopback so that it sounds seamless. You can then import into Director and incorporat it into your animation.

Session

J3 Digitizing Video

"Garbage in, garbage out," is also true when digitizing video. Start from the highest quality source. If you use a professional video camera or player, you'll get the best quality input. However, currently most consumer level video cameras offer Hi-8 format and S-video output. These levels of quality are better than the older 8mm and VHS standards, and are sufficient for Web video.

ADOBE PREMIERE 4.2

STEP 1: CONFIGURE EQUIPMENT

Connect your video camera or player to your video digitizing board, or directly into the computer (if your model supports video input). Almost all video digitizing boards support video cables with RCA connections. RCA cables are the standard cables used between a television set and VCR. An RCA cable transfers *composite* video, which is all the video information combined into one signal. One level of quality higher than the composite format is *S-video*. The S-video format consists of separate signals which can create a better quality video image. If your digitizing board and camera/player support S-video, use an S-video cable to make the connection and maintain better quality.

TIP: *If you have a video source that supports S-video, and can't find an S-video cable, a regular Mac keyboard cable works in a pinch.*

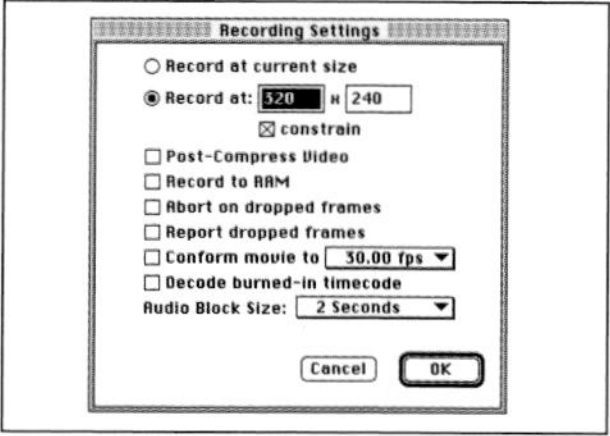

STEP 2: DIGITIZING SETTINGS

Test your video connection by previewing your video footage. In Adobe Premiere, choose Movie Capture under the File menu. This displays the Movie Capture window, which shows you a preview from your video source—digitizing starts only when you hit the

Record button. Before you start digitizing, make sure the digitizing settings are properly set. When digitizing video, you want to *over-sample*, or capture more information than you're going to use to maintain the best quality.

Choose Recording Settings in the Movie Capture menu. If your final movie will have a pixel resolution of 160 x 120, set the digitizing option to 320 x 240. Click in the checkbox next to Report dropped frames; this helps you digitize the best quality video. Most video sources display extra lines of video at the bottom of the screen. This is due to a video process called *overscan*, which crops the edges and limits the size of the video signal on your television set. In the process of digitizing video, you may see extra pieces of video on the edges of the footage. Crop these out later.

Now choose Video Input from the Movie Capture menu. Here, you select video options specific to your system configuration. Choose Source from the pop-up menu at the top. In the Source window, select your digitizer, input, and format. If you are able to see a preview of the video in the Movie Capture window, you have set these setting correctly. Switch to the Image window using the pop-up menu. Adjust the hue, saturation, brightness, contrast, sharpness, black level and white level for the incoming signal, depending on the options supported by your hardware.

The last group of settings is specific to compression and frame rate. Choose Compression using the pop-up menu. Select the compressor suggested by your hardware's manufacturer, and then choose the desired frame rate of digitizing. If your system is fast enough, you can capture a full 30 frames per second, which also will generate a final movie file of the best quality. If, however, your system cannot handle 30 frames per second, set the rate to 15 frames per second.

STEP 3: DIGITIZE AND VIEW

Now that Premiere is configured for your session, start digitizing. Close the Video Input window by hitting OK, and click Record in the Movie Capture window. Digitize a couple of extra seconds at the beginning and the end of your selected clip (you will edit these out later). Click again to stop the digitizing process. At this point, Premiere may display a window notifying you of dropped frames. If this is the case, change the desired frames per second from 15 to 10, and digitize again. After you have successfully digitized your selection, save the clip to your hard drive and play it back for content and quality.

TIP: *If your video looks choppy, and it like you're dropping frames, make sure you have plenty of hard drive space, and optimize and defragment your hard drive.*

Session

J4

Editing Video and Adding Transitions

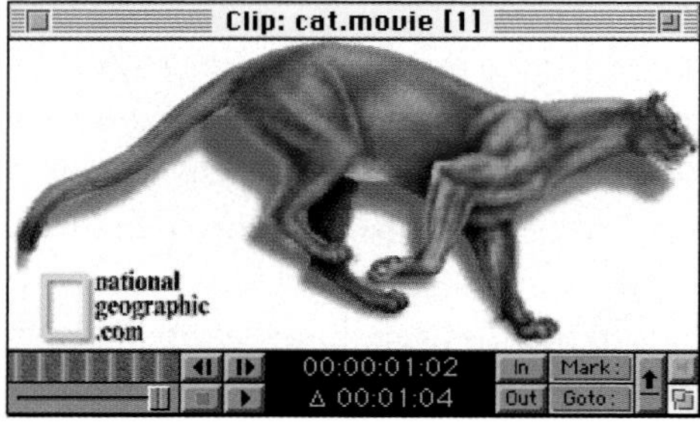

ADOBE PREMIERE 4.2

The most creative part of working with digital video can be editing and adding transitions. This session assumes that all of your video and audio clips have been digitized, and that you've already created the still graphics you will need to make your movie. The specific example in this session is creating a movie of the inner workings of a cat, dissolving between its skeletal system, its muscular system, and its exterior appearance. In this example, you will edit still images into the final movie. But the same principles apply if editing video clips.

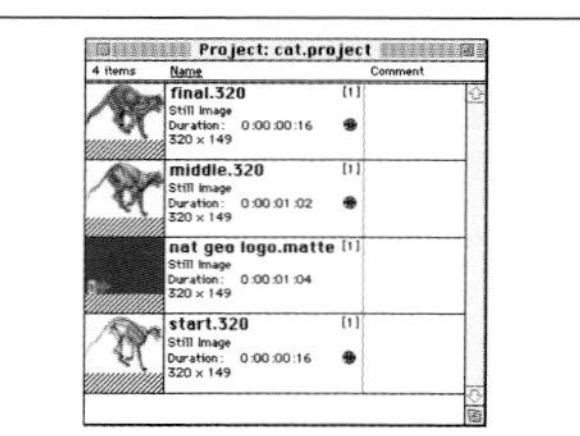

STEP 1: IMPORT ALL OF YOUR ELEMENTS

Starting Adobe Premiere automatically displays the New Project Presets window. Here, select one of the default presets for your new project. The presets automatically choose the optimum settings for each type project, but you can change any of these settings later. Among the six new windows that appear, you will see a new Project window, which you can think of as your cast of characters. Import all of the elements you will need in your project, including video, stills, mattes, and audio, using the Import command under the File menu. Then choose one of the following options: file, multiple, and folder. Keeping all the elements you need organized in one folder saves time when it comes to importing, as well as archiving.

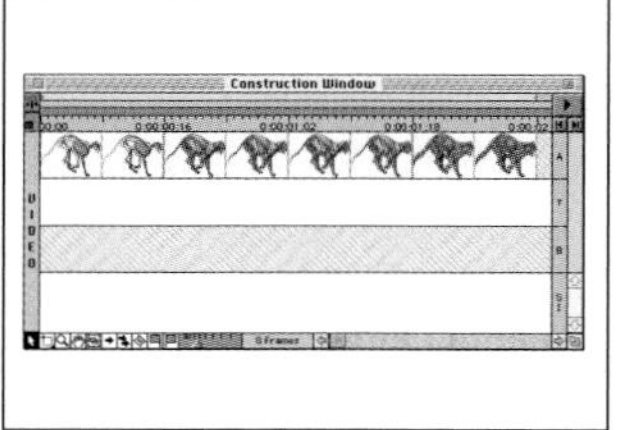

STEP 2: SEQUENCE YOUR ELEMENTS

Place your video clips and stills into the Video tracks A and B of the Construction window. Do this by clicking on the elements in the Project window and dragging them into the Project window. The Construction window is organized left to right, according to time. A typical technique in video editing is that of using *jump cuts*, which means that there are no transition effects between elements. If you'd like to try this, use only one video track, and align the edges of the elements next to each other. The Return key on the keyboard to automatically display a preview of your edited video.

By first placing all of your elements into the Construction window, you'll have a rough cut of your movie, and a general idea of the movie's length. Then you can preview the movement, and start focusing on the timing of the clips. This gives you a good idea of what needs to be adjusted or cropped.

STEP 3: EDITING A SINGLE VIDEO CLIP

If your digitized video contains a few frames that you don't want to use, now is a good time to set in and out points for the clip. Double-click on the video clip in the Construction window, and step-frame through it in the Clip window, using the frame Forward and Back buttons. When you arrive at a good starting point for the video, click the In button at the bottom of the Clip window to set the beginning frame of the video. Again step-frame through the video and click the Out button when you reach the last frame of the video.

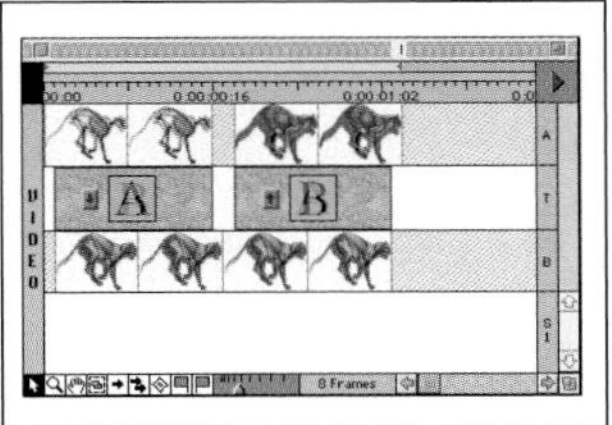

STEP 4: EDITING MULTIPLE CLIPS TOGETHER

Jump cuts are one way of editing a video. If, however, you choose to use the multitude of transition effects offered in Premiere, try to limit your project to just one type of effect. Otherwise, the transitions can distract from the content of the video. Cross-dissolves between clips of video are professional-looking and unobtrusive.

Position one clip of video in Video Track A of the Construction window. Position another clip of video in Video Track B, slightly overlapping in time. Drag and drop the cross-dissolve transition from the Transition window into the T Track, exactly where the two clips of video overlap. Double-click on the transition in the T Track to set the direction of the transition. Make sure the direction is from the first clip of video to the second clip of video by looking at the vertical arrow in the lower right-hand corner of the Settings window. If the transition moves in the wrong direction, your final movie displays unexpected results.

In this example, our Construction window displays the following timeline:

- Skeletal image of 16-frame duration, about 1/2 second
- Cross-dissolving, 15-frame dissolve into
- Muscular image of 32-frame duration, just over 1 second
- Cross-dissolving, 15-frame dissolve into
- Coat image of 16-frame duration, about 1/2 second

The project is then compressed and outputted to a movie that briefly displays the skeletal image, which then dissolves into the muscular image, which, after pausing for one frame, dissolves into the cat image.

Session

J5 Compositing Graphics

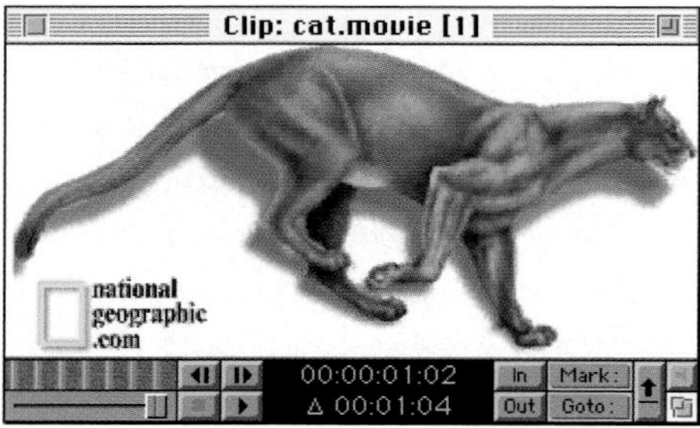

ADOBE PREMIERE 4.2

Premiere does a great job of compositing graphics onto clips of video This session focuses on compositing a corporate logo on top of video clips and still images in Adobe Premiere. If you plan to offer copyrighted material on your site, you should consider adding this kind of mark. As users all over the world can download and save your clips, you might want to mark them with some kind of branding and copyright. This session shows compositing of the National Geographic logo onto the cat video from the previous lesson.

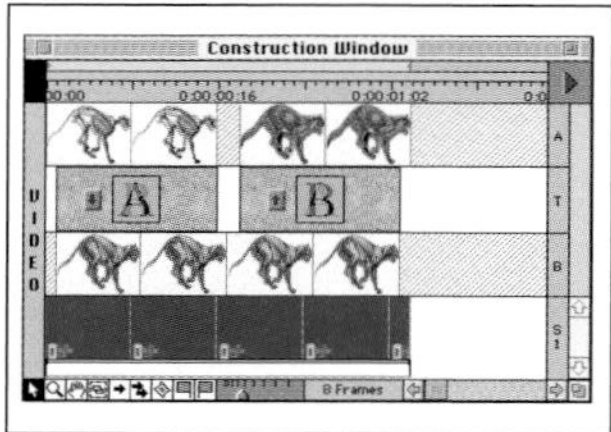

STEP 1: EDIT VIDEO, IMPORT GRAPHIC, PLACE IN CONSTRUCTION WINDOW

Starting with your current project, and associated Construction window that already includes placed and edited video clips, import the still image you'd like to composite on top of the video. The still image should include a solid, one-bit background that is later made transparent. Import your still image, and drag and drop the image from the Project window into the Construction window in the S1, or superimpose track. Position the graphic for timing and duration. If the graphic should last the duration of the entire movie, click on the right side of the image, and drag the edge of the clip until it reaches the end of the entire movie.

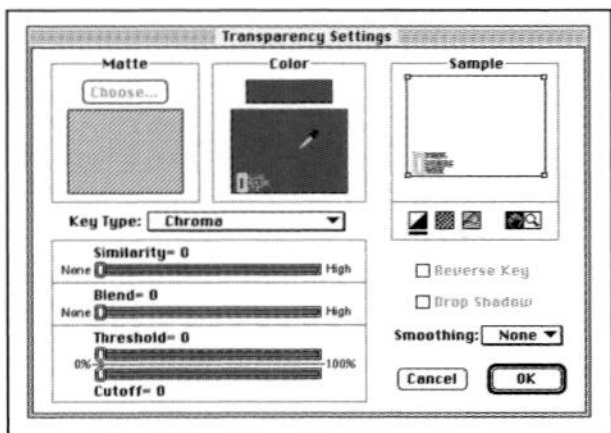

STEP 2: TRANSPARENCY SETTINGS

Select the image in the superimpose track, and choose Transparency under the Clip menu to access the Transparency Settings window. Choosing Chroma from the pop-up window associated with Key Type, changes your pointer to an Eye dropper tool. With this tool, choose the background color of the image that you want to make transparent. Premiere offers many ways to set transparency of video and images; the Chroma option works very well if your image has a solid one-bit background. View the results of the transparency settings in the Sample portion of the window. If you are pleased with the results, click OK to apply the settings.

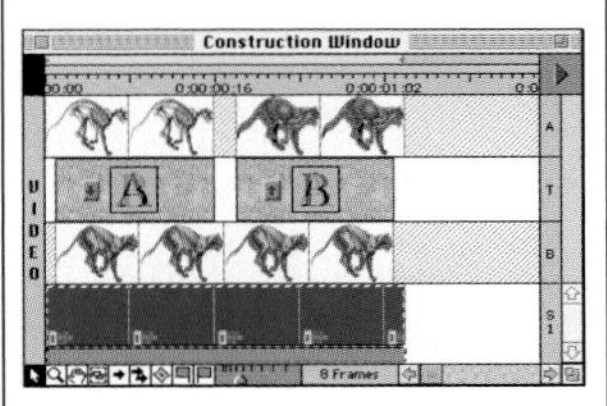

STEP 3: PREVIEW YOUR TRANSPARENCY

Preview the settings of the key for the duration of the entire movie by adjusting the Work Area Bar at the top of the Construction window and hitting the Return key on the keyboard. To see a preview of an individual frame, position the cursor in the Time Ruler at the top of the Construction window. When the pointer changes to an arrow, the corresponding frame appears in the Preview window. Click on other areas in the Time Ruler to view other frames.

Session

J6 **Synching Video to Audio**

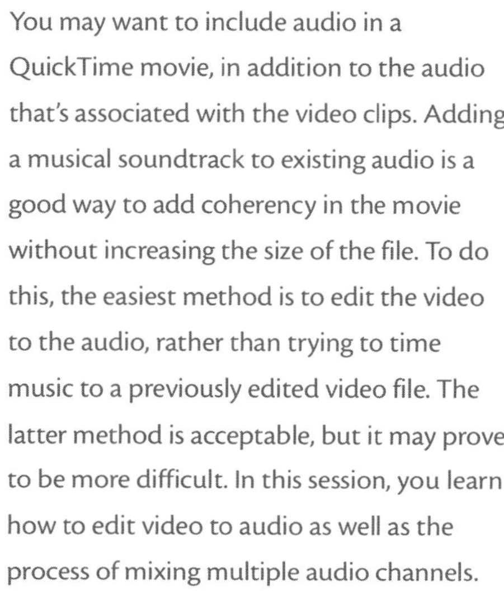
You may want to include audio in a QuickTime movie, in addition to the audio that's associated with the video clips. Adding a musical soundtrack to existing audio is a good way to add coherency in the movie without increasing the size of the file. To do this, the easiest method is to edit the video to the audio, rather than trying to time music to a previously edited video file. The latter method is acceptable, but it may prove to be more difficult. In this session, you learn how to edit video to audio as well as the process of mixing multiple audio channels.

ADOBE PREMIERE 4.2

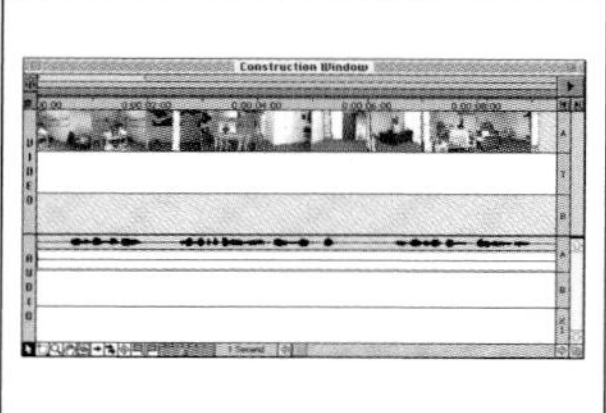

STEP 1: PLACE AUDIO IN CONSTRUCTION WINDOW

After importing all of your elements, place the video clips you want to use in Video A and B tracks of the Construction window of a new project. Drag and drop the audio clips from the Project window in Audio tracks A and B. Without altering the clips, hit the Return key on the keyboard for a quick preview to check the placement and length of the clips. This helps to synch any sound effects to activity within the video clips.

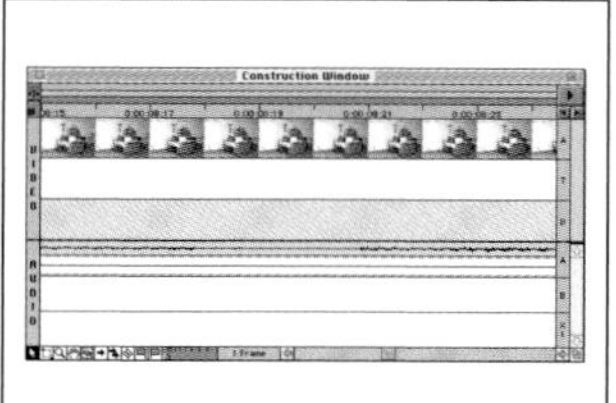

STEP 2: CHANGE THE VIEW OF THE CONSTRUCTION WINDOW

Once you have previewed a rough of the video and audio combination, zoom in on the files to make more detailed adjustments. To zoom into the files, drag the time unit selector slider (in the lower left corner of the Construction window) to the left, changing the view from 1 second to 8 frames. This means that each thumbnail in the Construction window now represents eight frames of video. One second chosen in the time unit means that each thumbnail in the Construction window represents 1 second, or 30 frames of video. The closer detail allows you to see the waveform of the audio file to better edit the video to the audio.

STEP 3: MARK AUDIO AND VIDEO ELEMENTS

Premiere allows you to specify or *mark* elements within the Clip window of all files. You can access these marks immediately within the Clip window, and they are instantly recognizable within the Construction window. If the audio and video files contain specific sounds and actions that should coincide, mark each one separately, and then match the marks in the Constructions window. Double-click on the audio file, to display the Clip window. Step forward and back through the audio to find the specific sound. Click the Mark button and select a number to represent that sound. Now double-click on the video file to display the video's Clip window. Follow the same process to mark individual frames of the video clip. Close both Clip windows. The marks display in the Construction window and allow you to easily align them.

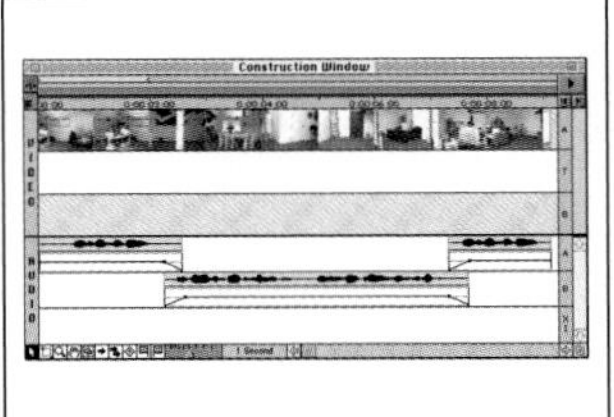

STEP 4: EDIT AUDIO LEVELS

Once your video and audio clips are placed and edited in the Construction windows, you can adjust the volume of the audio. Drag the time unit selector slider to zoom in to the Construction window to maintain accuracy in your settings. Each audio clip placed in the Construction window contains an Audio Fade control that allows you to set the volume at various places in the clip. The Audio Fade control is the section of the clip that is directly below the waveform. The control is set to a default of mid-volume for all clips. Click and hold in the selection to create a handle that you can drag up or down, to adjust the volume of the audio file. Dragging the handle to the bottom of the window allows you to fade the sound in or out.

TIP: *Slightly fading the audio in from the beginning of the clip, and out at the end of the clip is a professional-sounding effect.*

Session

J7 Output and Compression

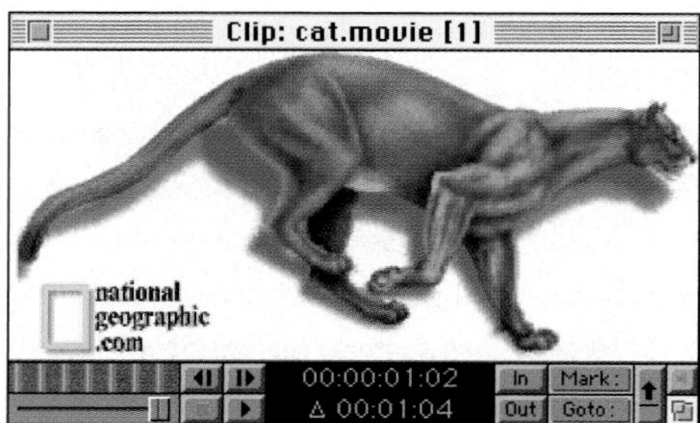

ADOBE PREMIERE 4.2

Your output and compression options can greatly affect both image quality and file size. The key to these options is a good balance for your particular clip. For example, the best quality for some video clips may be a high frame rate. Others may require fewer frames, but a higher image quality and a larger frame size. In general, the standard 160 x 120 pixels, 15 frames per second, highest quality setting creates a good quality movie as a reasonable size. However, be prepared to try several options to finalize your output settings for the best quality. This session focuses on the output and compression settings for the movie created in Session J4.

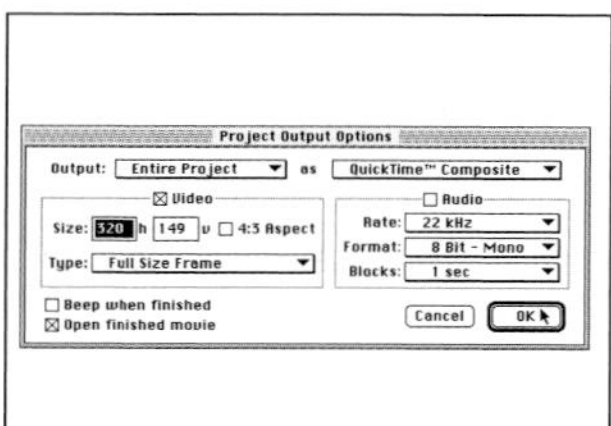

STEP 1: OUTPUT OPTIONS

Under the Project menu, choose Make Movie. This displays a window with three options to set: the name of the movie, Output Options, and Compression Settings.

First, name the movie and decide its placement on your hard drive. Then click choose the Output Options button. The Project Output Options window enables you to compress the entire project or only a part of it. You can choose to output a QuickTime movie, numbered PICT files, or a filmstrip file. In this example, you output the entire project as a QuickTime movie.

The options you chose when starting this project automatically determine the height and width of the output, but you can alter these numbers if you choose. In this case, the height and width are 320 x 149 pixels. This example movie does not contain audio, leave that box unchecked. Click OK to move on to Compression Settings.

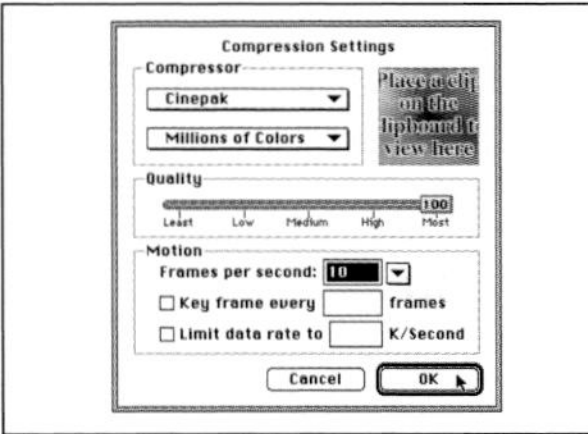

STEP 2: COMPRESSION SETTINGS

The standard, most reliable and best quality compressor is called Radius Cinepak. The Compression Settings window allows you to choose Radius Cinepak in 24-bit color, and also offers a slider bar for quality of the image. In this example, leave the quality at best; you should do your own tests regarding different levels of image quality, and how that impacts the size of the final movie.

The Motion settings let you choose the number of frames per second, as well as placement of key frames. By choosing Cinepak, the limitation of the data transfer rate for your movie becomes available. For this movie, set the output to 10 frames per second as there isn't that much movement within this particular video. Click OK in the Compression Settings window, and then OK in the Make Movie window, and Premiere starts compressing and outputting of the movie.

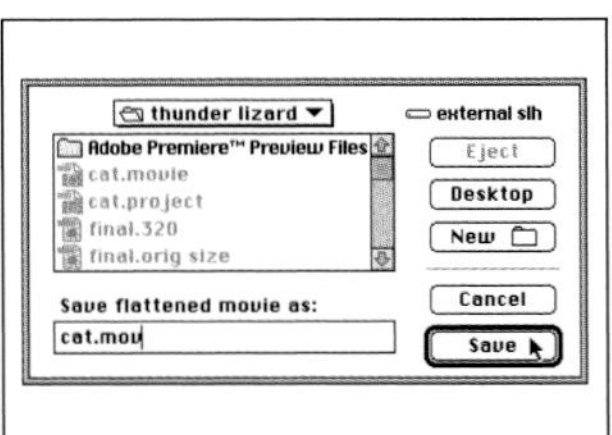

STEP 3: FLATTEN YOUR MOVIE

When choosing the command Make Movie in Premiere on the Macintosh, you create a movie that plays on a Macintosh. To ensure cross-platform playback from the Internet, flatten your movie. Choose Export Flattened Movie from the File menu, and select your file. This automatically, and very quickly, creates another file that is now cross-platform.

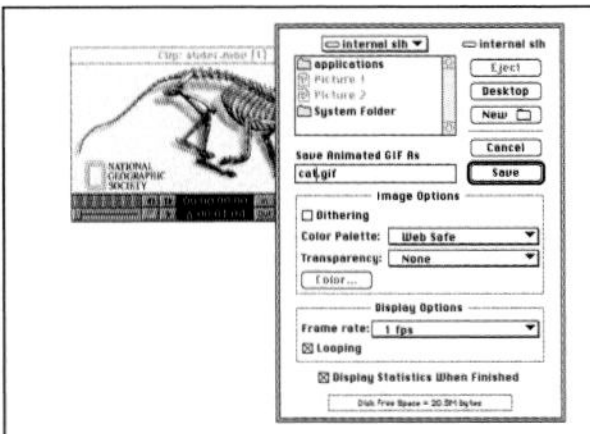

OPTION: EXPORT TO ANIMATED GIF

Adobe Premiere also offers an export to animated GIF feature. Generally, video files are not optimized for GIF compression (see Chapter F, "Preparing Graphics for the Web"), the Premiere editing capabilities allow for interesting effects in an animated GIF. This is also an excellent way to create a thumbnail file of your video clip that you can use inline as a representation for the user to click.

Make sure the plug-in is in your Premiere Plug-ins folder and start Premiere. Open the file you want to export; you can export from the Construction window or the Clip window. Choose Export Animated GIF from the File menu, and the Save Animated GIF window appears. Enter the name for the new movie and its path, then check the settings below.

Image Options give the choice of dithering or indexing to a color palette, including the Web-safe palette. You can also choose different transparency options along with a color wheel to choose the transparent color. Display Options allows you to choose the frame rate of the final animated GIF, and whether or not it loops when played. After setting these options, click Save, and your animated GIF is created.

Session

J8 Animating Layers in After Effects

Adobe's After Effects is a great program for creating animations from various layers of source files. As After Effects does an excellent job of keying transparencies and creating smooth, realistic motion of moving objects, it makes a great companion to the video editing capabilities of Adobe Premiere. This session walks you through the steps for making a simple animation from layered files.

ADOBE AFTER EFFECTS 3.1	Object Gear, Culturals: Piñata Object Gear, Design Elements: Magnet Object Gear, Design Elements: Gold Frame #2

TIP: *Before starting this lesson, open the images in Photoshop and convert the background to transparency.*

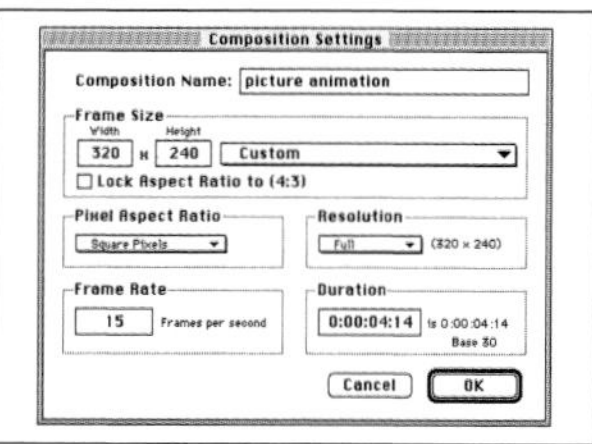

STEP 1: CREATE A NEW COMPOSITION

Import the three images into After Effects, the Import Footage File command under the File menu. The Project window then stores all of the imported files for your composition. Choose New Composition under the Composition menu and fill in the variables—the more critical being height and width, frames per second, and duration of the movie. For this animation, choose the resolution of 320 x 240 pixels, 15 frames a second, and a duration of 4 seconds and 14 frames.

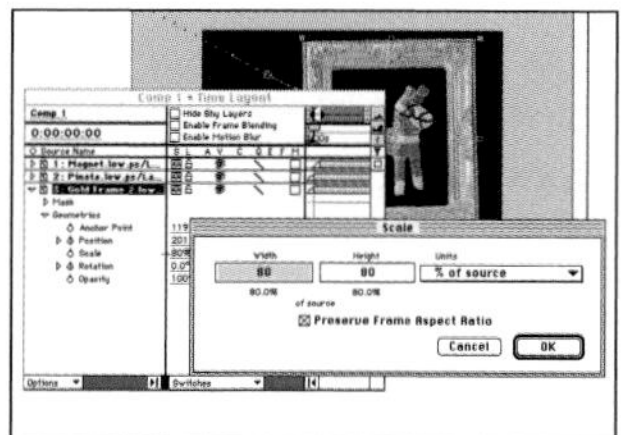

STEP 2: PLACE AND SCALE ALL ELEMENTS

Place the picture frame image in the Composition window. The image is too large to fit in the current window, so scale it down. Select the picture frame layer in the Time Layout window, and click the triangle next to the layer to expand the outline. Click the triangle next to Geometrics and choose the underlined Scale value of 100% to open the Scale window. Change the value in the Scale window to 80%.

Place the piñata image in the Composition window, and follow the same procedure to scale the piñata to a value of 40%. The magnet image requires a few different settings. Position it off-screen at the beginning of the movie, and then have it animate into the frame. When you place the image outside the frame, you see only the bounding box for the image. Once placed off-screen, go ahead and follow the same scaling procedure as the two other images, and scale the magnet to a value of 20%.

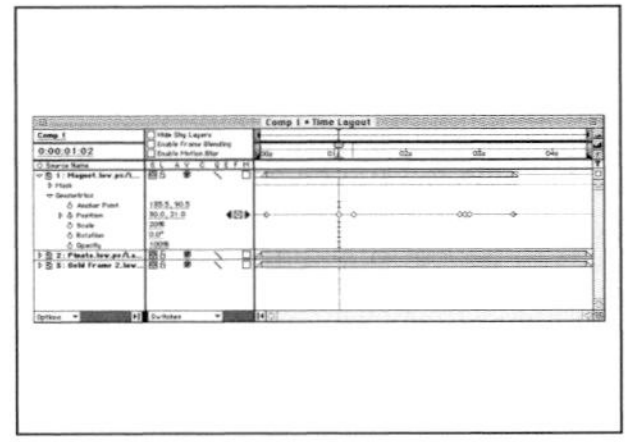

STEP 3: CREATE KEY FRAMES

Key frames allow for controlled movement of elements. Setting them automatically generates the frames in between the key frames. We want the magnet to move in from off stage and stop at the timing of 1 second. At the beginning of the Composition, click the Geometrics triangle to reveal the options for the magnet. Now, click the stopwatch next to the Position option to create your first key frame. Now, to create another key frame, choose Go To Time, under the Composition menu, and enter 1:00. Click the stopwatch again next to the Position option to create a keyframe, and move the magnet to a position on stage. Test your key frames by hitting Rewind in the Time Controls, and then hit Play. The magnet should move smoothly from its position off stage into its new position at 1:00.

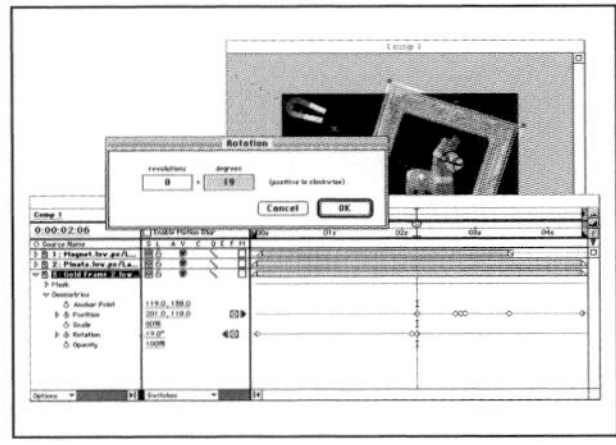

STEP 4: KEY FRAME OPTIONS

Between key frames, you can also affect the rotation, scaling, and opacity of the object. To rotate the picture frame from one key frame to another, create two key frames specific to the picture frame. While creating the second key frame, click on the stopwatch next to the Rotation option, and then click on the Rotation value. Change the Rotation value from 0 to 18%. The picture frame now rotates to fit the angle of the magnet image.

Now, create the rest of your key frames to animate the picture frame moving with the magnet out of the frame of the Composition. Because the piñata image layer is on top of the picture frame image layer, the picture frame animates behind the piñata.

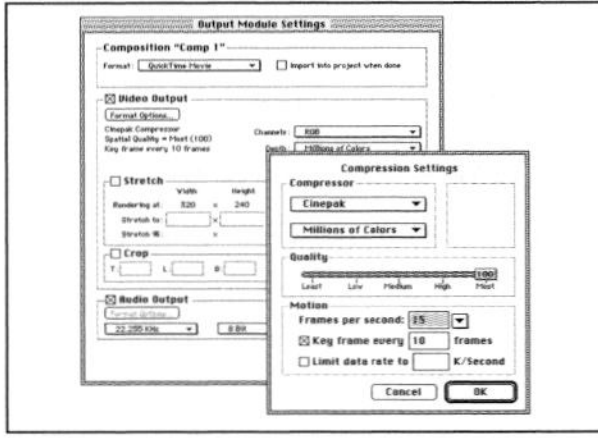

STEP 5: MAKE MOVIE

After your animation is complete, you are ready to compress and output your QuickTime movie. Choose Make Movie under the Composition menu, and your movie appears in the Render Queue. Make sure you are outputting a QuickTime movie, and click the Format Options button under Video Output. Choose the Cinepak compressor at the Most Quality setting, and verify the frames per second. Click OK, to render and output.

Session

J9 Linking Audio and Video in HTML

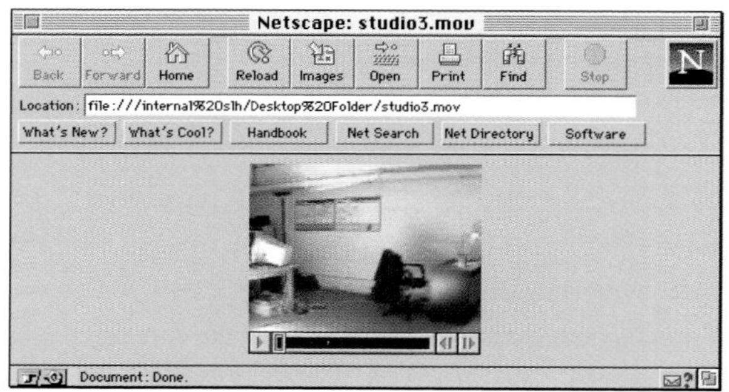

Now that you've created your audio and video files, you need to reference them in the HTML to allow users access. You can offer audio as a simple download to the user's hard drive, and played with a helper application configured in the browser. Another option is the *<bgsound>* tag (see Session J8 for specifics of the *<bgsound>* tag). You can offer video files two ways: as an optional download, or as an inline QuickTime movie. When referencing your files within HTML, it is a good idea to include an indication of the file size, so the user knows how long a download to expect. This session demonstrates the HTML necessary to offer downloadable audio and video files, as well as inline QuickTime movies.

SIMPLETEXT OR NOTEPAD

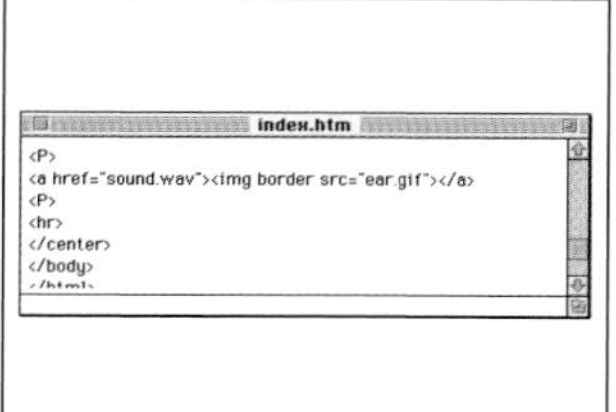

DOWNLOADABLE AUDIO

The standard *<a href>* within the HTML is an easy way to handle a downloadable audio file. You can write a simple description of the file, or include a graphic to represent the content of the audio. The following line of HTML starts downloading the sound *.wav* file when the user clicks the file called "ear.gif."

```
<a href="sound.wav"><img border=0 src="ear.gif"></a>
```

Depending on the user's browser settings, the file then plays with the help of a helper application, or it is simply stored on the user's hard drive.

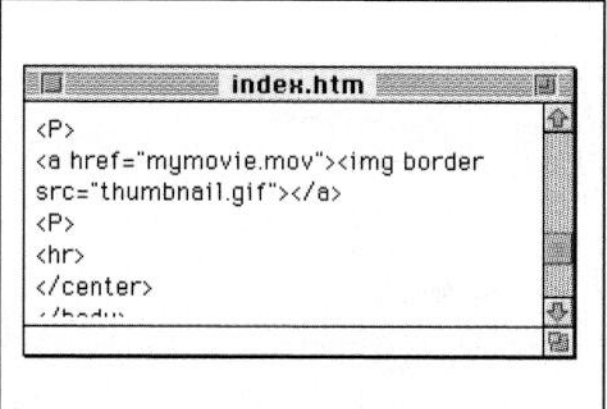

DOWNLOADABLE VIDEO

The standard *<a href>* within the HTML is an easy way to handle a downloadable video file too. Consider representing a video download with a thumbnail graphic. This, along with the file size of the download, gives the user an idea of what to expect. The following line of HTML starts downloading the movie, "mymovie.mov" when the user clicked on "thumbnail.gif."

```
<a href="mymovie.mov"><img src="thumbnail.gif"></a>
```

Once again, depending on the user's browser settings, the file then plays with the help of a helper application, or it simply is stored on the user's hard drive.

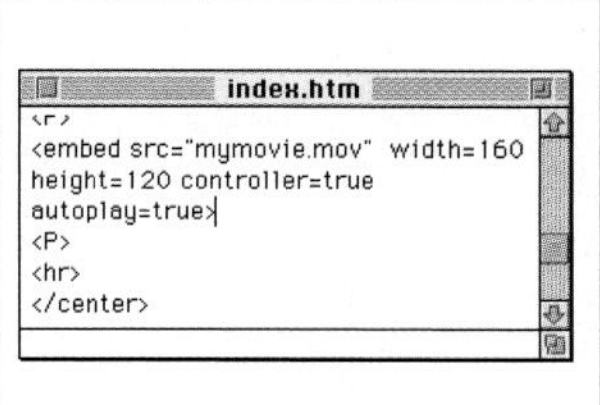

INLINE QUICKTIME

When referencing video, you have the added option of downloading a video clip *inline*, or within the design of the page. This means that while the HTML page is downloading, the movie will start downloading as well. Rather than using the *<a href>* tag to download the file, use the following line, including the *<embed>* tag.

```
<embed src="mymovie.mov" width=160 height=120
   controller=true autoplay=true>
```

The *controller=* variable refers to the QuickTime play bar, the setting of "true" means that the play bar is visible. The setting of *autoplay=true* means that the movie starts playing once it's downloaded on the page.

Chapter K

Creating PDF Files with Adobe Acrobat

Providing Acrobat PDF (Portable Document Format) files is a great way to allow others to see your work, especially if formatting and page layout are important. PDF files combine the best of print capabilities and interactive media to create rich, low-bandwidth documents that retain their original design. Adobe Acrobat creates pages that are formatted with fonts and images that are ready to print. Interactive documents, including linking, multimedia elements, and presentation capabilities, are also easily created with Acrobat. The beauty of PDF files is that they retain their design and formatting perfectly, without the burden of the original application, or linked images and fonts. Your users only need Acrobat Reader to view and print any PDF files. With the PDFViewer Plug-in you can view and interact with PDF files within your Web browser.

CHAPTER SESSIONS

- K1 *Conversion to PDF and Adding Interactivity*
- K2 *More PDF Bells and Whistles*
- K3 *Incorporating Scanned Documents*
- K4 *Cataloging and Indexing PDF Files*
- K5 *Referencing PDF files in HTML*

CHAPTER TOOLBOX

Adobe Acrobat Distiller 3.0

Adobe Acrobat Exchange 3.0

Adobe Acrobat Catalog 3.0

Simple Text or Notepad

ADOBE ACROBAT 101

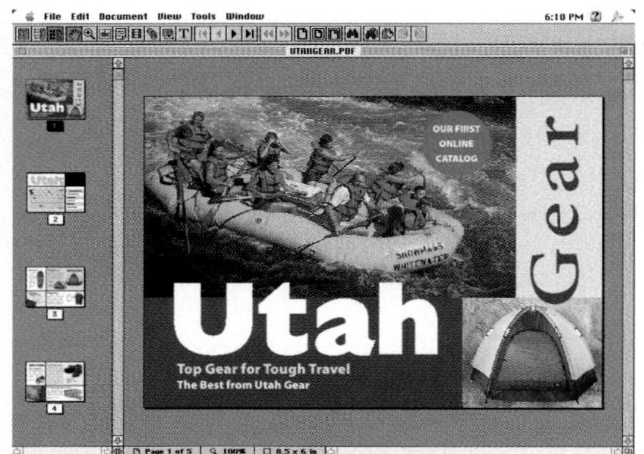

Acrobat consists of an integrated set of applications that allow you to convert PostScript documents into PDF files, enhance the files with interactivity, and index multiple files to allow user searching. Adobe Acrobat consists of:

- Acrobat Distiller and the PDF Writer
- Acrobat Exchange with the optional Capture plug-in
- Acrobat Catalog and Search
- Acrobat Reader and the PDFVeiwer browser plug-in

ACROBAT DISTILLER AND PDF WRITER

The two utilities that easily create PDF documents are Acrobat Distiller and PDF Writer. Distiller converts a normal PostScript file, from any application that outputs a PostScript file, into a PDF file. Use Distiller when you've created a file that includes any embedded graphical elements. The PDF Writer is a printer driver that you can access using the standard application Print command. The PDF Writer can be used for fast, easy conversion of less-complex documents.

ACROBAT EXCHANGE AND THE OPTIONAL CAPTURE PLUG-IN

After creating a PDF file, use Acrobat Exchange to incorporate interactivity, including password protection and linking, as well as inclusion of multimedia elements such as video and audio. The Capture plug-in for Exchange allows you to convert scanned documents of text and images into PDF files. Acrobat Capture uses OCR (Optical Character Recognition) capabilities to convert text, and to optimize and embed images.

ACROBAT CATALOG AND SEARCH

Acrobat Catalog creates an index of PDF files that can the user search using Acrobat Exchange and Acrobat Reader. The Acrobat Search plug-in needs to be installed with Reader to access these indices.

Acrobat™ Reader 3.0

ACROBAT READER AND THE BROWSER PLUG-IN

Users can download both Acrobat Reader and the browser plug-in from *www.adobe.com*. Acrobat Reader is a little over one megabyte, and the browser plug-in is about 150k. When viewing PDF files in your browser, the plug-in launches Acrobat Reader in the background to render the files into the browser.

Session K1

Conversion to PDF and Adding Interactivity

ADOBE DISTILLER 3.0
ADOBE EXCHANGE 3.0

The greatest benefit of PDF is that your documents can be created in almost any application; you don't have to give up your favorite page layout program. Just make sure the program can output a PostScript file—they all do. This session covers the process of outputting a 13-page document that was created in QuarkXPress, converting it to a PDF file, and then adding some interactivity.

The original publication document, including all images and fonts, takes about 20.5 megabytes, not including the application. Our final outcome a PDF file under 1 megabyte that can be offered as a downloadable on the Web, and viewed using the Acrobat Reader or the Acrobat browser plug-in.

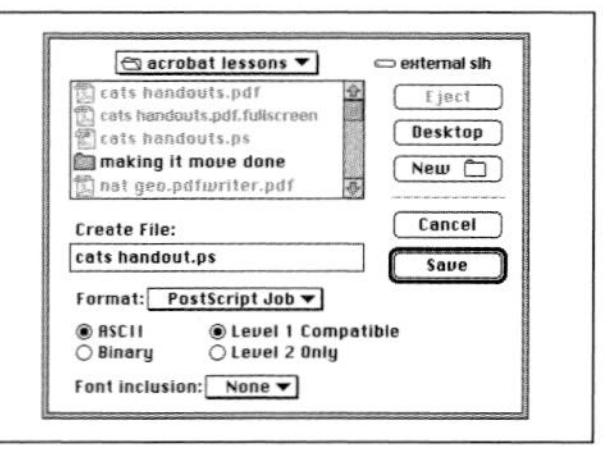

STEP 1: CREATE A PDF FILE

With the file open in QuarkXPress, choose Print from the File menu. In the Print window, check the radio button for File (to create a PostScript file) rather than Printer (in the Destination area of the window), and then hit Print. A dialog box prompts you for the file name and location of the PostScript file. Click Save to write the file.

Now, launch Acrobat Distiller and verify that Distiller can find the fonts used in the original document by choosing Font Locations under the Distiller menu. Make sure that the folder storing your fonts is present in the list. Also under the Distiller menu is a choice called Job Options. This is where you set preferences for sizing of the pages, downsampling and compression of the images, and color management. Under most circumstances, the defaults work fine. Distiller gives you the option of controlling these settings to maintain high resolution of images; for example, if you are sending the files to a professional printer for publishing.

Open your newly created PostScript file; Distiller prompts you with a Save dialog box. Hitting the Save button automatically starts the distilling process to create the PDF file. While this is not an instantaneous process, it doesn't take very long. Our 13-page Quark document distilled to 450k.

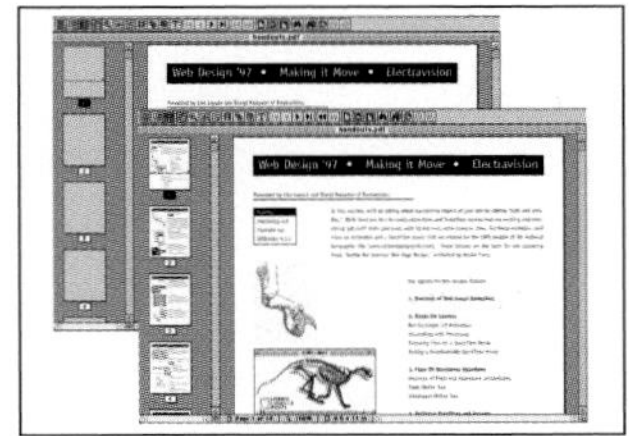

STEP 2: EDIT THE ORDER OF PAGES

After distilling, you can open your document in Acrobat Exchange, and make final touches. First, you may want to put the document in Thumbnails and Page view by choosing the command under the View menu, or the button on the toolbar. Next, create thumbnails to more easily navigate through and arrange your pages. Under the Document menu, choose Create All Thumbnails. Exchange automatically creates thumbnail images of all the pages in the left frame of the document window.

With these thumbnails, you can now easily and quickly navigate between pages, as well as change the order of pages simply. By clicking on the number 3, representing page 3, and dragging it to the space between page 1 and page 2, you've changed the order of the pages.

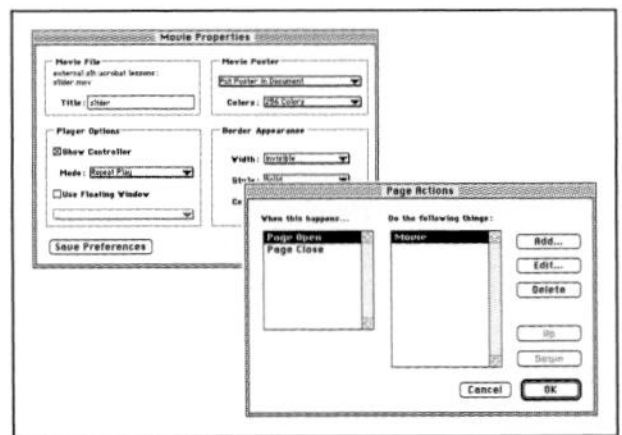

STEP 3: ADD A QUICKTIME MOVIE

Click on the Movie tool in the toolbar, and go to the location where you want to add a QuickTime movie. Draw a rectangle in that location, which prompts you with a window that asks for the location of the movie file. Choose your movie, and another window appears. In this Movie Properties window, set options such as show/hide controller, play once, or back and forth, or repeat play, show/hide movie poster (by default, the first frame of the movie), and border options. You can always change these settings later, by double-clicking the movie with the Movie tool.

STEP 4: SET AN ACTION ASSOCIATED WITH A PAGE

In this file, we want the QuickTime movie to automatically start playing when the user reaches that page. Under the Document menu, choose Set Page Action. This allows you to set automatic actions when a page is opened or closed. Choose Page Open, and then hit the Add button. This opens a dialog box with a variety of options to set. Choose Movie, and when your user comes to this page, the movie you've selected automatically starts playing, according the options you have set in the Movie Properties window.

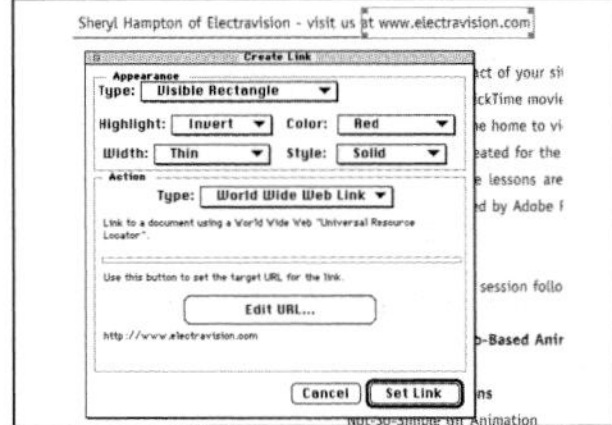

STEP 5: CREATE LINKS

Links can be created in a PDF file, switching from page-to-page and zoomed views. External links to a URL are also possible, for example. To link a piece of text to a World Wide Web URL, click on the Link tool in the toolbar, and draw a box around the text or image you would like to be clickable. In the Create Link window choose World Wide Web link and enter the destination URL. In order for URL links to work, your user needs to configure her copy of Acrobat Reader to launch a Web browser.

Session

K2 More PDF Bells and Whistles

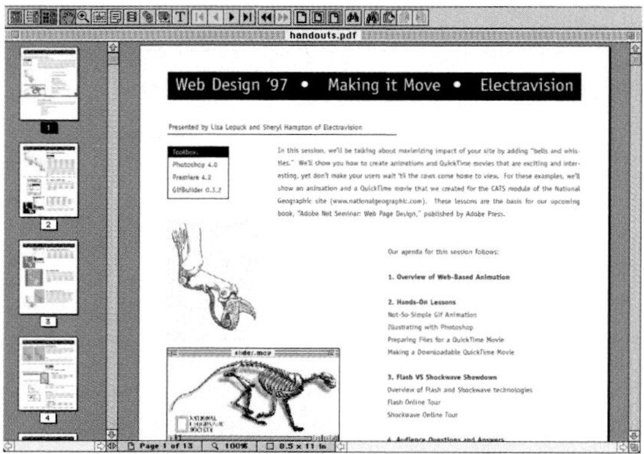

This lesson focuses on providing interactivity for your users, via a variety of features. PDF files can include notations, so that others, including clients and co-workers, can give you feedback on the content of the PDF. A PDF can have internal links (links that offer interactivity within the PDF document), switch to specific pages, or chang views. Additional methods of navigation are also possible, offering a different method of information retrieval. Exchange also offers simple presentation features that can make your PDF file work well as a slide presentation.

ADOBE EXCHANGE 3.0

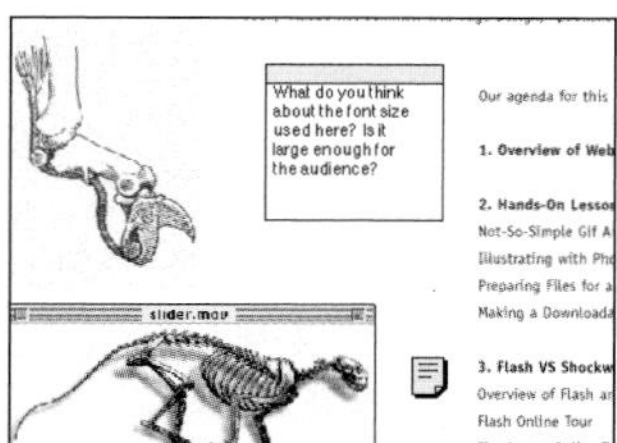

STEP 1: USE NOTES TO GET FEEDBACK

The notes feature is especially useful for getting feedback from a number of users in a controlled group environment (e.g., an intranet). All of the members of a project team can view and respond to individual parts of the PDF file. Notes can then be sent back to the creator of the file and summarized for updating. This can be extremely helpful when finalizing a PDF file for output.

Using the Notes tool selected from the button bar, click next to an area you want to annotate. This opens a Notes window with an area for typing. All others viewing your document with Acrobat Exchange can add their own notes, but cannot change or add to your notes.

To view all notes, choose Summarize Notes under the Tool menu. This creates a separate PDF file with the content of the notes and corresponding page numbers and creation dates.

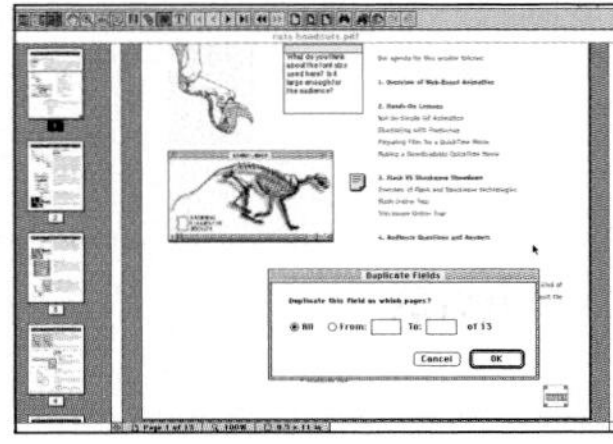

STEP 2: ADD INTERNAL LINKS AND COMMANDS

In this example, you create a button that automatically takes the user to the next page within the PDF file. Using the Form tool, draw a rectangle around the area you want to be clickable. This opens the Field Properties window where you can select the options for your field. Choose Button in the Type pop-up menu.

The Appearance tab in this window allows you to choose background and text options, while the Actions tab reveals the real power of this feature. With the Mouse Up option selected, click the Add button. In the Add an Action window, choose Execute Menu Item from the pop-up menu. Choosing this option allows you access to all the menu commands within Exchange, including Print, View Next Page, and even Quit. Click on Edit Menu Item, and you are prompted with a representation of the menu bar of Exchange. Choose Next Page from under the View menu, and click Set Action. Click OK in this window, and again in the Field Properties window. Your button is now active on that page. You can choose Fields > Duplicate under the Edit menu to automatically copy that button to every page within the PDF file.

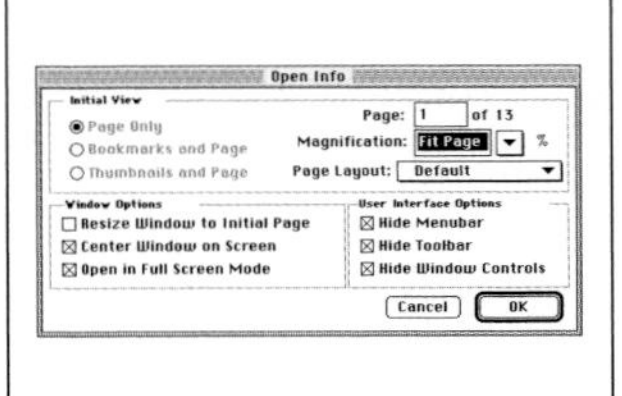

STEP 2: CHOOSE OPTIONS FOR PRESENTATION

Acrobat can easily make your PDF file work like a slide presentation. Simply choose Full Screen from the View menu. You can use the arrow keys and other commands to move through youy document. To get out of Full Screen mode, use the Escape key.

Session

K3 Incorporating Scanned Documents

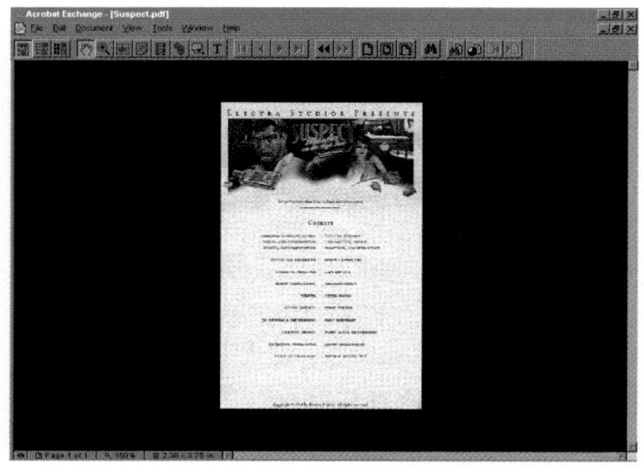

Importing and capturing scanned images with Adobe Exchange's Capture plug-in is a great way to get traditional printed documents online. The Capture plug-in comes with Exchange, and allows you to connect directly to your scanner for one-step conversion to PDF.

ADOBE EXCHANGE 3.0

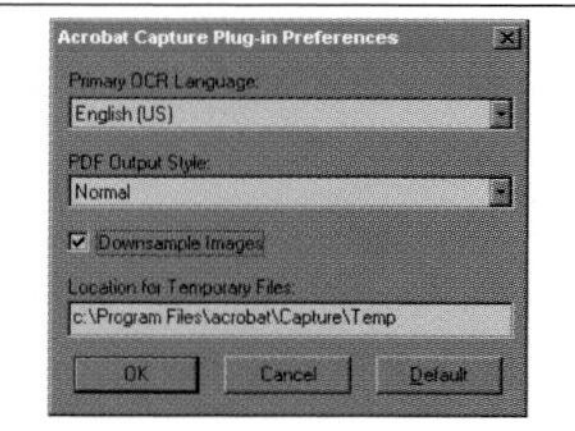

STEP 1: CONFIGURE THE CAPTURE PLUG-IN

During installation of Adobe Acrobat, you can select the scanner that connects to your machine. And, if you have already scanned images, you can convert them to PDF too. Open the Preferences Capture window under the File menu. Here, you can select the OCR (Optical Character Recognition) language, whether or not images should be downsampled, and the location of a temporary storage folder.

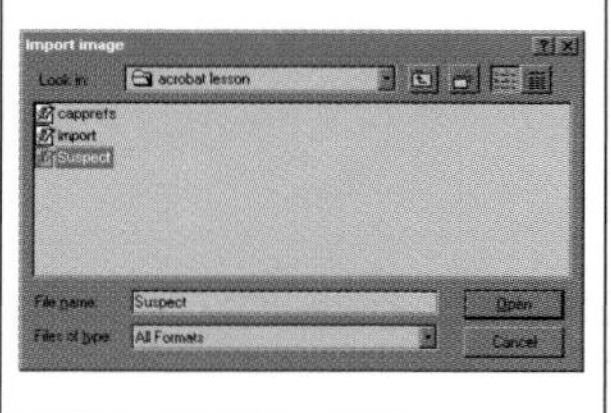

STEP 2: CONVERT TO PDF

Use the Import Image command under the File menu to choose the image you want to convert. This automatically converts a bitmap image into a PDF file.

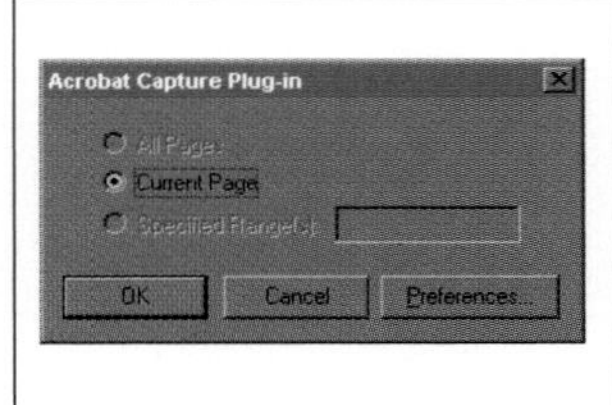

STEP 3: CONVERT TO EDITABLE TEXT

Once the image is a PDF file, use the Capture Pages command under the Document menu to convert all the elements of the PDF into images and text that you can edit.

TIP: *Your image must be between 200 and 600 dpi if it's black and white, or 200 and 400 dpi if it's color. Otherwise, the Capture Pages command displays an error message, and does not convert the image.*

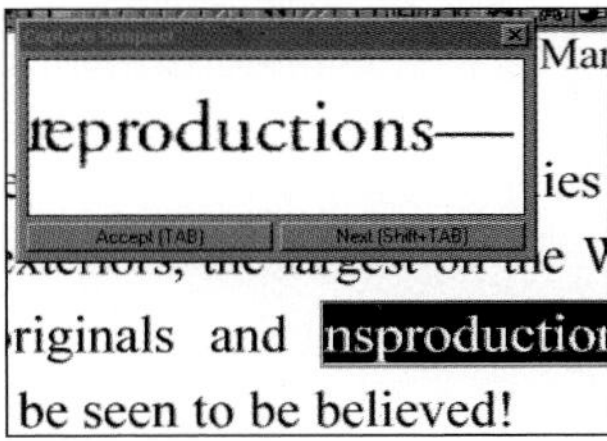

STEP 4: EDIT AND VERIFY ACCURACY OF OCR

Under the Edit menu, choose Show Capture Suspects. This command shows all of the text and images that the OCR software couldn't determine. In many cases, these are bits of text that were unclear in the scan. Exchange makes its best guess for the suspect text, and allows you to either accept or edit it. In other cases, Capture Suspects may be graphics that should remain so in your document.

Session

K4

Cataloging and Indexing PDF Files

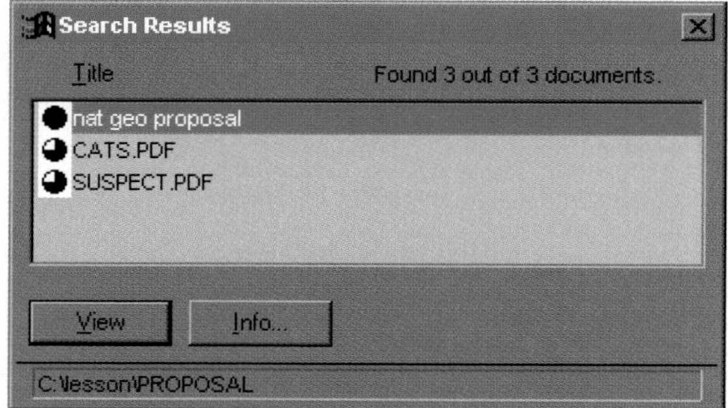

The Find command under the Tools menu search enables you to within one PDF file for an individual word or phrase. Adobe Catalog allows your user to search for a word or phrase throughout multiple PDF files. The index created by Catalog contains a listing of every single word in all of the PDF files, less any common words you've chosen to omit. This index, or list, then becomes searchable to your users through the use of either Exchange or Reader with the Search plug-in.

ADOBE CATALOG 3.0

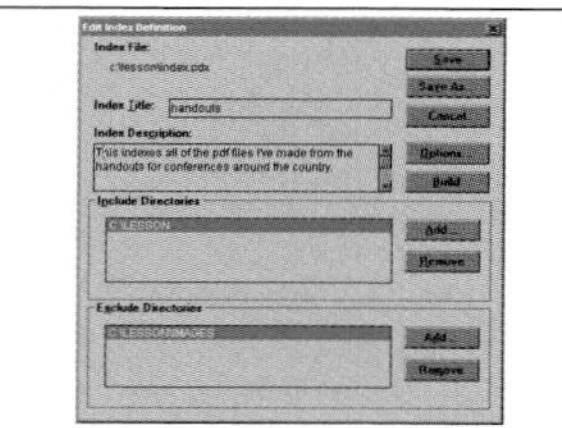

STEP 1: CREATE THE INDEX

Choosing New under the File menu opens the Index Definition window that enables you to set options for your new index. Type a name and description, and then select the directories to include where your PDF files are located. Catalog also offers the ability to Exclude Directories, in case there are folders within the Included Directories that you don't want to include in the index.

Cataloging is a pretty fast operation. Three PDF files consisting of 37 pages and multiple graphics on each page takes about two minutes to catalog on a relatively slow computer.

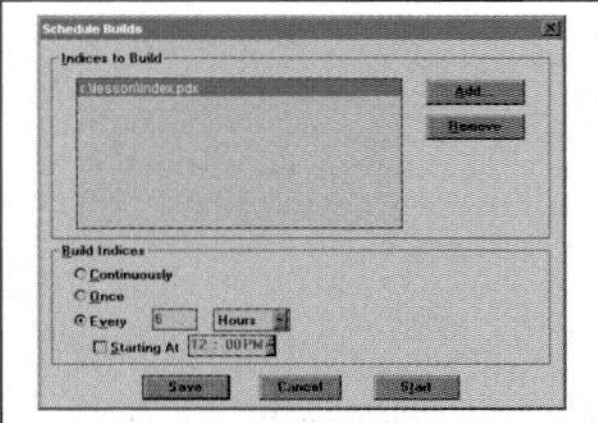

STEP 2: SCHEDULE OPTION

Cataloging can take place in a batch, as well as at regular intervals that you can set in the Schedule Builds window. Choose Schedule under the Index menu, and select the pre-defined index files. Scheduling the indexing of PDF files is useful when you want to maintain an updated index on a server or volume where the content changes often.

Select your choice of building indices according to your desired schedule, including continuous, once, or at any specified interval of days, hours, or minutes.

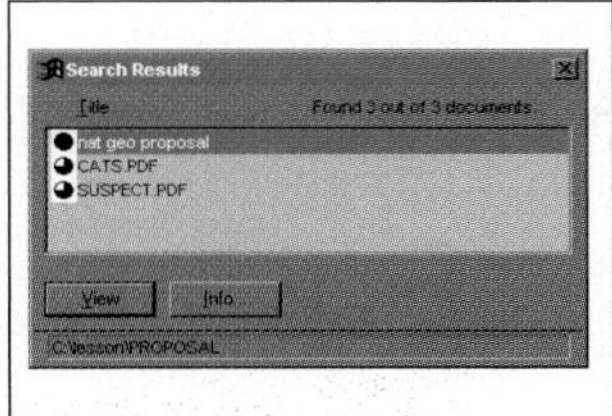

STEP 3: SEARCHING AN INDEX

Once you have indexed your PDF files, your users can perform full-text searches in either Adobe Exchange or Reader. By choosing the Search > Query command from the Tool menu, or by clicking the button with the small binoculars and Document icon, the user can select the indices to be searched and specify how to search them.

First, they may need to add the index to the viewer's list of available indices by clicking the Indexes button, or using the Search > Indexes command in the Tools menu. With an index specified, a word or phrase can be typed in and search options selected.

Clicking Search quickly performs a search of the index and generates a list of PDF files that match the criteria. The PDF files included in the list are clickable, and take the user directly to the page, highlighting the matching occurrences. The results can be returned by choosing Search > Results from the Tool menu, or by clicking the appropriate button in the toolbar. There are also buttons to move to the next or previous occurrences.

Session

K5 *Referencing PDF Files in HTML*

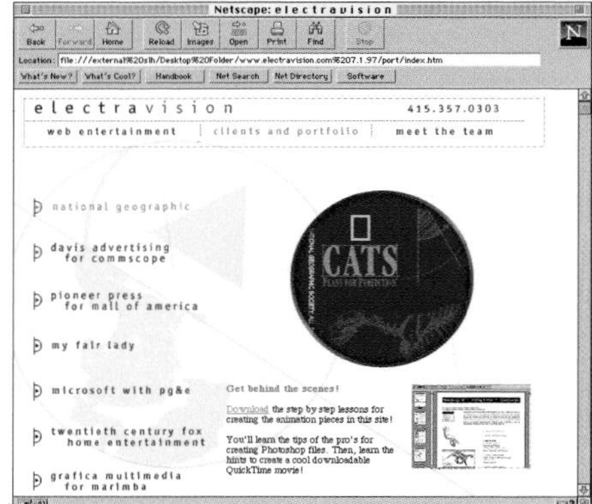

Offering a PDF file on your Web site means first determining how you would like your users to access it. If you want your users to view the document inline on the HTML page, they will only see one page and cannot interact with it, which may be just fine for that particular document. Alternatively, you can offer it as a downloadable file to view by itself in the entire browser window using the PDFViewer plug-in, or to view separately in Acrobat Reader. This later method is accomplished using the usual*<href>* tag to link to the *.pdf* file, while the *<embed>* tag is used to incorporate the file inline as a static image.

SIMPLETEXT OR NOTEPAD

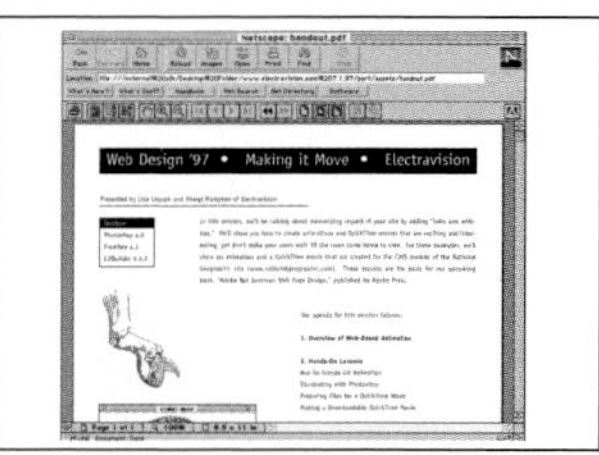

OFFERING A PDF AS A DOWNLOADABLE FILE

To offer a PDF as a downloadable file, link to the PDF file with the *<href>* tag. The PDF file can then fill the entire browser window, or launch Acrobat Reader or Exchange as a helper application, depending on how the user's browser is configured.

The following line of HTML downloads the PDF file "Brochure.pdf" when the user clicks on the graphic "thumbnail.gif."

```
<a href="Brochure.pdf"><img src="thumbnail.gif"></a>
```

INLINE PDFS WITH THE PDFVIEWER PLUG-IN

The *<embed>* tag tells the user's browser to display the PDF file inline on the HTML page as an image.

```
<embed src="Brochure.pdf" width=600 height=350>
```

The above line of HTML places the PDF file "Brochure" inline on the HTML page. Using the *<embed>* tag, you can scale the size of the PDF file as a percentage; if you don't, it displays at actual size. Internet Explorer, however, ignores the scaling information in the *<embed>* tag, and reads it from the PDF file's Document Info Settings.

Chapter L

BEHIND THE SCENES

During the design and production of your site, you should never lose sight of important challenges behind the scenes, and the issues that you need to consider prior to launching your site. At the top of this list is your choice of server. You'll need to decide the location of your server and how to interact with it. This chapter presents a series of questions that will help you determine how and where to host your server. We also consider the advantages of the latest personal Web sharing software that allows you to easily serve Web files directly from your desktop. Other useful tasks that add to the capabilities offered on your Web site are explored, as well as investigating servers themselves. Session L5 offers a CGI script for gathering information about your users. Closing the chapter is an introduction to the basic principles of a database, as well as a step-by-step session on the creation of a database.

CHAPTER SESSIONS

- L1 *Choosing a Server*
- L2 *Working with Your Remote Server*
- L3 *Mac Personal Web Sharing*
- L4 *Internet Explorer Personal Web Server*
- L5 *Simple CGI Script for User Feedback*
- L6 *Introduction to a Database*
- L7 *Creating a Database*

CHAPTER TOOLBOX

Fetch 3.0

NCSA Telnet 2.6

Simple Text or Notepad

FileMaker Pro

Mac OS 8.0

BEHIND THE SCENES 101

Every Web site resides on a server, which is a computer of any platform. The most common servers are UNIX, Windows NT-based, and Macintosh-based. There are many varieties of server software, ranging from the freeware Apache to the Netscape Secure Commerce to the Microsoft IIS software. The choice of server software depends mostly on the capabilities you want on your site. Many companies choose to house their server at an ISP (Internet Service Provider), or a *server farm* (a company set up to "rent" you server space and allow high bandwidth access to your site). They can recommend platform and server software according to your needs. See Session L1 for choosing server farm options.

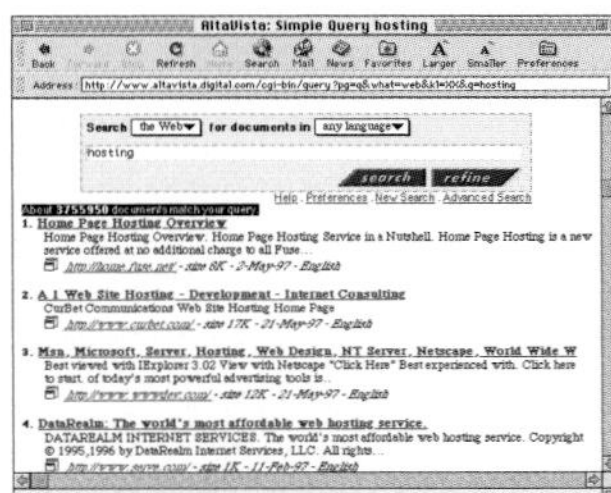

INTERNET ADDRESSES

Every Web site has two pieces of information associated with it: a domain name, like *www.adobe.com*, and a unique number called an IP address. (See Session L1 for information on registering a domain name.) An IP address is a set of four numbers, each set can be up to three digits long, separated by periods (e.g., 205.134.233.1). This unique number represents one individual computer connected to the Internet. Frequently a server, if partitioned, is associated with multiple IP addresses. This is the case with most server farms, which allow a single server to access multiple domain names.

PERSONAL WEB SHARING

The new Macintosh operating system (Mac OS 8) enables Web browsers to recognize your Mac as a server. Mac OS 8 includes a control panel and extension application that, like file sharing, allow others to see your Web site that resides on your hard drive. When you access the Web through your dial-up account, you are given an IP address that can be accessed remotely. Internet Explorer, on both Macintosh and PC, also allows this capability.

CGI SCRIPTS

The most common method of interactivity and user feedback on a Web site is through the use of a CGI (Common Gateway Interface) script. A line of HTML code references the CGI script, and the script is then executed. CGI scripts are written in the scripting language Perl.

Session

L1 Choosing a Server

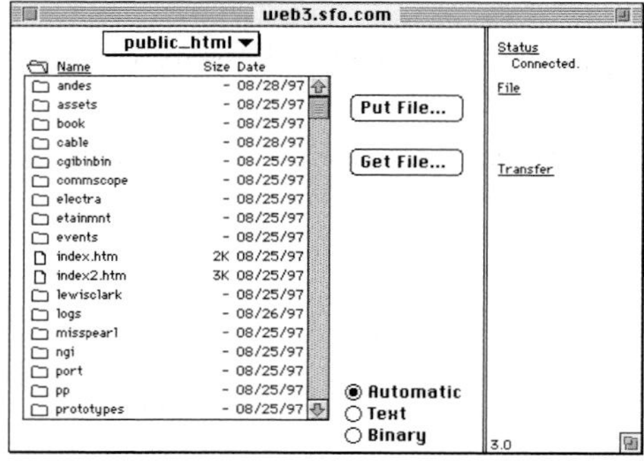

The first technical question to answer before producing a Web site deals with hosting. Should you host your own site? Should you contract with an ISP (Internet Service Provider) or a server farm for Web server space? What are the ramifications of these decisions? This session looks at the options available to you and how to make the best decision. Also included in this session is the step-by-step process of registering your domain name.

HOUSING YOUR SERVER

First, you need to decide if you want your server in-house. While this gives you ultimate control over your site, the up-front investment can be rather large. In addition to the cost of the machine, you need adequate bandwidth, which may require an additional investment. Security, and perhaps a firewall, are issues you should also consider—especially if you plan to connect your server to an internal network.

If you decide to buy your own server, however, you do have the option of location. Many companies have emerged lately that offer to house your server. The serving machine resides at that company, and they provide adequate bandwidth and security. While this option means investing in the server machine, it saves you the cost of hiring a Webmaster and a full-time support team.

PICKING AN INTERNET SERVICE PROVIDER

If buying a server is out of the question, you still have plenty of options. Many ISPs offer Web server space to their customers. Generally, this amounts to about 10 megabytes of space devoted to a personal Web site. In this case, the ISPs generally don't allow you to offer your own domain name. So, rather than pointing your users to *www.janesmith.com*, you would send them to *www.isp.com/~janesmith*.

Server farms, on the other hand, usually provide a more professional front to the world. Your ISP probably also offers this service, but there is generally an additional charge. There are a couple different pricing structures for server farms, which combine some—if not all—of the following criteria:

- Amount of server space – Pricing is usually based on increments of 10 megabytes of space.
- Number of downloads – Your price can increase with the number of files downloaded from your site.

- Bandwidth offered – Generally, the higher the bandwidth offered, the higher the cost.
- Platform – A UNIX-based server may cost a different amount than a Windows NT-based server.
- Client control – You may be charged a higher amount for the ability to house CGI scripts on the server, or to have a higher level of access to the server.
- Number of POP accounts – Pop accounts are email accounts for people wanting to receive email at your domain name; generally, one POP account is included in the price.

Make sure you investigate your options to determine which pricing method is best for you. Some server farms require a setup fee and a three month contract just to initiate the service. Get references or check the client list to see if you recognize any well-known companies. Just keep in mind that you don't have to a server farm that's in your area. You can just as easily FTP your files to Timbuktu as send them around the corner.

REGISTERING YOUR DOMAIN NAME

First, you need to determine where your site will reside. This isn't absolutely necessary to register a domain name, but it makes it easier and quicker to get your site up and running. Eventually you need to inform InterNIC of your server's location, by telling them the computer's IP address. The IP address then is linked to the domain name.

Next, register a domain name with InterNIC, the agency that is responsible for all domain names worldwide. You can find them at *www.internic.net.* This is a relatively fast process, taking anywhere from 10 minutes to 24 hours, according to InterNIC. *Propagating* the name throughout the Internet (or having every computer connected to the Internet know about your domain name) usually takes a couple of days, so to make sure you've done this prior to your desired launch date. To ensure that users don't receive an error message prior to your launch date, create and upload a page that lets users know that your site is under construction.

When your site is live, you should start a marketing campaign to make sure people on the Web know to come to your site. This can be as easy and inexpensive as registering with various search engines, or it can be as complex and costly as including your URL in print and television ads, direct mail pieces, and buying advertising space on other Web sites. Your budget determines the scope of your campaign. Realize that users won't visit your site unless they are aware of it. (See Session A6 for in-depth ideas on how to market your site.)

Session

L2 Working with Your Remote Server

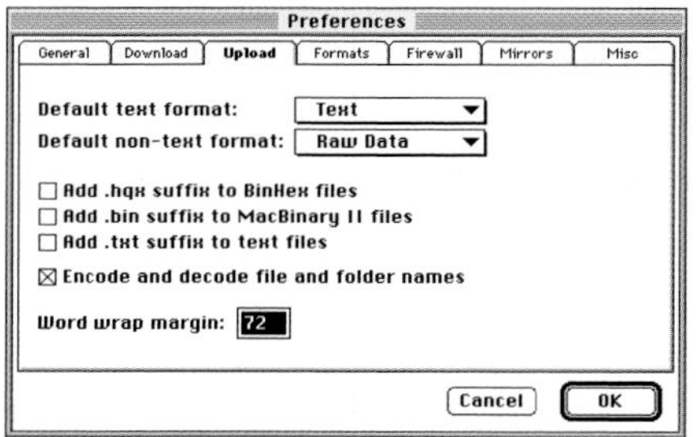

Understanding how to interact with your server is as important as producing a well-designed site. You need to know how to upload and download files and understand how to access and control your site. In addition, prior to creating your site, you need to make some decisions regarding file management, updating, and maintenance of your site.

UPLOADING AND DOWNLOADING

File Transfer Protocol (FTP) is the standard for uploading and downloading files to your server. You'll need three pieces of information to log onto your server and start uploading files: the domain name or IP address of the server, user name for you or your company (provided by the server farm), and a password for your user name (also provided by the server farm). After you log onto your server, find the appropriate directory for your files and start uploading. Upload text files, including HTML and CGI files, in text format. You should upload other files, including graphics, animations, and movies, in binary format. Make sure your preferences are set according to file types, or your newly uploaded files will be useless.

Downloading is the same process in reverse. Log onto your server with your user name and password, select the files you want and download them. Once again, text files, including HTML and CGI files, should be downloaded in text format. Other files, including graphics, animation, and movies, should be downloaded in binary format.

TELNET CONTROL

In some cases, you'll need the control to do more than just upload and download files. For example, in order to make a CGI script executable, you'll need to *telnet* into the server. This is another type of communication protocol, and your server farm grants you telnet access for this type of communication. Contact your server farm or ISP to get telnet access to your site. In some cases, you won't be allowed this much control over your server. If that's the case, the ISP should perform these tasks for you in a reasonable time frame.

DIRECTORY STRUCTURE

When producing your site on your hard drive, establish a directory structure for your files. Creating a structure makes production easier, and greatly eases the process of maintenance and updating. Some producers like to keep all HTML files in one directory, and all graphic and accessory files in another directory. Another method is to organize by categories of the site, and within those categories create a directory unique to the files of that area. The most important aspect is consistency in the way you choose to structure your directories.

Within any directory, most servers are configured to look for a *index.htm* or *index.html* file. It is the uppermost directory or page that is served when your user requests *www.yourdomainname.com*. You can configure the server differently, but the easiest method is to name the default page in a directory.

FILE NAMING CONVENTIONS

Along with the standards for the directory structure, you should generate standards for file names. Consistency in file naming makes it easier for those involved in production to reference files and graphics, as well as replacing these elements. If your server is UNIX-based, keep in mind that UNIX is case-sensitive with respect to file names, and replaces spaces with an underscore. An easy way to avoid problems with accuracy is to name files with all lowercase letters and no spaces.

Limitations left over from the early days of DOS also rear their ugly heads when naming files. Downloadable files that are accessed with helper applications should be named according to the DOS 8.3 naming convention. Otherwise, the user may have to perform an extra step during the download process in order to rename the file. You should also follow the 8.3 naming convention if you plan to burn a cross-platform CD-ROM of your project.

NOTE: *The 8.3 naming convention consists of an eight-or-less, character file name with no spaces or punctuation, followed by a period and three characters denoting file type. For example, "image.gif" follows the 8.3 naming convention.*

Session

L3 Mac Personal Web Sharing

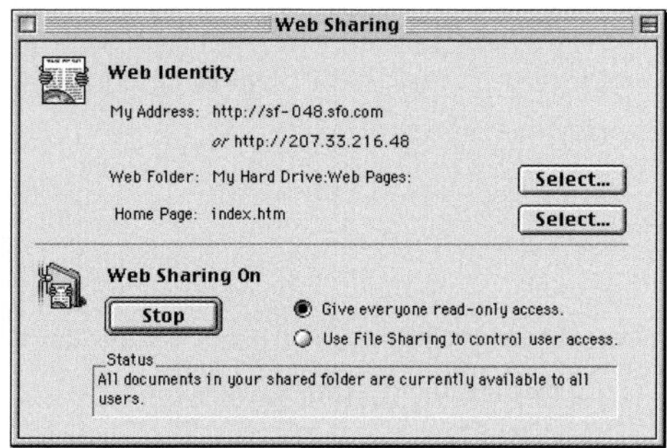

Personal Web Sharing on the Macintosh is an excellent way to offer HTML files that exist on your personal computer to others on the Web. Similar to the standard Macintosh File Sharing offered in Mac OS 8, Personal Web Sharing enables others to access your computer remotely, via your dial-up connection. This can be very convenient, in terms of getting approval on a design direction or discussing a detail of information architecture.

You probably wouldn't want to use this method, however, to serve your entire site in perpetuity. The speed at which your files are served is limited by your computer's speed and connection to the Web. In other words, if you usinge an older computer and a 28.8 baud modem, that is the server speed. You should also consider the cost of leaving the computer on and connected to your dial-up account 24 hours a day. If you're working in a business environment, the company is probably paying the ISP for unlimited usage of a dial-up connection to the Web. Most likely, they are also paying the business rate through the local telephone company for local calls, which can cost up to $.60 per hour. This works out to almost $15 per day—just to leave the machine connected to the Web.

COMPONENTS OF PERSONAL WEB SHARING

Installation of Mac OS 8 gives you all the components needed for Personal Web Sharing: the Web Sharing control panel, the Web Sharing extension, and a Web Pages folder on the root level of the startup drive. During installation, a variety of configuration, help, and example files are copied into the Web Pages folder to get you started. Also included in the help files are a few links to sites that give good advice about Web design, interactivity, and user interface.

By default, all of your files to be accessed by the outside world resides in this folder. You also have the option of choosing another folder. Keep in mind that only one folder is recognized by Personal Web Sharing, so localize everything within one folder.

CONFIGURE THE CONTROL PANEL AND EXTENSION, THEN START

Macintosh programmers have made it very simple to activate Personal Web Sharing. To start, launch your dial-up connection to the Web. When you open the Web Sharing control panel, it automatically queries your dial-up and returns an IP address to you. Two options for Web access, an IP address and a domain name, are presented.

Next, if you want to keep your files in a folder other than the Web Pages folder created during installation, click the Select button next to the Web Folder option. Locate your Web Folder and click OK. To select your home page, click the Select button next to the Home Page option; this displays a listing of every available HTML page within that folder. Select your home page document, and you're ready to start sharing. Click the Start button to turn on Web Sharing.

TIP: *Each time you log into your dial-up connection, you probably will be given a different IP address. Most ISPs assign an IP address randomly upon accessing the dial-up account. So, if a user is looking at your site, schedule the time with her to ensure that the site is live.*

Session

L4 Internet Explorer Personal Web Server

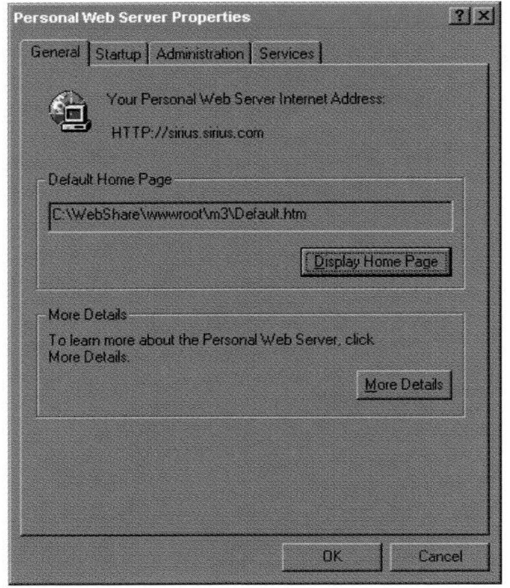

Internet Explorer (IE) users on both the Macintosh and PC can also take advantage of serving Web content from their personal computer. Like the Mac Personal Web Sharing, IE Personal Web Server allows others to access your computer remotely, via your dialup. Personal Web Server, however, is a built-in component of Internet Explorer—not the computer's operating system. Performing a full install of the current version of Internet Explorer installs all files needed for this feature. Currently, configuration of the Personal Web Server involves a few more steps than the Personal Web Sharing feature of the Mac operating system, but it is still well worth the effort and will continue to become easier and more stable. This session focuses on the configuration of Personal Web Server on a PC running Windows 95.

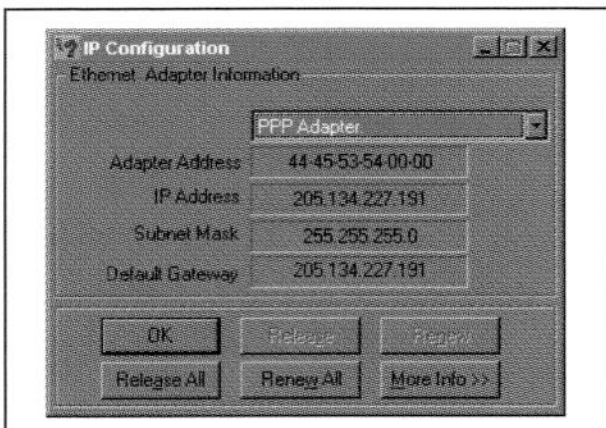

STEP 1: FIND YOUR CORRECT IP ADDRESS

First, open Personal Web Server in the Control Panel directory. The IP address or domain name listed at the top of this window may or may not be correct. To verify the IP address, open the IP Configuration File. This is the file "winipcfg" located in c:\windows. This window displays the accurate IP address for your machine.

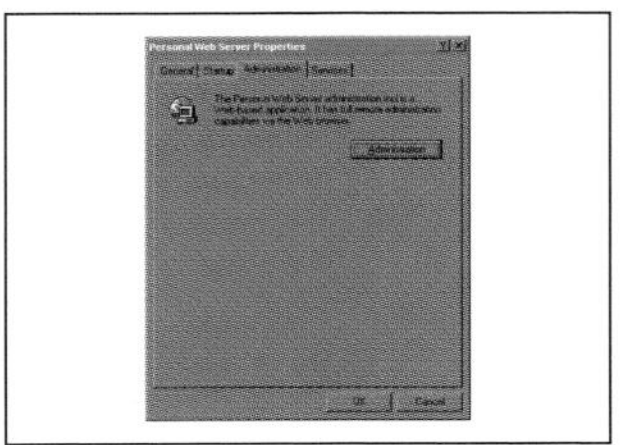

STEP 2: CHANGE THE DEFAULT HOME PAGE

From the General tab in the Personal Web Server Properties window, you can Display your Home Page; unfortunately, you cannot change it from here. The Default Home Page defaults to a directory on your hard drive, c:\WebShare. If you' want to change the location of your Default Home page, select the Administration tab. Clicking the Administration button opens Internet Explorer and a browser-based tool called the Internet

Services Administrator. Under the heading Personal Web Server Service, choose WWW Administrator. Select the Directories tab, and the first alias in the list, <*Home*>, has an Edit button next to it. Click the Edit button and select the path and files you want to serve.

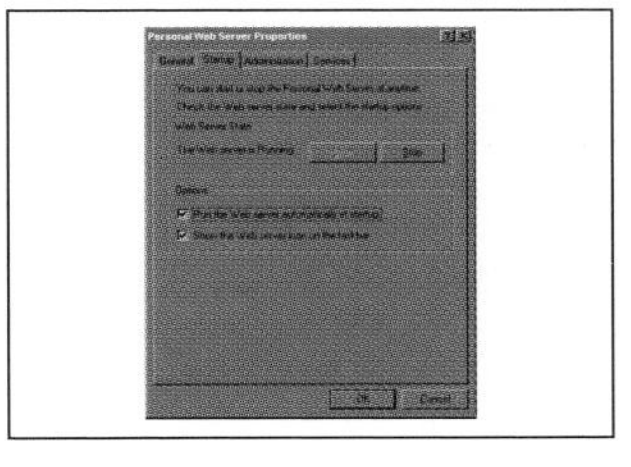

STEP 3: START PERSONAL WEB SHARING

Now that your Personal Web Sharing is configured, click on the Startup tab, and then the Start button to start serving your files. Occasionally, one additional step is required. Click the services tab, and in the services text box click on the HTTP listing. If its status is not running, click the Start button and close the window.

Session

L5 Simple CGI Script for User Feedback

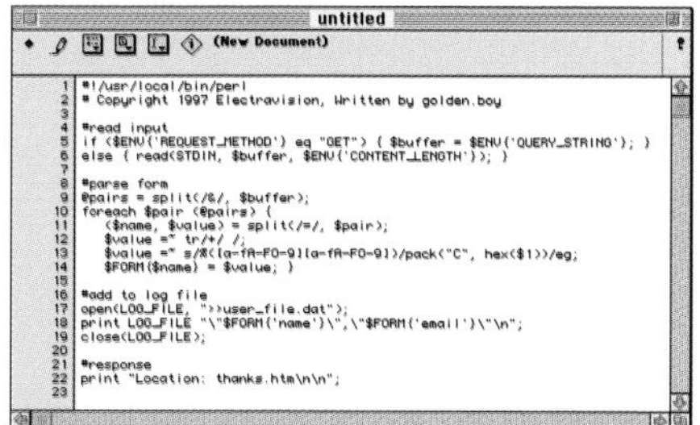

To get feedback from your users, you can either use the simple *mailto:* HTML command referenced in Session H5, or you can write a CGI script that gives more directed, specific feedback. This lesson provides an introduction to CGI scripts and presents an overview examination of a script with a description of its elements.

This particular script reads user input and stores it in a log file on the server for later use. The script then delivers a page to the user thanking him or her for their feedback. In a CGI script, the character # is used as a comment, and allows you to identify processes within the script.

The CGI Script Code:

```
#!/usr/local/bin/perl
# Copyright 1997 Electravision, Written by golden.boy

#read input
if ($ENV{'REQUEST_METHOD'} eq "GET") { $buffer =
   $ENV{'QUERY_STRING'}; }
else { read(STDIN, $buffer, $ENV{'CONTENT_LENGTH'}); }

#parse form
@pairs = split(/&/, $buffer);
foreach $pair (@pairs) {
 ($name, $value) = split(/=/, $pair);
 $value =~ tr/+/ /;
 $value =~ s/%([a-fA-F0-9][a-fA-F0-9])/pack("C", hex($1))/
   eg;
 $FORM{$name} = $value; }
```

```
#add to log file
open(LOG_FILE, “>>user_file.dat”);
print LOG_FILE “\”$FORM{‘name’}\”,\”$FORM{‘email’}\”\n”;
close(LOG_FILE);

#response
print “Location: thanks.htm\n\n”;
```

INITIAL COMMENTS

The first line of every CGI script defines the location of the Perl application on your server. This is also the area where your programmer can make general comments about the script and its purpose, as well as any copyright information.

READ INPUT

This part of the script reads the text input by the user. The text is now stored in the buffer.

PARSE FORM

These lines separate the input from the user into distinct variables.

ADD TO LOG FILE

The file on the server, called *user_file.dat*, opens and the new data, consisting of the user's name and email address, is added to the end of the file. The log file is then closed.

RESPONSE

After the user's information is stored in the log file, the page *thanks.htm* is returned to the user.

Session

L6 Introduction to a Database

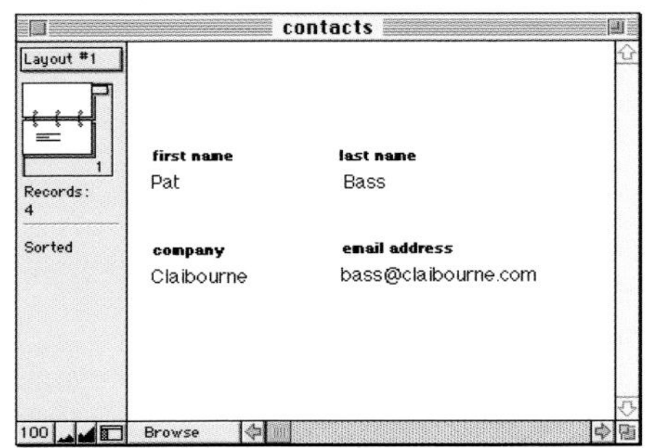

A database is simply a way to store and view a wide variety of information about a group of similar items. Say, for example, that you have a collection of music CDs organized by dance, romantic candlelit dinner for two, wake you up, and atmosphere for cocktail parties. You also may want to organize them alphabetically by artist, title, or even by predominant color on the cover. A database allows you to sort your CD collection in a variety of ways. Accessing a database online can be a powerful feature to offer your users, especially if you have an existing database that you want to share with your users.

APPLICATION

If you are designing and producing your own personal Web site, you can create an individual page for each one of the CDs in your collection. Or, your company can create a page for each one its products. These Web pages can all be generated from a database. Then, your Web site can have an internal search engine, giving your users direct access to each product or CD.

APPLICATION

In database-speak, following the example of your CD collection, each CD is a record, and each aspect of the record is a field. Each record can contain a great number of fields; the only limitation is your database application. The fields in a database can be text, numeric, or a calculated number (like a serial number within the database).

After you have entered all data for all the records, you can perform complex, multi-criteria searches for the exact information you want. Database applications also allow you to perform multi-criteria sorts that generate a report listing the information in exactly the order you choose.

In these applications, you also have the option to create new layouts for the information. These layout can include any combination of the fields, so you are in essence creating your own custom reports for the data. Keep in mind that when you create a new report, you are not deleting information from the database if you choose not to display a field. You simply are not accessing that bit of information for that specific report.

ACCESSING A DATABASE

There are two ways to access database information online. If the actual database resides on your server, you can access the data in real time. In some cases, however, it makes more sense to output data from the database, generating HTML pages that can be accessed on the Web. Generally, if your database is huge and constantly changing, and you want your users to have access to up-to-the-minute information, you should consider locating the database on your server.

If, however, the data does not constantly change, you may want to consider outputting information to static HTML pages that can be accessed on the Web. Keep in mind, however, that direct database access takes additional server time. Applications also exist that compile the database information from a schedule that automatically uploads the static pages to the server. Your choice in these two methods ultimately depends on the type and usage of the database.

TIP: *If you choose to locate the database on your server that is in turn connected to your internal network, you should consult a Web security expert.*

Session

L7 Creating a Database

FileMaker Pro is a great, inexpensive, cross-platform database application. The default layout and interface of FileMaker Pro is a notecard metaphor whereby one card represents one record, making it a very intuitive and user-friendly interface. It can accommodate an unlimited number of records with an unlimited number of fields. This session focuses on the creation of a simple database that consists of your business contacts. You enter all the typical information from a business card, including address and contact numbers, then sort the information and create new layouts for custom reports.

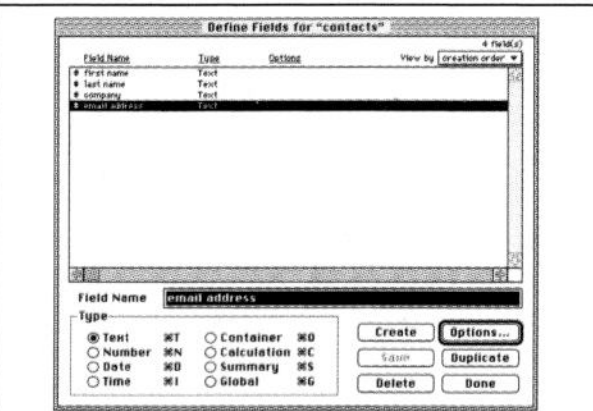

STEP 1: DEFINING FIELDS

First, define the fields that you want to include in the database. This can be as simple or as complicated as you want. Keep in mind that if you want to track an aspect of a record, you first must assign a field to it. You should create the following fields: name, company, address, city, state, and zip code, work phone number, and email address.

In FileMaker Pro, select New under the File menu and name your new database. The Define Fields pop-up window automatically displays to allow you to create your fields. Define the fields of information you want to track. Keep in mind that each piece of data you want access needs to be a separate field. For example, if you want to sort by last name of the contacts, you'll need a field for just that information.

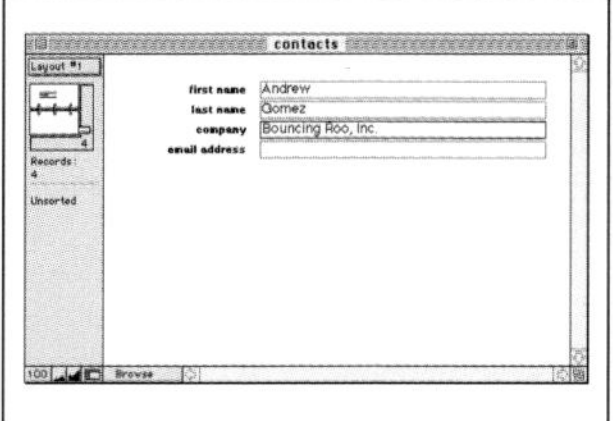

STEP 2: ENTER INFORMATION FOR THE RECORDS

This is the most time-consuming part of the database creation process, but after the information is entered, finding and sorting is very easy. And, you don't have to retype anything to view the information in a different way. Enter all the information from your business cards and scraps of paper. If you find a person with multiple phone numbers, you can easily create another field.

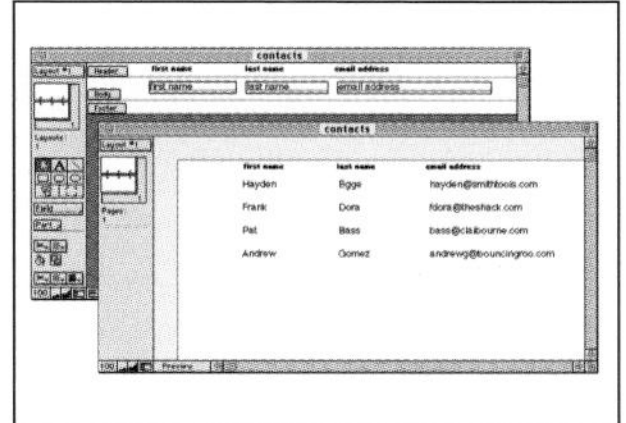

STEP 3: CREATING A NEW LAYOUT

This step allows you to create your own custom report. After your information is entered, you can display all, or a limited selection, of the fields in a variety of different layouts. Choose Layout under the Mode menu, and select the fields that you don't want in this layout, and delete these fields. The remaining fields may consist of the first name, last name, and email address fields.

Now, rearrange the fields and their titles within the layout page. If you move the field titles above the line associated with the Header, they will appear only once at the top of each page. Choosing Browse under the Mode menu allows you to view only one record at a time. Preview the output of all the records in the database by choosing Preview under the Mode menu.

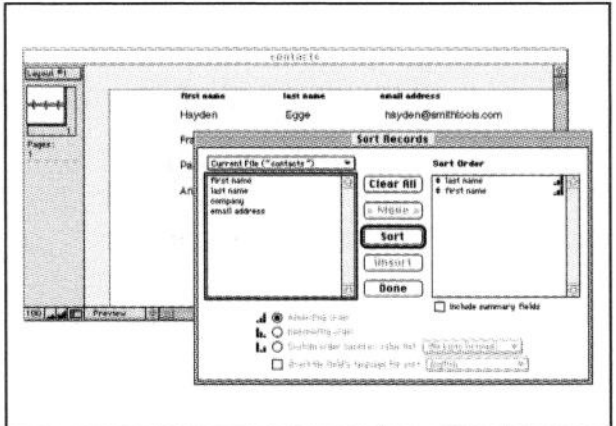

STEP 4: SORTING RECORDS

To find a record at a glance, you can sort the records alphabetically or numerically. Choose Sort under the Mode menu, and select the fields that you want to sort. FileMaker Pro allows for multiple sorting criteria, which enables you to sort first by, for example, last name, then by first name, if you choose.

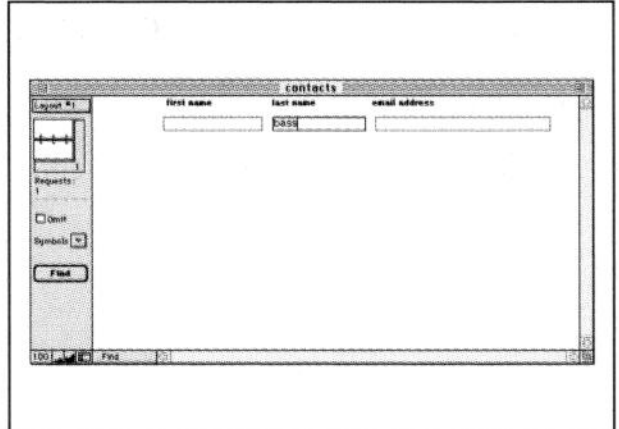

STEP 5: FIND A PARTICULAR RECORD

All database applications allow you to search for a particular record, or a series of records that match your search criteria. In FileMaker Pro, choose Find under the Mode menu, and type into the field text boxes your criteria. If you fill in more than one field, your results will be a cross-section of the records that mach both criteria.

TIP: *After you've performed your search, choose Find All under the Select menu to continue browsing all of your records.*

LISA LOPUCK

The Creative Director and co-founder of Electravision, Lisa Lopuck is a well-known expert on user interface design. She speaks around the world at Web conferences, and teaches interactive media seminars at universities and colleges, including Stanford, UCLA, University of Hawaii, and San Francisco State University.

Lisa's first book, *Designing Multimedia*, has been translated into multiple languages, and is used as a new media reference around the world. Her second book, *Kid's Web Kit*, is a CD-ROM book and software set that steps kids through a fun, animated process for creating their own Web site.

Prior to forming Electravision, Lisa's interactive multimedia career included working with such companies as the Apple Multimedia Lab, Voyager, film producer George Lucas, Kidsoft, Kaleida, United Nations, Sony Corporation, Microsoft, vivid studios, and Clement Mok designs.

Lisa holds a B.A. in Communication Design from UCLA.

SHERYL HAMPTON

As Executive Producer and co-founder of Electravision, Sheryl Hampton pursues and evaluates new technologies, and advises clients on online media trends. Sheryl's technical R&D findings are incorporated into Electravision and client projects, and form the basis of seminar sessions. She also designs and builds customized training sessions for individual clients. Sheryl addresses audiences at various national multimedia and Web design conferences.

Prior to founding Electravision, Sheryl was a producer at top design firms, with clients that included Twentieth Century Fox Home Entertainment, Apple Computer, Columbia TriStar Television, Levi's, Harper Collins Publishers, and divisions of Sony Corporation.

Only in social situations does Sheryl get to use her degree in Political Science from the University of Kansas.

ELECTRAVISION, LLC

Electravision is a San Francisco-based Web development company, offering years of industry experience. With an eye toward the future of interactive technology, Electravision develops highly versatile, entertaining, and informative original content that utilizes the Internet market of today and tomorrow. Visit Electravision online at *www.electravision.com.*

About the CD-ROM

The enclosed Image Club Graphics Web Sampler CD-ROM includes the graphics used in this book's examples, over a thousand Web-ready clip art graphics, and tryout versions of Adobe's popular software applications.

The CD is both Windows and Macintosh compatible.

IDE

multimedia guide to the contents of the CD-ROM launch pplication. If you need QuickTime, it is included in the '.

IN THE BOOK

ectory on the CD contains all the graphics used in the he book. You can use these sample images to follow along rated steps, or for your own projects. The graphics are nter and session.

RE

ctory on the CD contains tryout versions of many of the plications used in the techniques described in this book, PageMill 2.0, Adobe Photoshop 4.0, Adobe After Effects tor 7.0, and Adobe Premiere 4.2.

TRAS

ectory on the CD contains free Web clip art from Image d Letraset including over a thousand Web-ready back- ers, buttons, bullets, dividers, and much more.

gy of digital communications. Produced by Adobe Systems Incorporated and published by Macmillan Computer Publishing USA, Adobe Press books are available wherever books on computing or digital communications are sold. Visit the Adobe System web site (*www.adobe.com*) for the most recent releases within the Adobe Press library.